"I spent last weekend reading *With You There Is Light* ~~—~~ er to cover and was deeply moved by the lives of Sophie Scholl and Fritz Hartnagel and the spiritual journey they shared as they both struggled to be faithful. Alexandra Lehmann has given us an important and complex story which put flesh and blood on the German Resistance, making these important historical figures live for us." – GREGG MAST, President, New Brunswick Theological Seminary

"Growing up in West Germany during the 1960s and 70s, I learned very little about those brave individuals who had decided to act against the National Socialists. One reason why Germans found it so difficult to acknowledge these "heroes" had to do with the uneasy psychological effect that the existence of resistance fighters had on the wounded collective soul of Germany: if these individuals could muster the courage to stand up against evil, why then were there so few of them? Every act of resistance is therefore a reminder of the widespread enthusiasm for Hitler, assimilation to his murderous policies, and obedience to a totalitarian regime among ordinary Germans.

Alexandra Lehmann's book *With You There Is Light: The True Story about Sophie Scholl and Fritz Hartnagel* confirms how important it is to include the stories of resistance fighters in our educational work in order to strengthen awareness of human rights and tolerance as the foundation of a just society.

It takes a gifted writer like Lehmann to create an emotional bridge between those brave people and us. This novel creates a beautiful portrait of Sophie Scholl as a spirited young woman with a strong Christian identity. It is her faith in the existence of God that lends her conscience the power to resist Hitler's evil empire of nihilism. I could not put Lehmann's book down without asking myself some very important questions."
– ROLAND DOLLINGER, PhD. Princeton University. German Department Chair,
Sarah Lawrence College

"Alexandra Lehmann's book chronicles the relationship between Sophie Scholl, founding member of the White Rose Group, and Captain Fritz Hartnagel.

Under the sway of Sophie's intelligence, idealism and burgeoning womanhood, Fritz comes to question his sworn allegiance to Hitler and to see with moral clarity the true nature of German wartime atrocities. With flawless writing and delicate prose, Lehmann renders her own voice indiscernible, letting the people she brings to life speak for themselves. Coupled with meticulous adherence to actual events, she provides the reader with a deeply moving narrative.

With You There is Light is a masterful work, powerful for its realism and touching in its intimacy. Sophie's and Fritz's story along with the White Rose Group is highly significant, not only for the study of totalitarianism - its impact and responses - but also for its universal appeal and relevance. This small group of young people had the wherewithal to see beyond their childhood indoctrination and grew to challenge the machinery of the Nazi state amid widespread obedience and moral decay.

Lehmann, with her exceptional talents as a researcher and writer, has done the world a great service in making their story accessible to all." - REBECCA ODESSA,
The Wisdom Daily

"A compelling read and fascinating story of courage, nurtured by faith in God and in the dignity of each human being. An unescapable power! A complex story of a maturing conscience midst the horrors of World War II in Germany. Deeply moving. Most appropriate for any era and indeed for this early decade of the 21st century. We are called to search out, speak and live our deepest convictions. "Summon All the Powers That Be!" - as the Family Scholl did, quoting from Goethe. Alexandra Lehmann has captured these tremendous spirits and the context of this devastating history."
–REVEREND JOE BAXER, PhD, MDiv/President of United Nations Association of Connecticut

"In Germany, Sophie Scholl is celebrated as one of the most influential people of the twentieth century. Yet, sadly, her courageous spirit is barely known to the English-speaking world. In 1942-43, as Hitler's brutal political and military campaigns raged on, Sophie, just 21 years old, joined her brother, Hans, and several other Munich university students, to form the White Rose—a resistance group that published and disseminated a series of leaflets critical of Hitler and the Third Reich. In 1943, the core members of the group were arrested and executed for treason.

These are the historical facts. What Alexandra Lehmann's novel does is flesh out the people involved, focusing on Sophie and her sweetheart, Fritz Hartnagel. When their relationship begins, in 1937, Sophie is a lovely, independent girl of 16. Fritz is a 20 year-old cadet at a military academy, and goes on to become a communication's officer in the German army. Their curious romance developed largely through their letters to each another. Unfortunate for them, but fortunate for us. For these documents, many of which are translated into English for the first time in the novel, reveal the intimate thoughts and feelings of two young people living in the nightmare world of National Socialism.

Fritz describes to Sophie the horrible destruction and carnage he experiences, first in Holland and France, and later, in Russia. These accounts were certainly among the motivating factors in Sophie's ultimate revolt against, and critical attack upon, National Socialism. On the other hand, Sophie's descriptions of the stifling government control and paranoia of civilian life led Fritz to question his own commitment to the war and his participation in it.

The pacing of the book, from the pathos of Sophie's experiences of the brutal Nazi terror of Kristallnacht, to Fritz's seemingly hopeless rescue from the German defeat at Stalingrad, is done with extreme artistry and control. Her descriptions of the characters' psychological and emotional insights convey to the reader a sense of real, thoroughly believable, flesh and blood people in extraordinary circumstances.

Writing good historical fiction is a unique challenge. Overemphasizing the historical can make a book informative, but lacking in charm. Overstressing the fictional can make it charming, but fantastic. In this novel, Alexandra Lehmann has struck a masterful medium between history and fiction. From the book, you will learn much. And you will feel deeply." – DENNIS SWEET, PhD. University of Iowa.

INTRODUCTION

———

AN ESTIMATED TOTAL OF OVER 50 million people died by the end of the Second World War.

Germany's Führer Adolf Hitler led this cataclysmic destruction on humanity with an ideology proclaiming a so-called superior race. Elected into office in 1933, Hitler and the National Socialists systematically dismantled the legal protections of the country's newly established democracy. A resulting dictatorship imprisoned the German people as the Nazi Party deported Jews, political opponents, members of the Church, and all those deemed "inferior" into concentration camps. With the Germany Army invading countries all over the Western hemisphere and in Africa, paramilitary troops perpetrated the Holocaust which is responsible for the murder of an estimated 11 million innocent people, six million of them Jews.

The Scholl siblings, Hans and Sophie, along with sixteen of their fellow students in Munich, began a resistance movement against this tyranny, known as The White Rose.

This book is inspired by their true story.

With You
There Is Light

With You There Is Light

BASED ON THE TRUE STORY
ABOUT SOPHIE SCHOLL
AND FRITZ HARTNAGEL

———

Alexandra Lehmann

Chapter titles are excerpted from Sophie Scholl's letters.
All translations from German are by the author;
Sample Chapters translated by Heinz Tophinke.

Excerpts from the letters of Sophie Scholl and Fritz Hartnagel are translated by the author from Sophie Scholl, Fritz Hartnagel, *Damit wir uns nicht verlieren. Briefwechsel 1937-1943.* © S. Fischer Verlag GmbH, Frankfurt am Main, 2005. Used by permission.

The title is from a prayer poem written by Dietrich Bonhoeffer, *Gott, Zu Dir Rufe Ich*

ISBN: 0997826118
ISBN 13: 9780997826111
Library of Congress Control Number: 2016911631
Published by L&L Media
Third Printing/Kapitel Auf Deutsch
Printed in U.S.A.

Book's website and blog designed and maintained by Swikee

Kindle e-book and print book available at amazon.com, Nielsen BookNet Web and IndieBound.org
Signed print book available at www.alexandralehmann.com
See compendium including historical context and relevance at alexandralehmann.com/blog
Engage on https://www.facebook.com/SophieSchollFritzHartnagel/

Cover design: David Drummond, Salamander Hill

For my mother

DONETS RIVER, UKRAINE, JUNE 26, 1942

Yesterday I had to put up with another evening in the
officer's canteen. It is horrifying with the conviction
and cold-bloodedness that my commander speaks
about the slaughter of *all* the Jews in occupied Russia.

—*GERMAN ARMY CAPTAIN FRIEDRICH
HARTNAGEL TO SOPHIE SCHOLL*

MUNICH, JULY 1942

Sabotage!
Sabotage in factories!
Sabotage in rallies and meetings!
Sabotage propaganda posters!
Sabotage wherever you can!
Everyone is in the position of helping
to destroy this government.

—*LEAFLET III, CO-WRITTEN, PRODUCED, AND
DISTRIBUTED BY SOPHIE SCHOLL AND THE
WHITE ROSE (LATER THE GERMAN RESISTANCE)*

AND YE SHALL KNOW THE TRUTH, AND THE TRUTH SHALL MAKE YOU FREE.

-JOHN 8:32

Shed the veil of indifference!

———

MUNICH, FEBRUARY 18, 1943

SOPHIE LOOKED UP AT THE clock looming over the main foyer. 10:53 a.m. She had two minutes to meet her brother downstairs. Moving quickly, she covered the university's floors with leaflets, careful to be quiet. Setting a few stacks on the interior balcony's ledge, she glanced at her favorite line—*"Shed the veil of indifference!"*—and pushed them over. Sheets of paper fluttered down into the atrium like white birds, drifting over the statues of Bavaria's King Ludwig and Prince Leopold.

February's morning sun streamed through the glass cupola, proving that spring was possible after the fierce winter. Sophie paused for a moment to give thanks to victory over silence. She had never given up her dream to study in Munich at one of the oldest and most prestigious universities in Europe. Classical architecture graced the elegant city and enhanced its reputation. The Nazis had tried everything in their power to stop women from studying and now she was risking it all.

They were fighting to help the Jews and all the others. The German men sent to slaughter. They were fighting for freedom. A warm wave swept through her, and for one brief moment she knew that they had succeeded. She thought about her boyfriend, Fritz, badly wounded in occupied Poland. He had barely survived Stalingrad. Only two men remained from his company. She was fighting for him too.

CHAPTER 1

Anyone who wants to be an artist

———

ULM, SOUTHERN GERMANY, 1936

AN OAK TREE BRISTLED IN the summer breeze. Sophie studied the stolen razor blade from her brother's shaving kit. Ten-year-old girls played and laughed in the sunlit meadow, filled with cornflowers and daisies poking through the tall grass. Sophie clapped her hands to get their attention. Unlike the younger girls who kept their long blond hair wrapped tightly in braids, Sophie Scholl, at 15, wore her dark brown hair cut short in a bob. She had seen this style in magazines and asked her older sister to cut it. Modern women wore their hair like this. She liked the way one piece dangled over her eyes. With an athletic build, she didn't mind if she sometimes even appeared like a boy.

"*Kommt hier her*, come here," Sophie shouted. They ran to her immediately because obedience was a sacred German virtue.

"*Blutgemeinschaft!* We are a community joined together by blood!"

She flashed the silver blade. A ray of sun picked it up and reflected back into the bright sky. The girls looked around nervously as they stood to attention in their uniform of brown skirts, white shirts, and black ties.

One by one Sophie took their thumbs, cutting skin. She continued to lecture.

"We must keep our bloodlines pure. Everything that the Führer wants for us begins with the protection of our superior race."

Petra started crying, setting off a reaction. Disappointed by their weakness, Sophie ordered them to sit down, cross-legged in a circle. She began to sing a popular folk song from the League of German Girls' handbook, raising her hands up in the air, signaling them to join her.

It worked. A melody rose up into the sky. The girls' voices sounded like angels heralding in a supernatural power. Its simple tune and lyrics calmed them. They looked up at their leader in awe. This encouraged Sophie. Her intelligent eyes grew wide with enthusiasm. She was going to instill in these girls the German traits that were listed in the Nazi training booklet. Someday they would be grateful to her for it. *Toughness. Responsibility. Comradeship. Physical fitness. What doesn't kill you makes you stronger.*

With her troop following behind in rows of four, waving the black flag with white lightning bolts, Sophie began the march back into town. Despite what Sophie's father said about the Nazi sickness sweeping through the country, and even her older brother's secret defection from the Hitler Youth, Sophie supported the New Germany. It hadn't been easy moving to the city two years ago. The other girls liked her. She was a natural leader.

With long hands, Fritz Hartnagel poured his beer into the tall glass, tilting it to the side to avoid too much foam. He wondered at the host's choice of music. Its rhythmic cadence of drums, brazen trumpet and singer's raspy voice was so different than the music they knew. The Minister of Propaganda—the little man with the tin voice and limp—just banned American Jazz. They could get in a lot of trouble for such a subversive act. Suspension from school, work or even jail. But there was no stopping it now, the partygoers twisted and turned, enjoying the new improvised way of dancing. Still, Fritz wasn't leaving. Judging by the already elevated mood, it was going to be a memorable party.

He took another sip of beer and leaned his lanky frame up against the living room wall. He was a handsome young man. Dark features of brown hair and eyes were also congruent with Southern German traits and his physical attributes—height, sinewy thinness, natural upright posture—fit well with his person. The even expression on his face indicated here was a man with few inner struggles. He hummed the song's catchy tune, admiring its lyrics: "Dancin' into heaven with you, it's like dancin' into heaven with you."

Fritz turned his attention to the center of the room. He recognized one of these pretty girls. She smiled, swiveling her hands to the left and right. What a modern way of dancing, he thought, and not sure he liked it, he waited until she moved off of the makeshift dance floor.

"Fritz. Fritz Hartnagel," he reached out his hand to her, addressing her formally. "Do you remember me?"

His heart pounded harder than when he concentrated hitting the bull's eye in target practice.

Sophie wiped her brow. Large, expressive eyes defined most of her face. A trusting smile welcomed his question.

"Sophie Scholl." She laughed, taking his hand at once, returning his firm grip.

He reddened. Was he being too rigid? Fritz was instantly relieved that he wasn't in his cadet's uniform. They were, after all, at a Saturday night house party in their hometown. He straightened himself out, allowing his tallness to tower over his peers. Sophie stared back at him.

"Yes, Fritz. I remember you."

Sophie scrutinized his kind face.

"Please use *du* with me, I am only sixteen."

She laughed again. Her voice didn't match the girl who had been dancing. He hadn't learned anything at the academy about handling emotions like this.

Sophie rolled her eyes up at the ceiling, avoiding his. When their brown eyes met, she said, "You and my little brother Werner used to be in the Ancient Free Masons." They were both in Germany's oldest youth fraternity until the Nazis banned it.

With the waxing of the summer moon, cheers of *Prost* accompanied the sound of clanking beer glasses. More and more smoke filled the room and laughter competed with the illegal music which had started up again. Fritz threw his head back and chuckled. Although they continued using the formal form of "you" with one another, they spoke in Schwabian dialect.

"Please. Use the familiar form with me. I am only twenty," he joked, smiling back at her.

Sophie raised an eyebrow. Four years her senior seemed a lot. She tucked her bobbed hair behind her ear and moved her long bangs to the side so that she could look at him more clearly. Open windows revealed the universe of stars. Their host, Anneli, couldn't help looking at them through the crowd. She covered her mouth in awe and nudged their friend Lisa. Sophie was talking to Fritz Hartnagel, the handsome, dark-haired cadet who attended the Potsdam Military Academy way up north, one of the most elite schools in all of Germany.

"Put on a waltz! Hurry up! Save them," Lisa admonished Anneli and together they rifled through her father's record collection. Finding Strauss, Anneli put the black shiny disc onto the record player. It worked. This time couples flocked to the middle of the living room.

Fritz lifted his arm for Sophie's hand and led her out onto the floor. They turned in the smallest of circles. One-two-three, one-two-three.

Just for a moment Sophie lost her feelings of separateness. Fritz's walls began to crumble.

"Would you like to take a hike with me on Sunday afternoon?" he asked.

Sophie gazed up at him as if he had just asked her something in Russian and then she nodded yes.

Fritz sped up to Olgastrasse, swerving into a parking spot by the Scholl family's apartment building at Münsterplatz. Hearing footsteps on the creaky wooden steps, Sophie threw open the front door of their apartment.

"I can come," she burst out, forgetting to first say hello. "But my father says I have to bring Werner with us."

Fritz held back the impulse of kissing Sophie hello on both cheeks. Instead he bowed his head and cursed the stiff gesture. She was getting the wrong impression of him. Soldiers, he learned repeatedly at Potsdam, had to hide their feelings like the stoic silence of trees.

Blond-haired Werner bolted out of the kitchen and stretched out his hand to Fritz. Werner couldn't wait to ride in a new car. Germany was becoming prosperous again, and even the Hartnagels had a *Wanderer*.

Careening into the mountains, Sophie rolled down the window and stuck her head out, letting the air rush over her. When Fritz pulled over, they hiked into the fields towards the river. Together they admired the flowing Danube, swelling from melting snow on the Alps. Surrounded by a bluish-grey chain of white-capped mountains, the river's brilliant sparkle mirrored the congeniality of friendship. As July turned into August, the circle of friends grew, sometimes Sophie's sisters Elisabeth and Inge, or brothers Hans and Werner joined them.

Although Elisabeth was a year older than Sophie, she didn't try as much to impress others. She was tall and thin and wore her hair in two long brown braids. Just being was fine with her. Some of their friends mistook this quietness as plainness, but Fritz didn't doubt that she too had a world of thoughts going on in her intelligent mind. He liked the balance she provided. Inge, the oldest sister, was outspoken too, but nothing compared to Sophie. Together they put up with their youngest sister's outbursts or impulsive acts. One morning she even jumped from the highest tree limb into the river.

As summer finally gave up and turned into mid-September, Sophie and Fritz took their last walk. Fritz was leaving for Potsdam in a few hours. As usual, hiking loosened their thoughts. Summer was finally letting go and soon they would have to say good-bye. The Ulm forest still smelled sweetly of fir needles from the hundreds of sky-high skinny pine. This was their kingdom, as all the greatest German poets and philosophers had affirmed to them. Sophie stopped their silent, steady cadence in the middle of the trail. She had to tell Fritz what was on her mind. Here alone in the middle of the woods, she could tell him without the fear of anyone listening. When had this fear become so pervasive? Since when did she have to be so careful?

"Fritz," Sophie paused. He stayed quiet until she was ready to speak again. She had to tell him about how her older brother changed his mind about the National Socialists after attending a Hitler Youth rally in Nuremberg. They demoted Hans from group leader because of his refusal to carry their flag. Hans insisted on his own flag and didn't want to carry the same one as everyone else. They punished him by taking away his duties. Was she supposed to step down too? What about all this propaganda about Germans being a superior race? Could any of that be true, anyway?

Sophie knew that her father always thought the same way about the Nazis as Hans did now. Robert Scholl listened to his illegal radio station in secret. Their father hated everything that the New Germany stood for. All that was left of him over the last year were wisps of cigar smoke coming from behind his closed office door. The Nazis were an unnegotiable subject.

Fritz took her hand and together they sat down on a fallen tree lying across the trail. He turned to face her, reading her mind.

"I don't know about all of this, Sophie..." He trailed off and stroked her hand as he struggled with the right words. He had chosen to become a career officer because he wanted to fly planes. Plain and simple.

She put her face in her hands. He continued.

"Soon I'll be graduating as an officer—sworn to defend our country." For two years now the Prussian officer oath to God and country had been replaced with a personal oath of loyalty to the Führer. Fritz didn't tell her that he would promise unconditional obedience, swearing both to God and Hitler.

For a few moments neither of them spoke. They looked up through the trees and admired the serenity offered by the woods, changing now from multitudes of green to shades of brown. She turned to him and smiled for the first time. Sophie thought about what she wanted to do when school finished.

"I don't have a sense of a vocation yet, but anyone who wants to be an artist must become a human being first and foremost. From the bottom up. I'm going to try and work on myself," she said, wondering how she could become an artist in a place that disallowed her to speak freely.

Fritz could never lead his men to safety if they were in battle and he questioned his convictions. Military men were not supposed to get involved in politics. His duty would be to his men, although the new oath worried him.

Because words couldn't define their situation any further, he took her into his arms playfully. She was much more herself when she was laughing. But these were strange times and neither of them could fully understand the hatred taking over Ulm. Offering his hand, Fritz helped Sophie up off the fallen tree, and together they started walking again for the last time that summer. A yellow leaf broke free and drifted down lazily over the worn and broken path.

POTSDAM, OCTOBER 1937

Fritz gazed out of the classroom window at the sky as if his life depended on it. Soon he would be a pilot. Bronze statues of Friedrich and Wilhelm, I and II, flanked a graveled pathway that led up to the Academy's grand classical entrance. Built during the reign of the King of Prussia MDCCCLXXIII. Troops marched past the classroom. *Eins. Zwei. Drei.* Hup. Eyes to the right. Eyes to the left. He heaved a sigh of relief and opened his book on military tactics. In an attempt to focus himself, Fritz readjusted his grey uniform and bumped his long legs on the bottom of his desk. Being a student of one of the most decorated generals of the Great War, Erwin Rommel, would give him every advantage should he ever need it.

"Here," Field Marshal Rommel announced and traced a line on a map of Europe with a pointer. "This sophisticated maneuver of Army A forms a successful offensive attack from the east."

Rommel finished every class with the same mantra. "Remember," he admonished them. "It is not the strength of the army that matters but the brain."

Fritz's friend and classmate, Otto, was nodding off when Rommel came up from behind him and slapped him on the back with the pointer. Otto barely grimaced. Another Prussian military philosophy relentlessly drilled into them. *You shall know obedience in order to later be able to command.*

When the bell finally sounded, Fritz headed for the pool. Dark blue tiles reminded him of his favorite river at home in Ulm. Thoughts about Sophie never completely stopped. He didn't like how over time they had become almost physically painful. He missed her way of speaking and how she questioned most things. The memory of soaking in the sun after swimming in the Danube while she painted or drew sustained him in the world he found himself in now, devoid of her kind of artistic expression.

Diving into the pool, he let the water embrace him and in the weightlessness he finally felt free. Into his fifth lap, his mind turned again to the rumors going around about Adolf Hitler and the Nazis. The hysteria was overcoming everything, sweeping through Germany like a sickness. As he glided in the smooth water, he lifted his face and drew another breath, but his political worries followed him. The recent ill-fated military revolution of 1934 failed to stop Hitler.

As Fritz swam effortlessly through the pool, he thought how enough cadets and officers supported the Führer and believed Hitler could make the promise of Germany come true again.

Approaching the wall, he did a flip turn and pushed out against it with strength. He didn't really like to think about all of this. Fritz substituted his worries with the inner command—pull—and the water obliged, soothing him.

With his dark hair slicked back and wet, he met his friends again in the mess hall where oil portraits of the great German Field Marshals in dress uniform—von Zeiten, Seydlitz, Schwerin, and Winterfeld—surrounded long rectangular tables. Along with the clanking of white ceramic plates, pewter pitchers of water and utensils, the cadets swapped stories about women. Fritz kept his mouth shut. He had vowed himself to secrecy. Gentlemen did not exchange such vital information. Inevitably, the subject turned to the National Socialists' recent attack on the Catholic Church.

"I heard the Nazis just put nine hundred priests into one of those camps," Cadet Otto von Fritsch announced, speaking too loudly. A hush enveloped the long table. Spontaneously, they all looked over their shoulders to see if anyone had heard him. Fritz, in a desperate attempt to help his friend, changed the topic to the next fencing match.

From then on, they kept their opinions to themselves.

CHAPTER 2

It is not this or that, it is everything

———

ULM, NOVEMBER 1937

SOPHIE'S MOTHER, MAGDALENA, KNEW WHAT to do. She hurried down the hallway into her son's room. The voices in the living room grew louder and louder. She grabbed a basket and started tossing books into it. Thomas Mann. Heinrich Heine. Georges Bernanos. George Bernard Shaw. Ernest Hemingway. She trembled. This was her fault. All of her children were sneaking around with these books and she hadn't stopped it. This household was last on their search list, and in this apartment they would smell treason.

Magdalena remembered what she had read in the paper. *Agents will be inspecting houses at random.* She laughed when she read what was considered subversive: reading books written by the Reich's enemies, belonging to an unsanctioned organization, listening to an illegal radio station, traveling to a foreign country without permission.

"Why isn't a photograph of the Führer hanging on the wall?" The younger man asked, pointing to the vacant space above the fireplace. She didn't answer. They moved quickly into Hans' bedroom.

Magdalena spoke without thinking, "My eldest son isn't here."

She stood in front of Hans' empty desk, crossing her arms across her chest. "You should know. He's in Stuttgart; he's been called up into the cavalry regiment there."

Pushing her to the side, they started pulling out drawers and dumping them out onto the floor. She closed her eyes and prayed. *Please don't let her husband hear them.* He was downstairs in his office, working as usual. God knows what would happen if he found out what they were doing. He would lose his temper. Her husband's open disdain for the National Socialists worried her. She admired the way he encouraged their children to think for themselves, but she heard rumors of what happened to those who protested against the Party. Robert wasn't being careful enough. It was every family for itself.

Magdalena watched the Gestapo tearing her son's room apart. She knew that the Hitler Youth demoted Hans. It hadn't concerned her because he seemed more pleased about it than disappointed. He hated how their leader stripped all individuality. He had not even been able to carry his own flag at the rally. Hans couldn't stand not being able to have his own opinions. She suspected that he joined another club with his new friend Ernst, but that too hadn't concerned her. There were new laws against belonging to a non-Party organization. She cursed herself for being negligent. Now the police were searching their home for evidence to arrest a nineteen-year-old boy.

She needed to pray for these people. Magdalena raised her high cheek bones. Her hair fell out of a bun. She was still beautiful when she was angry. She was the mother of a very unusual boy, and Hans needed special protection. All of her children were a part of her daily prayers, but her oldest gave her the most concern. He had such a need to prove himself. She sometimes wondered if it was because he was slightly ashamed of people always admiring his appearance. Hans wanted to be acknowledged for something other than that.

"I got it," one of them shouted loudly, waving a gray and red notebook in the air. They had found what they needed in Hans' overflowing shelves. On its cover, someone had drawn a crest of two swords, a dove, and a white flower.

"It is all in here," the agent flipped the pages of the notebook, reading the names of secret club members by their nicknames and duties. It was enough evidence to arrest Hans Scholl.

Magdalena found her four other children hiding in the kitchen.

"What's going to happen to us?" Inge begged her mother for an answer. Magdalena hid her fear and gathered her children around her. She stroked Werner's hair. Inge, tall and broad shouldered, helped her mother with her siblings. This time, however, Inge was just as scared as her younger sisters and Werner.

"I don't know what is going to happen," Magdalene spoke so softly that they could barely hear her. Instinctively they gathered closer. She fought back tears. She never lied to her children and she wouldn't start now.

The secret police moved to the indoor porch and, now having also discovered Hans' diary, sat on the swing and began to read from it out loud.

"Listen to this garbage," the larger man boasted as the swing buckled from too much weight. He began to read out loud, feigning an affected tone: "Only now am I fully alive to my father's desire, which he himself possessed and passed on to me, to become something great for the sake of mankind."

Elisabeth and Sophie exchanged glances, confirming admiration for their brother. Elisabeth could no longer stand it. Breaking loose from her mother's protection and without thinking, she ran out of the apartment with the door slamming behind her.

"Come back," Magdalena screamed and covered her mouth in horror. Inge and Sophie cowered by the stove. Fifteen-year-old Werner stood up, protecting his sisters with his face contorted in anger and fear. Magdalena positioned herself in front of her children and spread out her arms.

She started shouting, "They have done nothing! For God's sake, they are only reading books. They're just children! Leave them alone!"

Picking Werner up by his collar, the older one pushed the boy down the stairs. It was too late for Magdalena to yell for her husband. Stunned, she could no longer even speak. She watched from the window as they forced Inge, Sophie, and Werner into the back of an open truck. A cold November wind brought an unforgiving winter evening. A light snow covered the deserted sidewalk.

Sophie's teeth chattered. She inched closer to her sister and brother to try and keep warm. Werner hadn't spoken since being pushed down the stairs. He shivered from cold and fear. For over a year he attended the illegal meetings with Hans and his friend Ernst. Would he be sent to prison?

Suddenly the truck stopped.

"Get out of here! *Geh!* Go!" The driver screamed. Sophie's cropped hair had confused him. She wasn't a boy. She was just a girl and too young to be hauled in for questioning. Sophie looked back at her terrified brother and her older sister. She wanted to stay with them. Her heart beating with rage, Sophie turned and started running as fast as she could. Her father would know what to do. She had to go and find him.

Bursting through the front door, Sophie found her parents comforting Elisabeth in the kitchen. She found refuge in a church, escaping capture. Sophie's lips turned blue from the cold. Still filled with fear, she started yelling.

"What about Inge and Werner? Where did they take them? How will we get news to Hans that they're coming after him?"

Alarmed at her daughter's state, Magdalena drew Sophie a bath. Robert, quiet during his wife's and daughters' accounts, finally spoke. "If Hitler's henchmen touch a hair on my children's heads, I will go to Berlin and beat them senseless."

He stormed out of the room.

The truth struck Sophie with so much intensity that it forced her to sit back down. Her father had been right all along. Germany was in the hands of a madman. She shut the bathroom door and ran the hot water, sinking into the tub. As she thawed, the past unraveled before her. She had once believed all of it, even the nonsense about a master race.

And now? What was going to happen to them? She tried to scrub the shame off with a wash cloth. She immersed all the way under the cloudy water, trying to get rid of the feeling. Werner and Inge returned after a week at Gestapo headquarters in Stuttgart. Werner stared out of dull eyes. Inge woke up in the middle of the night, screaming. From that day forward everything inside of the Scholl household changed back to the way it was before Hitler came into power. They were one family again.

Sophie winked at Lisa.

"We are going to have some fun! Don't worry," she assured her best friend. Sophie needed some fun. That summer the Nazis had also declared Paula Modersohn Becker's work as degenerate. She and Fritz had admired her original colors and innovative portraits of children once up north at the artists' colony. She and Lisa were going to hitch hike to the Prince Heinz barracks, where Fritz was now stationed since graduation.

"What now?" Lisa asked as the last driver let them out at Augsburg's train station. Sophie pressed a coin into her best friend's palm and pointed to the phone booth.

"Call Fritz," she suggested and smiled. Without hesitation, Lisa dialed the barracks. Her friend wanted an adventure and she was not about to let her down. Clearing her throat, she pulled her long skirt up over her calf and laughed.

"Yes," she said softly. "Is Officer Ha-ha," she stumbled on purpose. "..ha-hart-nagel there?"

Sophie burst out laughing. Within minutes, Fritz drove up in a jeep. He said nothing, not even asking them to get in.

"Do you know what kind of trouble you could have had on the Autobahn?" he asked sternly. Fritz furrowed his brow. "Where do you intend on sleeping?"

Sophie hadn't said anything either, sensing his anger. Finally, she spoke.

"But your reputation will only increase, Officer Ha-ha-hartnagel," Sophie could not help but continuing the joke. "You not only will have one girl in your room, but two."

Lisa kept her mouth shut. Fritz started to give them instructions on sneaking past the guards.

"Do what I tell you, Sophie Scholl, for once," he said, his voice starting to break as the situation took on more levity.

He was having trouble not looking at her. With its walled fortress, identical square buildings made out of hand cut limestone, the Prinz Heinz barracks was a perfectly preserved medieval military installation. Lisa and Sophie ducked down in the jeep and waited for Fritz as he worked on getting past the guards. They held on tightly to one another's hands to keep themselves from giggling. He was her moral compass. She often admired how dedicated and loyal he felt towards his men. Now by seeing this quirky side of him, Sophie's heart swelled with the recognition of his humanness. He was actually capable of deceit. Fritz gave them the signal and they ran down the back corridor and tumbled into his room. An engraved brass plate hung outside of his door, "First Lieutenant Friedrich Hartnagel, German Air Force."

Sophie immediately started to read his bookshelves. She admired the bust of Friedrich Nietzsche peering out of its overflowing but neatly organized library. Gently she pulled out the volume of poems by Manfred Hausmann she had sent to him. He had dog-eared some of its pages. She read on. *I think of you even in my sleep. They call it a dream.*

A loud knock came at the door. Fritz entered the room. With the comic mood gone, he was stern again Sophie wondered if he was going to click his heels. Those damn Prussians, she thought and bit her tongue.

"Good night, Sophie and Lisa," he bid them good-night and promised money for a train ride back to Ulm in the morning. Before vanishing, he quickly took Sophie's hand and kissed it. Lisa's eyes grew wide with amazement. He really had been trained at Potsdam.

This gesture did not intimidate Sophie as much as her desire did.

BAD CANNSTATT, DECEMBER 1937

Bad Cannstatt's boundless meadows and carriage trails could be reached from Ulm in two hours by train. The German Army enlisted Hans for the cavalry because Scholl knew the language that horses spoke and understood their power and edginess. In Hans' presence the giant animals nickered and relaxed their tenseness. They trotted, cantered, and galloped together in perfect unison.

Squadron Nineteen outside of Stuttgart was not infested with Nazi ideology, and Hans' superior, Riding Master Scupin, concentrated solely on equestrian military practices. He needed his soldiers to be excellent marksmen and riders. He knew that many of his men were committing "crimes" and he didn't care. What mattered to him was that Scholl could settle down his horse after a thundering ride and could concentrate well enough to hit his target.

Scupin tried to hide his nervousness around Hans. This young man possessed an enigmatic power. He was the men's natural leader and the other men respected his ability to saddle, cinch, and tighten the horse's girth in a few seconds time. It was a wonder to watch Scholl and his horse. But this young man was always brooding, thinking about something. His dark coloring and features emanated an intensity that made the Riding Master uneasy. When Private Scholl wore his jodhpurs, the young man reminded Scupin of a prince belonging to the ancient traditions of Prussian nobility.

One early December morning Hans was already in the barn shoveling hay when a shadow appeared on the wooden stall. Without saying a word, the stranger emerged, putting his hand out to a horse's nose so that it could sniff him. Then he stroked the chestnut coat which had taken on a deep shine. The horse's eyes glittered.

"Fine creatures, eh?" The man in a tan trench and fedora continued, sneering with a crooked nose. "They know loyalty."

Hans snorted.

"What price will you have to pay for forgetting yours?" he asked without the expectation of an answer.

The horse pricked his ears and studied Hans, leaning up against a pitchfork. Sensing the growing animosity between the two men and noise coming from the outside, he started to retreat backwards. Hans could hear the commotion, too. It was getting louder. The Gestapo was arresting soldiers. His father had warned him that they would be coming since the raid on their home and took Inge and Werner away for questioning.

Hans was not prepared for the anger that rose up inside of him. For a brief moment he thought of driving a pitchfork into the sneering man's leg. Instead he turned, and faced him squarely. The agent grabbed his arm and led Hans out of the barn and into the truck full of soldiers charged with the same crimes:

Belonging to a subversive organization.
Listening to an illegal radio station.
Reading banned literature.
Traveling to a foreign country without permission.

Hans offered no resistance but thrust out his shoulders and grinned to his friends as he got into the truck. This reassured them. They knew that Hans had also attended the Nuremberg Rally in 1935 and had come back opposed to the Party. They also knew that they were not guilty of anything. Every man on the way to prison understood that this arrest was a badge of honor.

ULM, NOVEMBER 1938

The streets were filled with men carrying lit torches and sledge-hammers. Sophie saw a man from church with a rifle. She hurried through to Münsterplatz where a crowd began to gather, singing folk songs, waiting for Party Leader Eugen Maier to make a speech. When he reached the podium, a hush fell over the angry crowd. Herr Maier cleared his throat and started yelling into the megaphone. The gigantic Gothic Protestant Cathedral, Der Münster, loomed in the background. People came from all over the country to see the highest church spire in the world and testament to the Reformation.

"It's been three years since the Nuremberg Laws and now we are required to use force." Maier waved his fist. "We will Aryanize this city!"

The men in the crowd looked on hungrily, waiting for instructions. Maier's speech gathered momentum as it was met with cheers and clapping. He began to unleash his orders.

"Destroy all Jewish shops and close them down! By order of the Minister of Propaganda, Dr. Goebbels! Only Germans are allowed to make money in Germany! Whatever is Jewish property belongs to us."

Sophie froze in fear and started to retreat from the crowd as it chanted angrily and passed buckets of white paint and brushes as big as brooms.

Closed in by the growing crowd, Sophie thought of the Jewish families living in their apartment building. Would they set it on fire? Pushing her way through, she ran all the way home. She had to warn her parents.

Sophie rushed to her room, throwing clothes into a small suitcase.

"We have to leave. Now. They are coming after us. Jews live in this building."

Sophie ran into the living room where the family gathered. Completely silent and motionless, Inge, Elisabeth, and Werner waited for their father to tell them what to do. Sophie's mother tried to console them.

"They are going to set our house on fire!" Sophie was yelling now. Magdalena assured her that they were safe. She was upsetting her sisters and brother.

"And the Einsteins? The Guggenheimers? The Barths? What will happen to them?" Sophie insisted, naming the Jewish families and begging her mother for an answer.

"Your father is doing the best he can for them. Come, Sophie, and play us something on the piano," Magdalena hugged her daughter tightly.

When Sophie tried to play the way Herr Morgenstern taught her, and couldn't, she slammed the piano shut and went to hide in her room with Elisabeth.

Sounds of shattering glass and angry chanting came closer and closer until finally she could hear the crowd on Adolf Hitler Ring, surrounding their apartment building. Her father locked all the doors and drew the curtains shut. He forbade them to look out of the windows and ordered his wife to turn off the lights.

Sophie finally fell asleep in her and Elisabeth's room. Sometime during the night the fire trucks woke her and she heard voices in the kitchen. She strained to hear whom they belonged to.

"There's no more time," she heard her father say in a measured tone. "You have to leave Germany, now, while you still can."

It was Herr Einstein from downstairs. Sophie liked the way he always said hello. He pleaded. His voice broke and then he started sobbing.

"No," her father insisted now in a voice she had feared as a child. "You and your family must go. It makes no sense to think about your business or home now. Germany is not safe for anyone, not even us. We'll try and make it through as best we can. This country will never be the same again."

Sophie couldn't stand it. She put a pillow over her head and fell back to sleep. When she woke in the morning, her sister Elisabeth was the only one still left in the house. The two girls ventured slowly outside to see what had happened.

A warm autumn sun contradicted the horror of what they were seeing. Crowds had plundered Herr Fränkel's tobacco shop where Sophie's father bought his favorite cigars. Sophie stopped to look at the shattered empty cases. The dress shop on Hirschstrasse too had been rampaged, its carved glass doors with gold lettering painted shut with the Party's strange symbol.

The police had set fire to the synagogue on Weinhofplatz. Several townspeople stood outside the charred building. Frau Schultz, their father's client, stood among the speechless crowd. Many of them walked around in circles, shaking their heads, holding their hands to their mouths.

Frau Schultz saw it happen. Still in shock, she couldn't help telling the young girls. Maybe she shouldn't have. They were too young to know about this type of violence. The police took fifty Jews out of their homes and ordered them into the empty fountain in front of the synagogue. They set it on fire. The police beat them. The Rabbi, Dr. Cohen, lay in the hospital, barely alive. Someone ripped the beard off his face.

Sophie and Elisabeth turned to go. They walked for a long time without speaking. It was all too horrible to completely comprehend. In silence both girls were struggling to make sense of the beatings and the burned synagogue. Their witness would become a deeply buried psychic wound.

"Everything feels so strange," Sophie finally broke the silence. "As if there has just been some kind of war here and no one knows who the victor is. Everyone has gone into hiding."

Elisabeth, who deferred to her sister, nodded her head in agreement.

Fear permeated the air along with its opposite energy, pride. A few more red banners with black swastikas hung from a row of Tudor-styled houses near the train station. Burnt red geraniums hung on bravely, not ready to capitulate to winter. The state newspaper reported that the people in Ulm watched a bus full of Jews leave for a camp in Munich. Reportedly, they smiled as they pulled away, waving good-bye. Magdalena wondered out loud if that was true. Was the newspaper printing any truth at all? Party Leader Maier was also quoted in the *Beobachter*, "The city will be free from the Jewish pest!"

When Sophie and Elisabeth returned home to Adolf Hitler Ring, the entire Barth family was waiting outside. Their youngest daughter, Lotte, sat on top of a suitcase.

Sophie ran up the stairs and burst into her father's office on the second floor without knocking. She asked questions.

"Did you help the Einsteins, Father? Did you? Where is Lotte going?"

Robert scrutinized his daughter's face. He ordered her to calm down. He hated theatrics.

"Yes, I helped the Einsteins with the paperwork that they needed. Lotte is leaving for America, but her mother and father and sister have to stay behind. I don't know what will happen to them now. We couldn't get the whole family the paperwork that they needed."

Then he got up from his desk, shut the door, and switched on the radio, turning the dial to Radio Buromunster, the illegal radio station from Switzerland. He could go to jail for this but her father didn't seem to care.

"Listen with me, Sophie, please," and for the first time since the Party took over Germany, he was asking for her company.

The newscaster spoke in a heavy Swiss accent. Last night had a name—*Reichskristallnacht.* The Nazis destroyed Jewish shops and synagogues. There were reports that hundreds if not thousands of Jews were missing from cities. Father and daughter crouched next to the radio, turned down so low they had to strain to hear it. Sophie listened intently and looked back at her father with desperate eyes.

After that, Sophie went into her father's office regularly after school to listen to the illegal broadcasts. One night in an excitable voice the newscaster reported that the Nazis were burning books throughout universities. Sophie got up and went over to his bookcase where she pulled a copy of Heinrich Heine's poems from the tightly packed shelf. Her father hadn't acquiesced to her mother's request to remove his banned books. This time, she was going to see for herself what was so morally destructive about Heinrich

Heine, one of her mother's favorite Romantic poets. The Nazis had banned and burned his books in the bonfires. Sophie had trouble understanding why such a great poet—so admired and respected by her German teacher before the war—would suddenly fall out of favor in school. There never was any mention of his work at all anymore.

She turned to the back of the precious book and skimmed through Heine's biography. Yes, he was born to a Jewish father, van Geldern. She chuckled, of course, with that name. She called this fact out to her father, who scowled at her.

"Don't be so ignorant," he admonished. Sophie looked down at the book, embarrassed. She kept reading.

She was confused. Sophie knew enough about literature to know that his biography wasn't that important. His political statement was. Heine had once written "those who burn books will soon burn people." She gasped. The book burnings always bothered her and now, making the connection, she understood why. It struck her as premonition.

Horrified, she wanted poetry as a relief from these thoughts. Browsing through his titles and settling back into her father's reading chair, she read "The Return Home."

O, the eyes again,
One time they greeted me so lovingly,
And it is the lips again,
The ones which sweetened my life!
It is the voice again,
The one I once heard so fondly!

Only it is I who is no longer the same,
I am changed, returning home again.
With white, beautiful arms
Firmly and lovingly embraced,
I lie on her heart
With dull senses, numbed and drowned.

Sophie read Heine's poem over and over. It was about soldiers returning home after war. She thought about Fritz. If there was going to be another war, Fritz was going to have to fight in it. For many months they had been writing to one another almost daily. Fritz never mentioned fear, but it wasn't because he had a deep faith. He was trained in Prussian military traditions and once recited the great German poet Friedrich Schiller: *The soldier is the freest of men, the one who looks death straight in the face.* Everything would have to change now. What part of him would remain the same if he had to fight in a war like the last one? And how, she wondered, would he be able to fight for Hitler?

She remembered the time that they sat beside the Iller River and said nothing to one another, experiencing the same patterns of the earth. This was their natural language but now the talk of war overshadowed everything. Now Heine's poem also seemed like a foreshadowing. Sophie wanted to weep but no tears came.

His letters were hidden in a box under her bed where her two sisters couldn't find them. Sometimes when she was at school she looked out the window and daydreamed, remembering the things he had written to her.

"Do you know that I have a feeling that you are hiding things from me? You must not hesitate to tell me everything. I will not laugh."

She wasn't sure she could tell Fritz everything.

"When you look at me with your deep, dark eyes that suddenly become so sad," he wrote to her once, *"they are like an accusation, and even though I know that you are not accusing me, it still becomes urgent to know what you are thinking. I only wish to be able to help you. I know that one can't turn back from events in life, but I have learned as a soldier that a situation is dangerous as long as it is unclear. Therefore, you must tell me. You don't have to conceal anything, this will only lead to heartbreak between us."*

She understood what Fritz meant. But could she tell him what had happened after *Reichskristallnacht*? Could she confess to him that the entire Scholl family was in complete opposition to Hitler's ideas for Germany?

The hours slipped by until she heard her mother calling her to set the table. She put the leather bound volume down slowly, marking her place with a silk ribbon. Sophie sat at her regular place at the dinner table but didn't take part in the usually animated family conversation about politics. Hans pontificated. Inge argued. Elisabeth sided with Hans. Werner interjected. She was impatient for dinner to end so that she could climb back into the armchair and keep reading. In her books, like when she was drawing or playing piano, she could lose herself along with the thoughts that were starting to feel too dangerous.

Magdalena wondered why her daughter was so distracted. Then she remembered. Though he hadn't come over recently, the handsome officer, Fritz Hartnagel, visited the Scholl household enough over the past year for her to notice that the two might be forming something more than friendship. All of those letters that came from Augsburg. Of course her daughter was reading poetry.

"Heinrich Heine was unlucky in love," she mentioned to Sophie as they finished collecting the dinner plates.

"O mother," Sophie answered, exasperated. "Aren't we all?"

Magdalena sighed.

The next day after school Sophie walked to the League of German Girls meeting by herself. They were no longer voluntary. She had to attend at least one a week in order to finish school. Tonight was dedicated to German literature. Scharlo, their leader, started to take suggestions from the girls, sitting cross-legged on the church floor.

"Goethe, Schiller, Mörike, Novalis, Eichendorff." A stream of German Romantic poets' names cascaded into the room. This was not the moment to forget the poet who warned against burning books.

Unable to resist the temptation, Sophie got up, cleared her throat, and recited Heinrich Heine's poem from memory.

Bad weather,
Rain, storm, and snow.
I sit at the window and look out into the darkness.
A single light shimmers and wanders slowly forward,
A mother and her lantern out in the street.
She is buying flour, eggs, and butter

To bake a cake for her little daughter,
Waiting at home lying in an armchair.
Staring sleepily into the light.

The poet's words suspended in the air and then evaporated like soap bubbles. The girls grew still by the tenderness of the rhyme.

Scharlo pointed her bony finger at Sophie and ordered her to sit down.

"German girls don't read Jewish poets!" she screamed in a frightening pitch.

Sophie looked around the room at the girls who used to be her friends. Then she said, "Whoever doesn't know Heinrich Heine's poetry, doesn't know German literature."

They looked back at Sophie in bewilderment. A smile blessed her face and dark eyes shone with hope. Instead of sitting back down, she left the meeting without saying another word.

The next day Sophie hurried down the dimly lit street, slipping twice on dark wet cobblestones. Herr Morgenstern would be insulted if she was late. He would think that she didn't care enough about her weekly lesson. She could see him lift his kind eyes up from the weight of heavy gray eyebrows and shake his head in disapproval. She had practiced all week and looked forward to playing on his prize piano. This hour had become her only refuge. She could envision the ivory keys now, waiting, bright and ready, always in tune.

She hoped for some Bach. Herr Morgenstern spent most of his time in the music room, where sweeping silk curtains kept in the heat and his wife tended to long-stemmed pink roses in a blue and white porcelain vase. A white cat slept curled up on a settee. A marble bust of a long haired and frenetic Beethoven presided over all of their lessons. Herr Morgenstern's father had once been a famous concert pianist. Sophie felt his ghost presiding over their lessons.

"Come in child, you're late," he said, with his back towards her, hunched over from a lifetime of playing his instrument.

Sophie sat down next to him on the wooden piano bench. He requested some Bach. He was a master, a true artist and he could judge whether or not she belonged to the kingdom that he did and his father before him. She stumbled as she played, and stopped, bowing her head in shame. She interpreted the notes too rigidly. Herr Morgenstern gently corrected her. He put his soft hand over hers and guided her fingers over the keys.

"It is sometimes difficult to find harmony, my dear," he told her in a soft voice. "You will have to find the clarity within yourself."

She understood. She wanted to tell him that she could feel it like cool, clear, sparkling water. Music was his religion and her teacher had a reputation for once being one of the finest pianists in all of Ulm.

"Now. Beethoven, please," Herr Morgenstern flipped the lesson's pages to a sonata. He did not like to waste time on conversation. For him the true exchange between two people existed in the ability to interpret and appreciate music. When the hour ended, Sophie glowed with knowledge that music unleashed a special strength. She wanted to go home and write about it, but when she looked for a metaphor, she could not find it. Music itself could provide its best expression.

ULM, FEBRUARY 1939

Sophie jumped into Fritz's car and rubbed her thighs in a futile attempt to warm them. Fritz shut the car door behind her. He was visiting from Thuringen, where he was getting his driving instructor's license. They had the whole day together for themselves. Sophie and Fritz were glad. They had something important to discuss with one another. They wrote to each other almost daily. Something unnamable was growing between them that required clarification. The crisp air reflected that desire. Despite the freezing temperatures, Sophie and Fritz parked the warm car beside the side of the road and started their hike. The snow crunched under their boots. Fritz pointed out the deer tracks, and Sophie watched the cardinal perch in an empty tree.

The frosty air bit at Sophie's face.

"I can't feel my fingers," she complained. Fritz took her hands and rubbed them together with his. She looked up at him and found the courage to begin.

"Fritz, what is it that you want from me? You should tell me, because I don't know myself. I don't know what is right or wrong between us anymore."

He didn't let go of her hands. They looked at one another and didn't move. They were searching for the same answer to the same question.

He began in a voice so low and deliberate she had to strain to hear.

"Sophie, how can I express things that I myself don't understand? I only know that I am moved by something that must be bigger than me. I can't analyze and define it because it is not this or that, it is everything."

He paused for a moment, collecting his feelings. "What do I want from you? Nothing, nothing—only what you want to give to me and what you can give to me. I will treasure it as my most holy."

Passion claimed his normally calm dark eyes. She repeated what he said. *I can't analyze and define it because it is not this or that, it is everything.* Yes, this was the answer that they were both seeking.

They began to walk again. Dark clouds obstructed the sun, creating a grey and barren landscape. Sharp branches of leafless trees pointed into the colorless sky. Fritz was having difficulty continuing.

He turned and faced her directly.

"Sophie, we don't want to demand things from one another, but give them freely. I'm not sure if I can even give you what you want. Sometimes I have terrible insecurities about you. I don't know if I understand your question, even. I don't even know if I can help you sometimes. Can't we just show trust in one another anyway?"

Sophie slipped her hand back into his and nodded in agreement. He found the courage to articulate both their feelings for one another. He was right. They could trust. If there was only one person left in this mad world to trust, it was him. Even her teachers and most of her classmates seemed to have lost themselves in all the propaganda.

At the end of the trail, Sophie and Fritz approached the remnants of an eleventh-century castle where the Kaiser had once lived. Destroyed in the Thirty Years War, all that was left of the vast estate were broken stones and architectural ruins. They found shelter from the angry cold in a nearby café.

Pressing a coin into her hand he asked her to go inside and order something warm to drink. Then, without consciously willing it, he bent over and kissed her. But she didn't kiss him back. As he walked back into the woods to get the car, cursing the cold, he wished that he hadn't.

CHAPTER 3

The battle I wage with myself will be yours too

ULM, SEPTEMBER 1939

THE BELLS ON THE MÜNSTER Church clanged for hours. Germany was at war again. People gathered in the center of town and looked at the news plastered outside the post office. Sophie watched as the older men and women who survived the Great War shook their heads in despair. Young men cheered and hugged one another in the expectation of joining the fight.

School let out early. Sophie walked along the river. She sat down on a park bench newly stenciled *For Aryans Only*. The river flowed quietly southward, oblivious to the news. Sophie noticed the late summer light lingering as if holding back inevitable autumn changes. The last rays of the sun helped her to see what she had refused to see. The truth struck her with urgency.

Fritz was a willing part of Hitler's Army. He was going to have to fight in the *Blitzkrieg*. She took out her pen from her knapsack and began to write. She could always count on writing to clarify the truth, even though she agreed with the Eastern philosopher whose name she had forgotten. Truth couldn't be painted in black or white. It lay in the chasm. *Der Abgrund.*

Dear Fritz, Sophie pressed down hard on the paper against the book on her lap. *You and your men must have plenty to do now. It's unbelievable how a stronger force can willingly hurt a weaker one. I'll never understand it, and I find it terrible.* Without sparing his feelings and knowing that it was hurtful, she challenged him. *And don't dare say it's for the Fatherland.*

When Fritz received Sophie's letter, his first reaction was to crumple it up. Just a few days ago she sent him chocolate and a picture of herself. He was going to have to get used to these abrupt changes in mood. Fritz carefully folded her admonishment and put it in his chest pocket. They were getting to know one another through letters. Until the war was over. It was going to be a short one. What did a school girl know about it? Patting his pocket to see if it was still there, he dressed quickly, grateful that the Germany Army didn't censor officers' mail. He was worried. Why would she risk so much by writing like that? Of course, it was for the Fatherland. The Gestapo could have easily opened her letter. She had to be more careful.

Today was an important day. He had to plan the infrastructure of the central station and assure that the new amplifiers arrived for long distance communications. Fritz wasn't sure if the cables and batteries for continuous transmissions were compatible with foreign electrical currencies. Even though he hadn't yet been commissioned to fly planes, he liked the assignment as a lieutenant of a communications company. He knew that his role was absolutely vital to the success of any military operation. The skies would wait.

At the end of the day, stationed now in the Black Forest, he wrote to her.

Calw, September 13, 1939
My dear Sophie,
You create conflict for me when you ask me for the reason for this bloodletting. Two years ago I could have perhaps given you an answer, when I thought myself mature enough and clear about all these things.

But today I feel like a young boy, at the beginning of his development in these areas. You are the one guilty of bringing this about.

And I am glad about it.

He lifted his pen from the paper and paused. From his office he could hear artillery practice. Tanks and new troop maneuvers were increasing daily. The German Army was mobilizing all over the Black Forest.

Despite this, Fritz continued, *I can't agree with you because I don't have the courage to bear the consequences of such an opinion.*

He imagined that Sophie would call his response cowardly, but he wrote it anyway. How could he question the government he was meant to serve? His life, never mind his profession, would become impossible. If there were war, his death, certain.

Changing the subject, he wrote about the seasons. Their mutual love of nature solidified their connection, and he knew that he could write to her with abandon, use whatever language he could find, and she would be able to see and feel it as he did.

I think back with sad feelings about our past walks through the woods, especially lately since it is autumn now. I imagine how beautiful it must be in our woods and wish that we could walk through them together.

Although so many people hate autumn and see it as the end of the dying year, I find this time of year to be its consummation, its enjoyment, and above all, I love the colors, in their savageness, almost drunk.

Then their melancholy passes over into some other kind of madness called winter.

When he reached the end, he signed it deliberately, almost tearing the page. *Your Fritz.*

Sealing the letter, he remembered their vacation to the North Sea. For some reason, the innkeeper had searched through their belongings and found Sophie's copy of Thomas Mann's *Buddenbrooks.* Why did she take the risk of reading the banned author? That had irritated him. The innkeeper threatened to report them to the police.

He remembered how Sophie said good-bye at the train station. She even disrespected his profession.

"Your business will begin soon now," she had said in a mean tone of voice. "I don't like it. I hope it will all be done with soon."

Her angry words still burned in his ears, but this feeling wasn't stronger than the one they shared at the beach. The memory still felt new. Fritz loved dozing in the warm sun while Sophie collected shells. They walked along the surf together with the sea's rhythms echoing unending conversations. Together they rolled in the soft comfort of warm sand. Disturbed by their passion, the wicker beach cabana fell on top of them. They laughed at the moment broken by their force of gravity. It became a picture in his memory of falling in love. Their problems now could never compete with these memories. He would return to Ulm and visit her soon, and together take long walks in the woods and discuss all of these things in person.

ULM, MAY 1940

Sophie shuddered at the photographs in the newspaper. The German Air Force was destroying whole cities. Fritz was among the second wave of occupying forces in Holland. Everything was wrong. Hitler wasn't going to stop with Austria. Or Czechoslovakia. Poland. Belgium. The Netherlands. Which was worse—that her boyfriend was fighting for Hitler or that her family had to hide what they thought all the time?

Sophie began another letter. Her pen sped across the paper's surface. What came out this time wasn't anger for his profession. When she re-read it, she felt as though someone, something, greater than herself had helped formulate her feelings with compassion.

Ulm, May 16, 1940
Dear Fritz,

Our ideas are so different, I sometimes wonder if it's really so unimportant when it ought to be the basis of any relationship. But all this must be shelved for now.

Because what you and I need now is love, not friendship and companionship. We'll keep things between us that way until we can be by ourselves again.

My dearest wish is that you would survive this war without becoming a product of it.

All of us have standards inside ourselves, but we don't go looking for them often enough. Maybe it's because they're the toughest standards of all.

The enemy within their country was greater than the enemy he was fighting against.

You're all alone in an atmosphere that has nothing in common with the one I would like to win you over to. And at bottom you're already half on my side, and you'll never feel entirely at ease there again. The battle I wage will be yours as well.

She ended the letter with its most important request: *Don't just think of me as I am, though—think of me also as I'd like to be.*

The Scholl family recently moved to a larger apartment in the center of town, inside of the cobblestoned square abutted by the enormous Münster Church. Germany's largest Gothic church held over 20,000 Protestants inside during the Reformation. Sophie had stared up at its massive triangular vaulting, prayed to the central column's Man of Sorrows, and marveled at the tympanon's woodcarving of scenes from Genesis. Now, a giant photograph of the Führer hung next to the Italians' bald and round leader. Banners of red, white, and black flew in the wind alongside Italy's green, white, and red striped flags. Megaphones propped up all over town belted out Hitler's speech, "Together we will fight, shoulder to shoulder, until justice prevails!" Sophie watched in sadness from the window overlooking Münsterplatz and cringed when the crowd chanted "Heil Hitler" over and over in some maddening spell.

Suddenly a warplane screamed overhead followed by a massive explosion. It was louder than anything Sophie had ever heard. It made her head hurt. Crouching down low, she put her head in her hands and then, without thinking, she ran back to the window.

"Never by the window! Sophie!" Magdalena shouted. She couldn't understand her daughter's impulsiveness.

A few days later, Sophie's father registered the family with the nearest bomb shelter and made sure that his wife and children knew the fastest way to the church's cellar. Propaganda intruded on every aspect of their lives. Sometimes it was hard for Sophie to think straight about any of it.

Despite what the Nazis promised, the war was coming closer.

Magdalena brought in the *Feldpost* and studied its postmark.

"It looks like Fritz is in Belgium," Magdalena said, handing her daughter a little package. Sophie waited until her mother left the room to open it.

She took out some tightly wrapped coffee, inhaling its bitter smell. Her mother and father would be so glad to have strong coffee again. But as she read Fritz's letter, the world around her stopped.

Antwerp, May 18, 1940
My dear Sophie,

Pardon that I can't write you much. I have so little time now to write you because we have half an hour before we drive back to Germany, and I want to send something back to you. Hopefully this coffee from Belgium will arrive safely.

Yesterday I had enormous luck, if one can speak of luck and not of Providence. I was with Lieutenant Pfeiffer on a mission to scout out a landing strip in Tournhout. Close to 50 meters before a bridge we got a flat tire. We cursed and complained about it. Then, as a farmer and his equipment drove over the bridge, it suddenly exploded with an incredible blast into the air. The farmer's body landed 10 meters from us, in a meadow. A horrific lump of flesh. There was nothing left of his equipment. The bridge was probably rigged with a mine, meant for us.

The worst thing about all of this was that a few minutes later the farmer's wife came out, looking desperately for her husband.

It was my first experience of the horror of war. Later as I sat at my desk I listened to Mozart. O Sophie. Why can't people just listen to Mozart, why instead do they have to kill and mutilate one another?

The letter slipped from her fingers and it fluttered to the floor. She looked around in panic. Her heart started pounding and her palms began to sweat. Sophie paced back and forth in her room, running her hands through her hair. What could she do? Then she remembered. Like her mother had taught her, she clasped her hands together and closing her eyes thanked God for sparing his life.

Magdalena didn't force her religious beliefs on her children. Since the Hitler Youth, all of them stopped going to church as the Nazi leaders asked. Even since their secret defection from the Party's ideas, she still worshipped alone. Magdalena, in her quiet and un-imposing way, did not question why Sophie asked to come with her this Sunday. As they arrived at the Protestant St. George's Church, one of the newest in Ulm, the polished pine pews were more than half empty.

They sat up front. Magdalena shut her eyes. Sophie leafed through the worn Bible and tried to read the passage listed on the chalkboard, Exodus 17:11-12. It was from the Old Testament. Could Pastor Hofer get in trouble with the Party for choosing it? The organist launched into Bach. The music filled the little building, changing its mood from darkness into light.

"Thank you for coming," Pastor Hofer cleared his throat, unable to hide his disappointment at the few faces looking numbly back at him. Clear blue eyes and full head of hair gave him a youthful appearance, but there was something troubling him. He looked prematurely aged and a deep frown defined an otherwise kind and healthy face.

Sophie looked around at the mostly empty church and then back at him. She thought about Fritz's last letter and about how she had to get better at steeling herself against propaganda. She thought about Hans' recent deployment to France. When Werner would be drafted. About what she would study when she finally got to Munich. About what she would do when the war was over. She wondered if she would ever marry Fritz.

When she finally tuned back in, Pastor Hofer was wrapping up the sermon. Reading scripture had transformed him. With his whole body riveted against the pulpit, he was almost shouting.

"Moses is the mediator of God's law. He was chosen to lead the people out of Egypt to the Promised Land."

This lesson was relevant. Sophie's questions came quickly. Who was Moses now? Who would lead them out of Nazi Germany?

"But the essential point, and what I wish to teach you today, friends, is that when Moses held up his hands in prayer, they prevailed. When he forgot to hold up his hands in prayer, evil won over." Pastor Hofer was teaching them how to resist.

He paused, allowing the congregation to absorb the message. A few people, made uncomfortable by his urgent tone, and perhaps what he was asking of them, walked out of the Church.

"Prayer and petition are essential to the victory over sin and one's enemies." Their Pastor continued. Sophie closed her eyes and thanked Him again for sparing Fritz. She prayed for the Belgian woman who lost her husband.

"While our hands are stretched out and upwards, we are able to conquer our spiritual adversaries. If our hands are heavy, if we restrain prayer before God, internal corruption will win." The message had turned into hope.

Sophie looked to her mother and whispered, "Can we believe a story from the Old Testament?"

Magdalena paused for a moment, and although irritated by her daughter's question, she answered it patiently.

"You should think and answer this for yourself, Sophie. I can tell you a lot about how I feel about religion, but my feelings about these kinds of things are best demonstrated through action."

She minded her tone for a moment and then continued with more patience. At most she should be pleased that her daughter was finally curious about religion.

"Prayer is not something one learns to do overnight, Sophie. One must practice. Be able to ask for help. To receive. To listen. To be grateful. One must also be prepared to doubt, and often the hardest of all, to forgive. These too are necessary forms of prayer."

Magdalena's faith had been tested. During the first war she worked as a Diakonian nurse. She never spoke about it. Sophie had heard how bad it was when soldiers finally got to the field hospitals after the trenches. She knew these memories were the cause of her mother's sometimes faraway sadness.

"Go now, with the peace of God, which surpasses all understanding," Pastor Hofer dismissed them and smiled with his blue eyes lifting upwards.

The sermon was over. They stood up together and Sophie rested her head on her mother's shoulder. Hofer strode confidently down the aisle with his white robe flowing behind him. For the first time since she could remember, Sophie felt calm and capable. Perhaps merely believing in God wasn't enough. She had to pray more. Harder.

Together mother and daughter walked into town to buy some bread with the last of their food coupons. Townspeople were beginning to gather along the city's main streets to watch the parade of the first troops returning home from the Western Front. Fritz wasn't going to be among them and Hans had only just left for France.

Shopkeepers hung Nazi flags from Schillerstrasse next to the Hauptbahnhof all the way into Münsterplatz. Chairs were set up forming rows of bystanders, getting ready for the heroes' homecoming. The League of German Girls stood in the streets holding June's flowers stuffed in baskets. Hitler Youth rolled their drum sticks on tin drums. Even the tobacconists held out cartons of cigarettes.

Over the loudspeakers, Ulm's Party Leader Meier spoke hysterically as though he were broadcasting a horse race. When the train pulled in, spilling over with soldiers, the entire crowd of onlookers started to wave and sing. Grown men were crying. The crowd sang in unison, "Front and Homeland are one, we are one at last, one at last." Sophie shuddered. It was a spectacle worse than a circus.

Magdalena and Sophie stopped to watch the troops greet their loved ones. Many of the soldiers looked perfectly intact with uniforms as fresh as their faces. Some had their arms in slings or legs in casts, and even others seemed to stare with dead eyes. A soldier came up to Sophie, grabbed her and kissed her on both cheeks. His exuberance nearly knocked her off her feet. He smiled so intensely, seeming untouched by the war Fritz had described to her. He disappeared quickly into the crowd.

Fritz wrote often from France. His unit had finally settled on the coast in Wissant, a stone's throw from England. They occupied a medieval castle where he was in charge of setting up communications. They had been on long marches behind the infantry.

Sophie possessed images of war different from ones she was witnessing now. Fritz had given her the words in his letters. *Destruction. Ravaged. Ghastly. Disastrous.* He had seen dead soldiers lying on the road. He wondered if they had been starved by the very army he was serving.

Their stares, Fritz had written, *don't ever disappear from memory.*

There was no honor in this parade. It was a charade. If there were any rules in war, starving prisoners wasn't one of them. When Sophie finally got home, she went to her room and started another letter.

Ulm, June 22, 1940
Dear Fritz,

How long is it since I last wrote to you? Meantime, another of your letters has turned up. However much I always enjoy answering your last letter, I find it very difficult because it's hard to say things in writing that can only be resolved by conversation.

I'm perfectly prepared to believe that you simply argue with me for argument's sake when we get onto ideological and political subjects—the two go hand in hand. It's enjoyable, I appreciate that. Personally, though, I've never argued for argument's sake, as you may secretly believe.

On the contrary, I've always unconsciously made certain allowances for the profession you're tied to, in the hope that you'll weigh these things more carefully and perhaps make concessions here and there.

I can't imagine two people living together when they differ on these questions in their views, or at least in their activities. People shouldn't be ambivalent themselves just because everything else is, yet one constantly meets the view that, because we've been born into a world of contradictions, we must defer to it.

Oddly enough, this thoroughly un-Christian attitude is especially common among self-styled Christians. If it were so, how could one expect fate to make a just cause prevail when so few people don't sacrifice themselves for a just cause?

That doesn't mean I would put myself on the side of those who are single-hearted in the true sense. Scarcely an hour passes without one of my thoughts flying off at a tangent, and very few of my actions correspond to what I consider right.

Since school ended, she had a lot of time to think. She was like most of her friends in the League. They, too, didn't like the Party's new laws but no one ever said anything. She existed only like they did, paralyzed by fear. Writing in her diary and to Fritz was the only time she could be truthful. Slowly she learned to write her true feelings in between the lines. The memory of when they were taken away by the Gestapo never quite left her. She continued writing, letting the pen take control.

> *I'm so often scared of actions that all I want to do is cease to exist or become a grain of earth, or a fragment of bark. But this often overpowering desire is equally bad because it only stems from weariness.*
>
> *Weariness is my principal possession. It keeps me silent when I ought to speak out—when I ought to admit to you what concerns us both.*

Just yesterday she heard that the Party made it mandatory to serve the State for a whole year before she could study at the University of Munich. Her choice was either to teach kindergarten or work at the Nazi women's labor camps. Sophie chose teaching. Children were the closest thing to the truth. How hungry she had become for it.

The next day after school Sophie left for her last piano lesson before having to teach at the Nazi school. She did not want to be late again. Playing the piano had become her sanctuary. When she sat down to play, she could forget the expression of Lotte Barth's face, the story about the Rabbi, the sound of fear in Herr Einstein's face, and even the sound of the warplane crashing nearby. Playing piano restored her faith. With Mozart or Bach, she changed back into the girl who did not know that all of these things were possible. She skipped along the streets, humming. But when she arrived at Herr Morgenstern's house, it looked strangely empty. Had she gotten the day wrong? She knocked three times like he told her. She looked into the window and saw the closed and abandoned black piano gleaming in the early evening light.

The white cat suddenly appeared out of the darkness and meowed loudly. Where had they gone without telling her? Sophie looked up at the sky, trying to orient herself. A string of tears rolled down her cheeks. She turned away from the blue door and made a promise. Music could interpret this kind of vow. Herr Morgenstern had been the one to teach it to her and she would never forget it.

Bad Dürrheim, July 1940

The children's kindergarten was sequestered in a valley at the end of the forest. Its sole offering lay in the exploration of trees and meadows behind it. Sophie often took her five-year-olds for a walk through the giant pines and prickly overgrown meadows. Summer was brilliant this year. Sometimes she thought it was impossible to believe there was war anywhere. The little village tucked away in the mountains had the sharpest clear air. Every night when she finally finished cleaning the school, she stole upstairs to her room and found solace in Rilke or Fritz's letters. Stars shone brightly in the dark and quiet sky.

August 8, 1940
My dear Sophie,

You know how glad I am when I get mail from you, especially now since not much is demanded of us. For a while now I have been thinking over the feelings of opposition that you have for my profession and work.

I believe you sometimes see the soldier's profession from the outside and judge soldierly thoughts not for themselves, but for what these so-called thoughts represent.

It would be exactly as absurd as one would, for example, want to judge Christianity only after who we call Christians. During my military service I have met very few who have really been soldierly examples. Also the State and the Party have made the soldier's profession one of their tools and thereby have contradicted soldierly thoughts; therefore this is no reason to judge us.

Sophie sighed. Shouldn't he try and do something about the Party infiltrating the Army? Her bones ached from long twelve-hour days taking care of so many children. The giant moon shone into her room. What was it supposed to remind her of? What could anyone do? She read on, wishing everything were different. She could hear Fritz's firm voice, carefully articulating every word and equally convinced of everything he was writing.

I see the soldier's life as a standard that is expressed in a few sentences in the "Duty of the German Soldier": Self-confident, yet humble, upright and true, fearing God, discreet and unerring. Only achievement justifies pride. Character and achievement determine your purpose and worth. Or in Field Marshall Schlieffen's expression, "Be instead of appear."

I believe that this posture is worthwhile to strive for.

Moltke was always an example for me. He was neither arrogant nor boasting, neither brutal nor unspiritual—characteristics many people attribute to soldiers.

I see my responsibility as an officer less as training men in weapons but as an educator. I know that I must work harder on myself in this regard, but when I'm in the position to achieve something, this is what I see in my profession as one of its finest assignments.

Sophie paused again. She had become a teacher, too. These children taught her lessons she wouldn't learn otherwise. Mostly she loved how enraptured they were by life, living joyfully in the present moment. She missed telling Fritz everything about her day. Fate had dealt him a difficult card. To be an officer in Hitler's Army. She was a teacher in the Nazi State. The things they made her teach had become physically painful.

She finally understood his decision to be a career officer. He wanted to be an educator of young minds, but he had never calculated for whom or for what he would be required to fight. There was a problem in his logic. She got out a piece of paper. When she started writing, she couldn't stop. She noticed that she was running out of paper but she didn't care. She kept writing until the entire page was filled up.

Bad Dürrheim, August 19, 1940
Dear Fritz,

*I think you misunderstand my views on your profession.
Or rather, I think that the soldier's profession today is different from what you described.*

*A soldier has to swear an oath, after all, so his job is to
carry out his government's orders. Tomorrow he may have to
comply with a view diametrically opposed to yesterday's. His
profession is obedience. So the soldierly attitude isn't really
a profession. In your ideal conception of it, it really accords
with the moral demands made on every individual. I can
well appreciate that you regard your profession as an educa-
tive one, but I think that is only part of it.*

*How can a soldier have an honest attitude, as you put it,
when he is compelled to lie? Or isn't lying when you have to
swear one oath to the government one day and another the
next? You have to allow for that situation, and it has happened right now.*

*You weren't so very much in favor of a war, to the best
of my knowledge, yet you spend all your time training people
for it. You surely don't believe it's the job of the armed forces
to teach people an honest, modest, sincere attitude?*

*And as for your comparing this to Christianity, I believe
a person can be a Christian without belonging to a church.
Besides, a Christian isn't compelled to be anything other
than what his principal commandments require of him. If
a soldier's commandment is to be loyal, sincere, modest, and
honest, he certainly can't obey it, because if he receives an*

order, he has to carry it out, whether he considers it right or wrong. If he doesn't carry it out, he's dismissed, isn't he?

This was the whole problem in a nutshell. Fritz would have to take his orders from these Nazi criminals.

Sophie bit her fingernails. Running out of room and knowing that they could probably not resolve this conflict, she signed off, folded the letter and stuck it into an envelope. This time she didn't care who read it. She had to send it. She would take the consequences. When the next letter came, he wanted to know what she thought a soldier's duties should be towards his country. She answered back, quickly.

Sophie wrote to thank him for the gifts and didn't address the pressing question until she was halfway down the page. *As I see it, a soldier's position vis-à-vis his nation is rather like that of a son who vows to stand up for his father and family come what way.*

Sophie paused and glanced out the window, content with the metaphor.

If his father does another family an injustice and gets into trouble as a result, the son has to back his father regardless. Personally, I can't raise that much family feeling.

To me, justice takes precedence over all other attachments, many of which are purely sentimental. And it surely would be better if people engaged in a conflict could take the side they consider right.

I think it's just wrong for a German or a Frenchman, or whatever else that person may be, to defend his nation doggedly just because it's his.

It had to make sense to him. Nothing was stronger than justice, not even family bonds. Justice would always prevail. She made no attempt to spare his feelings. Wasn't this, after all, what true friends did? Once again, she hurriedly went to the post office box and dropped her letter inside. The Gestapo could censor her letters, but as an officer, not his. Still, she did not want to give herself any time to change her mind and not to take the risk of telling her best friend what she really thought.

Alone in the village without any friends, Sophie started to read the Psalms in secret. They were, after all, like poems. She dog-eared the one that she wanted to memorize. It had rhythm like a song. Its meaning, for her, lay in its call-to-action.

"Consider and hear me, O Lord, my God: lighten mine eyes, lest I sleep the sleep of death; lest mine enemy say, I have prevailed against him; and those that trouble me rejoice when I am moved."

Tomorrow was her day off. Sophie reached next for Rilke's *The Book of Hours*, which she kept by her bedside. She read for a little bit and drifted off into sleep. These homages to God written by one of Germany's finest poets gave her peace.

I am the dream you are dreaming.
When you want to awaken, I am that wanting.
I grow strong in the beauty you behold,
And with the silence of stars I enfold
Your cities made by time.

In the mid-morning, Sophie sharpened her pencils and found one of her pupils asleep during nap time. She drew until she lost herself in time illustrating the little boy with his hands curled tightly into his chest. Despite all these difficult conversations she and Fritz were having, art and poetry remained her lifeblood—even though the Nazis were taking that away too. She took her time, sketching slowly and deliberately. He was such a troublemaker. Sophie loved the way the boy wasn't afraid to speak his mind, and for this reason, he was her favorite but she wondered how he could ever survive living like this in Germany.

AMSTERDAM, FEBRUARY 1941

Despite the bitter cold, the Dutch demonstrators protested all day long. Hundreds of people flocked to the streets, lining up along the frozen canals, blocking the bridges. Stores shut down and the street cars stopped running. The city was on strike and the protests intensified. The German Army occupied Amsterdam for close to a year and they had had enough. Jews were disappearing from their city during nightly deportations. No one could deny it any longer.

Fritz stepped out of his hotel room onto the balcony on Prinzengracht. He felt the loneliness seize him like the cutting cold. The hotel's regal façade somehow survived the carpet bombings. He wasn't sure of what was going on below, and turning into his room, he began his shave in the mirror of the elegant bathroom. He eyed Hermann Hesse's *Journey Inward* lying on his unmade bed, and he remembered his favorite passage from the night before. He absorbed Hesse's wisdom in secret. He fought all the time to rid himself of Nazi propaganda.

"Where are we really going?" Hesse quoted Novalis, *"Always home!"* Fritz was supposed to forget that Sophie was his home. She

warned him against this type of feeling. She didn't want him to rely on her to be his everything. She wanted him to feel as though knowing God was always enough.

The protest was increasing, getting louder and angrier. He hated being here in Amsterdam, on a shopping trip for his superior officer, picking up silk stockings for his wife. Fritz finished dressing into his uniform and returned to the balcony.

Now he could hear it plainly.

"Get out of our city, you goddamn fascists. Leave our people alone!" They were chanting now.

He surveyed the enormous crowd. He would have to exit the hotel from the back door if he were to go out at all. With the stores on strike, he couldn't complete his assignment anyway. Rumors about the SS deportations were everywhere, but when he asked his commanding officer if they were true, he had been told to mind his own business.

The rat-a-tat-tat of machine gun fire was so short and abrupt that he wasn't sure he heard it until the screaming began. He hadn't seen the black uniforms approach the demonstrators. At first, Fritz couldn't move. His heart pounded. The crowd started screaming and fleeing in all directions. Very slowly, he retreated backwards into his room again and drew the curtains. Strangely, ambulance sirens didn't follow all the shooting. Only a dead silence ensued after the screaming subsided. Then he heard the muffled sounds of someone barking orders in German.

Fritz put his face in his hands and then looked up at the ceiling in desperation. The hotel telephone rang. He didn't answer it. Instead, he made his bed with trembling hands. He was in shock, uncertain of what he had actually seen. Then very slowly, he took out a piece of paper. She was the only one he could tell this to. He had to tell her. No secrets. This is what he expected from her.

> *Amsterdam, February 28, 1941*
> *Dear Sophie,*
>   *The civil population of Amsterdam just demonstrated against recent Jewish arrests. Street cars and many shops went on strike. The SS shot at a group of protestors. They supposedly killed twenty. The people are extremely angry.*

He thanked her for preparing him for this. She was the one who gave him the courage to open his eyes. She was the one who told him that living in denial was worse than not seeing the truth.

> *Dear Sophie, I thank you for everything that you have given me, especially courage and trust. By finally being able to realize all of this, I feel like I have just survived some kind of sickness.*

It struck him that the censors could read his letter, even though officers' correspondence was automatically exempt, or that is what they had been told. Fritz paused for a moment. Terrified, he thought about the consequences. He had seen how his superiors treated opposition, the "enemies within." He had to tell her. He knew that not telling her would be worse. It would be like denying to himself what he had just witnessed. She would help him now if she knew. Sophie would know how to help him. Then, suddenly, unable to control himself, he punched the wall. How could he be a part of this?

He would have to go out into this destroyed city, see these murderers—the SS and SA—on patrol on every street corner and look them in the eye. Perhaps even salute them. The sound of machine gun fire repeated over and over in his mind. The screaming. Then the eerie silence that followed.

He held onto the sealed letter tightly and prayed for Sophie to be its only reader. He knew only one thing for sure. He wanted them to get through the war the best they could. At this point, it meant coming out of it alive.

CHAPTER 4

Impervious to current influences

ULM, MARCH 1941

SOPHIE SIGHED AND LOOKED SKEPTICALLY at the photographs of calipers and rulers giving the proscribed measurements of the Aryan face. She put her hand up to her own face and tried to measure the wide space between her nose and eyes. Nonsense. People were not supposed to look like anything in particular. She frowned. Doctor Maier looked up from his clipboard and consoled her.

"It will be amusing, Fraulein Scholl. Sixty of your contemporaries, learning the same things. Community!" he belted out loudly. Then he lashed out again, "Heil Hitler!"

Half a year teaching kindergarten hadn't been enough. The Party just passed another new law. Women were being forced to spend a year at the Nazi propaganda work camps. No exceptions.

Without pausing Sophie returned the "Heil" and cast her eyes down in shame. Terrified, she remembered Fritz's recent letter in her dress pocket.

Wissant, April 3, 1941

We have a new doctor here. Arrogant and a boastful show-off. I can imagine that you would be horrified. I had an awful argument with him. There have been rumors that the SS didn't take any black prisoners, that they shot and killed those that were caught. Our doctor totally justified this—I argued that it was murder. He even supported the idea that all blacks in captivity in Germany were to be shot.

Sophie cringed as the doctor placed the cold stethoscope on her chest. Did he think like this too? What if he found something like an arrhythmic heart beat? Would he put her on one of those white trucks that were really gas chambers? Her mother found out about the Nazis' "euthanasia program" from a friend who worked as a nurse at the hospital. She had seen the mentally handicapped walk into the trucks singing songs. Sophie said nothing. She closed her eyes and prayed.

Doctor Maier finished examining Sophie and stamped his approval on her paperwork in four different places. This girl was a fine specimen of the German race. Of course, he couldn't tell if she had a genetic disease, but the scientists in Race Studies would get there someday. If she did, he'd have to sterilize her. Her strong and well-proportioned body was approaching the recommended age to bear healthy children. From the outside he could testify she was a perfect German woman, ready to provide service to the State. She could leave for the women's work camps immediately.

Doctor Maier continued to study his subject closely, putting his pen back into his lab coat's pocket. She was an unusual girl.

So shy and yet he could sense the thoughts coursing wildly in her pretty head. Sophie wouldn't even look at him.

She retreated behind the white curtain. He could see her figure's shadow behind it, putting on heavy wool stockings, slipping the dull-colored dress over her head, struggling with its zipper and slowly tying her broken shoe laces. She ran out of his office without saying a word.

A few days later Sophie received a letter from Ulm's Party Office. She was assigned to the National Socialist Women's Labor Camp at Krauchenwies, near Sigmaringen on the Danube. She had two days. No books were allowed.

Sophie's father said only one thing to her as she left. "Think for yourself and don't believe everything that they tell you." Then he retreated back into his office without even a smile. He was upset all the time now.

Sophie's mother and Inge walked her to the train station.

"Remember to go to church on Good Friday," her mother spoke so softly Sophie had to lower herself to hear. Easter wouldn't be acknowledged at the camp.

"Find a way to remember to thank Him for sending His only son who showed us how to love," her mother continued, and the tenderness swept over Sophie so that for a brief moment she couldn't fathom life without her.

Sophie boarded the train with the other girls. It snaked through giant boulders and along open fields. She gazed out of the window at the blue sky and harmless clouds, marveling at their innocence. Would the Thousand Year Reich someday rule over the world? This was Hitler's plan, and so far, he seemed to be succeeding. The Danube, no more than a wide stream, accompanied the train as it careened deeper into the Black Forest.

Sophie could see women, wearing long scarves, tilling the fields—foreign laborers who had been forced to come to Germany from Czechoslovakia. She wondered if they were being treated fairly, if they had enough to eat.

The thatched wooden fences divided the thawing fields, and ragged pine trees disappeared beyond sight. Rock cliffs suddenly peaked out of the woods and then vanished again. Sophie dug out a book from her knapsack. Deeply buried in it was her mother's copy of St. Augustine's *Confessions* and a Bible.

Fritz also was reading *Confessions* and was having trouble understanding it. She wanted to be able to talk with him about Augustine's thoughts on the nature of love. For God. Of God. They argued. Sophie didn't tell her mother that she had taken the books. She had had enough worry with her children reading banned books.

Sophie sat in the train and soothed the velvet seats with her hands. She was already feeling so alone. The books were the only refuge and a way to steel against the Nazi teachings. Morning, noon, and night, that was all they were going to be learning.

The Hohenzollern Castle came up on the left, and the chattering girls in the train suddenly quieted down. Sophie looked up at the red brick fortress and its countless pointed turrets and Gothic windows. Its high surrounding walls reminded her of the pictures she had seen of medieval times. The Danube wrapped around the castle, serving as a moat.

Wearing a brown pointed cap and uniform, Party Leader Gertrude Recknagel stood on the track with heavy arms jacked up on heavy hips. As the girls got off of the train, she belted out a "Heil Hitler" and issued her first command in a tone that sounded like she was issuing orders to soldiers to load their rifles. Sophie cringed and with the other girls got into the truck.

Schnell! Hurry up! Now!" she yelled, her throaty voice cracking.

Her tone did little to deter the girls drunk on giddiness and the new taste of freedom. It was the first time away from home for most of them. Sophie looked unsuccessfully around the truck for a suggestion of a friend. Inge, who had already been to one of these camps, warned her that it was unlikely that she would find any.

They drove along the deserted curved road through a forest of pine trees and turned into a pebbled driveway, stopping in front of a dilapidated two-story building with endless rows of identical windows. The dirty white paint was chipping and the black shutters were falling off of their rusted hinges. Only rodents live in a place like this, Sophie thought. One of the girls cried out in amazement as they gathered on the front lawn, which was beginning to thaw and show signs of its long neglect.

Recknagel began barking out rules, one after the other.

"Absolutely no men allowed!"

Sophie tuned the anger out. She would have to meet Fritz on her days off in nearby Freiburg.

"Tomorrow morning, and every day after that, we rise at six, salute the flag and exercise! Beds made with military precision! After that, we work on the farms, doing whatever is asked of us."

Sophie looked around again for a sympathetic face. Her peers stood proudly to attention. This was like a game to them. She received a room assignment and a neat stack of folded uniforms. At least she wouldn't have to waste time or energy wondering what to wear. With one rule after another, Recknagel dismantled the girls' individuality with the pleasure of a woman who wished she weren't one. Although her job was to train her recruits for marriage and childrearing, she herself acted like she had neither ambition nor temperament for what she regarded as subjugation.

"Remember! Proper German girls don't smoke, drink, wear jewelry or make-up!"

Embarrassed, some girls took off their necklaces and earrings. A pretty girl wiped lipstick from bow-and-arrow lips.

Recknagel issued yet another "Heil Hitler!"

It was answered with an obliging chorus. Sophie couldn't bring herself to say it. Her refusal went unnoticed.

The girls rushed up the crumbling stairwell, two and three at a time. Sophie found her room and claimed the top bunk. Her teeth chattered from the cold. Supposedly only the weak needed heating. This and incessant propaganda drilled into them all day long. From the room's small window, a spring snow's fluffy blanket covered the neglected bird bath. Sophie opened her journal in an attempt to block out the room's chatter. For how long now was she using these notebooks as vehicles for inner exile? Writing clarified everything to her. Made it right. She made sure she hid them under her mattress when no one was looking.

She wrote without pause in an almost undecipherable script. The fountain pen's nib skimmed over the page:

Kraunchenwies, April 11, 1941

   This evening I glanced quickly out of the window of our room, and I saw the yellow skyline through the bare trees. It suddenly struck me that today was Good Friday. Both the strangely remote and detached sky and all the laughing people who are oblivious to it made me sad. I feel so excluded, both from the cheerful company around me and from the indifferent sky.

   I'm glad that I'm finding it so hard to fit in. I'm trying hard to remain as impervious as possible to current influences. Not the ideological and political kind, which have ceased to have the slightest effect on me, but on the atmospheric influences.

Wasn't it strange that they weren't allowed to acknowledge one of the most holy days of the year? Sadder than that, Sophie realized that she was the only one who noticed. Christ had been betrayed by his friend, hadn't he? She closed her diary, said her prayers without anyone hearing or noticing, and curled up on the top bunk, drifting off into sleep. Working for ten hours a day baling hay, milking cows and feeding pigs was more exhausting than teaching six-year-olds.

The gong sounded at six o'clock, and with the other girls moaning against the cold. Sophie dressed quickly into her uniform. They formed a circle around the flag pole, clasping hands and singing. The folk song's innocent tune elevated their spirits. The bossy red-haired girl pulled on the mast and hoisted up the Nazi banner. Then they ran around the overgrown classical garden behind the estate in packs of four. Showers without hot water followed the classes about making a man happy in hearth and home. Raising as many children as they could for the Thousand Year Reich. Sophie wasn't sure which of all these alien ideas she hated more.

One evening in the mess hall, Recknagel pointed at Sophie, summoning her to her office. Sophie's stomach growled while standing at attention. There never was enough food.

"Tomorrow's class will be on our Leader's victory in Greece," Recknagel barked without looking up from her desk with neatly organized, tight piles of paper.

"I hear you have a talent for drawing."

This Scholl girl didn't fit in. The other girls excluded her in their games and conversation at dinner, and she didn't seem to mind.

"I need you to go into town, get some poster board and draw a map of the new German islands." Recknagel glared at Sophie so hard she felt like she would melt. She was concerned about this girl.

"We're all equal here and I will be watching you," she threatened angrily, dismissing her.

As Sophie turned to go, she spoke up forcibly, "We may be equal but we're not all the same."

Recknagel, infuriated by this insubordination, vowed to watch her closely and issued another "Heil Hitler." Sophie answered it back and shut the office door behind her.

The next day Sophie started down the road into Sigmaringen alone, hiding *Confessions* under her uniform. She walked on the beaten foot path into the forest thawing after months of withering cold. Birds chirped overhead, summoning spring. When she found a comfortable patch of moss, made warm from the filtered sunlight, she sat down and began to turn the pages slowly.

St. Augustine was difficult to read even translated into German from Latin. But there was also something simple in his spiritual message that kept her determined to understand it. Sophie paused and thought about Fritz and the insensitive letters she had written to him. She looked down at the leather boots with thick soles Fritz had sent earlier in the war from Albania. He was having so much trouble reconciling Augustine's teachings with his real life. She begged him to keep trying.

SMOLENSK, SOVIET UNION, JULY 1941

Guns jammed and jerked. Along with violent swearing, they were loaded and fired again and again. Through his binoculars, Fritz could count several enemy divisions. This was the first time he and his men were caught so close to the infantry lines since arriving on the Eastern Front. Nothing in the war so far had prepared him for this. Intense firing increased as the day wore on, bullets ripping by the communications company without ceasing. Field Marshall von Bock was leading the entire Army Group Center through Smolensk on to Moscow. There had been trouble with Hitler about this decision. Bock did not like it, arguing that the war couldn't be won on two fronts.

Fritz looked at his map to confirm his location. They were on the march through the endless steppe again. He folded the map carefully into his jacket pocket and started issuing orders.

Wiping the grime from his burning eyes, he saw that his men were having trouble carrying the heavy radio equipment along with their fifty-five pounds of steel helmet, rifle, ammunition, entrenching tools, knapsacks, and mess tins. They were responsible for reporting enemy positions and progress to Berlin. Fritz already knew that moving supplies over such great distances was going to be a problem. He had overheard his commanding officer say, "The vastness of Russia devours us." He hadn't been asked to lie about enemy position, supplies, and casualties, but he knew it was just a question of when.

The gunfire finally stopped. Although the Russians shot at them all day and night, they had only lost one. Fritz's men knew that the Russian soldiers would always fight to the last man. And not just men. Russian soldiers, to their surprise, were often women.

Stuck behind the infantry for two weeks, they were waiting for their marching orders. It was difficult not to listen to his men and all of the rumors. They were confused and everything was uncertain. Mostly he feared their staying out in the steppe in winter. How were they going to get supplies? The cold incessant rain came in sheets now. Followed by black flies, gnawing on their skin. While they waited, Fritz sat alone in his truck, safe from the flies and tried to figure out if he could predict which of his men would die. Was there a secret to survival? Or did it come down to pure, dumb luck? As of yet, he couldn't find a formula for survival from the men who lost their lives for *Volk, Vaterland and Führer.* He couldn't fathom a principle from any of this madness, none at all. The one thing that kept his men fighting under sheer terror and bad conditions was brotherhood. Theirs was an unshakeable fraternity based on death and horror. They weren't risking their lives for ideology or religion, and especially not a bizarre mixture of both. Neither were the Russians. In their poverty, what did they care about the Tsar or Stalin? Like in all wars, and on both sides, these men fought for one another.

The lines had been set for a week now. They were ready to move on. The burning roar of artillery and exploding grenades stuck in Fritz's ears. The dust continued to swirl in his face, making it almost impossible to see. His eyes felt as though they had melted into his ragged, unrecognizable face. He looked into the sky at the rising midday sun. The yellow ball would also fire upon them soon without mercy. The fierce heat was yet another enemy which, Fritz knew absolutely, could only be defeated if respected. He took out the map again from his breast pocket, trying to predict their next move. Either way, finding shade on the steppe at 16:00 hours would be absolutely necessary. He ordered his sergeant to check the water supply. Immediately.

His next thought turned to the night's cold. It was already too bitter for his men to continue to have to sleep outside. They had to start digging earth bunkers. And it was only July.

As night fell, and although he felt guilty about it, Fritz got into the truck. As an officer, he could escape the cold and flies. He was so tired. Good decisions required a clear mind. His men depended on him for that. He lit a cigarette.

Yesterday in the late afternoon he had gone to forage for raspberries in the woods after the shelling finally stopped. Four Russians spotted him. A warplane suddenly roared overhead, and then, as he threw himself on the ground and pressed his body into the shaking earth, a bomb went off 600 feet away. He lay there for what seemed like eternity. How strange it had been to realize that he wasn't dead. He had crushed the raspberries in his hands, and not knowing what else to do, he ate them. In this now quiet and beautiful summer oasis, while the crickets still chirped, he ate the red berries as if nothing had happened.

This experience had made him feel more alive. And instead of allowing the fear to set in further—clearly he and his men were in a terrible, unwinnable situation—he began to hope. Drawing deeply on the last of his cigarette, he got out his notepad and began a letter to Sophie.

Smolensk, September 2, 1941
Dear Sophie,

Right now I am dreaming of what it would be like if, after the war, I invested in a chicken farm and how many chickens I would need to live. I only want as many as I could handle by myself so I wouldn't have to have any strangers around me. Of course, the farm would have to be far away from any city, and not close to a village, either. Ideally it would be deep in the woods, in the meadows, or by a small lake. I would build a small wooden house. And a comfortable room for many books. During your semester vacation, I would invite you to my house in the woods with my chickens.

I even know what I would cook you for our first dinner. A farmer's breakfast. I know you might be thinking that I should use my time with more reasonable thoughts. But even though it is just a fantasy, there's a little bit of seriousness here. You must write to me how you see yourself occupying your time best. We have never talked about this, and maybe you see my abilities better than I can see them myself.

It was so good to think about these things. It helped to fortify his resolve to return from this madness, and in the morning he would teach his men everything he learned at Potsdam. Together they would get out of this hell. The cigarette had burned out on the truck's dashboard. Fritz closed his notepad and collapsed into the front seat.

KRAUCHENWIES, AUGUST 1941

German women must extend their service to the Volk, Vaterland and Führer. Due to the brave fight that German men are now engaged in against the Bolshevik enemy, German women are needed to support the home front for another six months. Your next assignment is listed below.

Sophie fell against the sign that Frau Recknagel nailed to the front door. With heavy footsteps she walked up the crumbling stairwell and returned to her room. The other girls were downstairs. They always left her out but it didn't matter to her. She thought again about the news. Six more months of this stifling misery. She cursed. She would be old before she got to study in Munich.

Feeling homesick and hopeless, Sophie fished out a pack of cigarettes from her rusty locker. How much more of this could she take? Gisela suddenly appeared at the door. She was oblivious of the impression her long blond hair and fresh face made upon others. Not too long ago, Sophie noticed the way she closed her blue eyes in defiance during propaganda training. She had been the only one to show any outward signs of protest.

"Let's go to the fields," Sophie suggested and flashed the illegal cigarettes. Gisela smiled widely with perfect white teeth. They walked for awhile, and then certain no one had followed them, and hidden behind enormous balls of tightly wrapped hay, they lit up, puffed, and blew smoke rings.

Sophie shouted out to the dusky pink evening sky, *"Götz von Berlichingen!"*

Gisela, also upset by having to stay longer because she wanted to study in Munich too, answered back.

"Götz von Ber-lich-in-gen!!" The great German poet, Goethe, had been the one to teach them this old swear word, and it was the best translation of their feelings—"Kiss my ass!" They shouted again in eighteenth-century slang, the words rolling off their tongues, and they put their heads together and laughed.

When they returned to the camp, Sophie looked up her new assignment on the list. Recknagel had never liked her. Sophie was going to Blumberg. She had heard things about the village at the end of the Black Forest. Cars didn't even pass through it. "State criminals" were sentenced to mine its one mountain for iron. Sophie wondered about their so-called crimes.

The other girls fell asleep easily that night, undisturbed by the news. For most of them, it meant more time away from their parents. The girl from the Saarland was snoring, and even Gisela was sleeping. Sophie tossed and turned. She hit her head on the steel bed post.

Unable to sleep, Sophie switched on her flashlight that Inge had sent to her and began reading St. Augustine again.

When a person's will is focused on finding himself or affixing itself to changing and temporary desires, either for enjoyment or in order to find true happiness, a person will destroy himself in this multitude of choices and lose his freedom and identity.

This helped. The camp was the worst experience in her life. She could forget being happy for quite a while. So she read on.

He will estrange himself from God through this search, because only God alone gives happiness and peace. Happiness is found only by striving for goodness, something that no one person can take away from him.

It was impossible to be good in this environment. Who could define "good" anymore? Were her mother and father good? It was almost too difficult to contemplate this any further. She thought about Fritz and his last letter about the chicken farm. She was worried by his writing to her like that. It seemed like some kind of foreshadowing. Was he genuinely contemplating buying a farm? It seemed utterly impossible to her that the German Army could conquer Russia. What did this mean for his chances of survival? Sophie threw herself down on the cold floor and prayed for him and without consciously wishing it, a whole flock of chickens flew by in her mind.

FREIBURG, OCTOBER 1941

Fritz waited for Sophie's train from Blumberg, pacing on the platform, putting out his cigarettes with well-polished black boots. Their shine belied his inner state; he felt worn and conflicted, tired and confused, in need of rest, her kind of conversation. He couldn't forget what it felt like to hold her. He clutched a bouquet of wilted flowers that mirrored his dismal condition.

The late autumn sun had been generous that morning, giving him no reason to wear his coat. He put on his uniform again with a surge of regret and wished that he could have greeted her in anything but officer's epaulets and Nazi pins. Wearing uniforms were mandatory now, even when he wasn't on duty.

He didn't know any more if he could look into her eyes in the same way he looked into them before. The things he had seen were reflected in his own eyes, had made them even darker. He felt the new lines on his face, altered in sadness. He had seen what men were capable of doing. He had seen the indescribable, unfathomable, unforgettable. He must not think of these things now. Fritz also knew that these memories would haunt him and become a part of his soul forever.

Another soldier on leave saluted as he passed, "Heil Hitler." Fritz responded coldly and cursed his luck, for at that moment, the train pulled in and Sophie, looking out from the window, saw it.

"Fritz!" She called out from the train's window and waved.

He walked quickly towards her compartment with his heart racing. As she came off the train, he saw immediately that she had changed too. Her face was etched in an unfamiliar seriousness, and her eyes no longer laughed the way he had remembered.

She hadn't calculated his change either. When they embraced, they held one another for a long time and she felt something different besides his new thinness.

"Tell me everything," she said and let go of him gently, slightly alarmed by his hollowness. He smiled and for the first time, he spoke her name softly, surprised by his own voice, breaking.

She hugged him again, this time even harder. He took her bag and they headed in silence towards the hotel. They were two strangers and it would take a while until they could find their common ground. Sophie would tell him everything about what life was like at the women's camp, and he smiled because he had missed her way of talking and telling stories. He couldn't wait to be alone with her again.

The years 1444–1655 were carefully stenciled on the hotel's façade, painted in a harlequin pattern of white and dusty pink triangles filled with reliefs of crests of lions and bears. The receptionist at the massive front desk glared at them after looking at Sophie's naked ring finger.

Fritz made a joke and for the first time since they met again, they laughed. But he wasn't sure anymore. He wasn't sure if he could love her in the same way he once had.

He heard things he never thought humanly possible and had done nothing to stop them. Fritz doubted now if he was worthy of her respect and trust. He couldn't tell her what he heard about the Eastern campaign. But he also couldn't lie.

Sophie opened the windows in their room that looked out into the cobbled street and the gilded Roman numeral clock on the medieval gate. She pointed out that the hands of the clock were a sliver of the moon and a star. When she returned to their bed, she rested her head on his chest and began telling him stories about the other girls at the camp.

"The girls keep copies of *Faust* for appearances and put on refined airs, but it's all so transparent, rather like their hairstyles worn only for purposes of self-adornment."

He wanted her to keep talking. Since September he had been ordered back to Germany and was setting up a communications regiment for his former teacher, Field Marshall Rommel, in Africa. But, in quiet times like these, he still couldn't forget the sight of thousands of starving refugees, the miles of columns of POWs, the dead stares and smell of decomposing soldiers, the incessant killing sound of artillery and explosions.

Sophie continued talking aimlessly about the ridiculous things Frau Recknagel taught and mocked the cooking, cleaning, and sewing classes. She sat up and when she did, he tackled her, grabbed her as if he were drowning and put his head on her stomach, finally allowing himself to fall asleep.

Sophie took the feather comforter from the floor and without daring to move him, covered him with it. When he woke, she was sleeping and he praised God. But he wasn't sure anymore if he believed in Him. He couldn't tell her this, either. Fritz gently moved her to the side and got up. For the first time in weeks, he took a hot bath in a clean bathtub. He submerged underwater for a long time, letting the water cleanse him, wishing that it could wash away the visions.

In the morning they decided to take a walk around the medieval city through its tight cobblestoned alleyways. A stream, a vestige from the ancient sewage system, flowed beside them. A woman and her child rushed past them wearing yellow felt stars of David sewed to their lapels. Neither Fritz nor Sophie commented on them.

Sophie wanted to visit the Gothic church in the center of Freiburg. The village square surrounded by a sixteenth-century *Rathaus* was lined with colorfully painted statues of dukes and princes. But when they arrived at the church's red triangle-shaped door, Fritz told her that he wouldn't go inside. She didn't force him. She only looked down at the ground and then at him with searching eyes.

He didn't speak about where he had been, and she didn't want to force him but his silence was unnatural. She was afraid that if she didn't ask, he wouldn't tell her and she wanted to know. Because she sensed that he was grateful that she hadn't asked, she couldn't bring herself to. He would tell her when he was ready. Wouldn't he?

Suddenly she remembered the poem by Heine about the returning soldier. It made her shudder and she pushed the thought out of her mind.

When they returned to their hotel room for the last time, Sophie finally asked.

"And what about during the fight for Moscow, what happened? What did you see on your way there? And what about Weimar? What is happening up there?"

Fritz's eyes glazed over as though she was no longer in the room. She read his letters over and over and responded to them immediately. It was too hard to tell whether or not he was protecting her from something unspeakable. Of course everyone heard the rumors. He could tell that she wouldn't be appeased by anything less than the truth.

"How far were you from Minsk?" Sophie asked. Even though she knew the truth wasn't printed in the newspaper, she read them anyway, and it was reported that it had been a particularly difficult battle. He knew that she wouldn't be satisfied with knowing that his communications company wasn't directly responsible. Fritz had seen soldiers in the infantry divisions. Some of them were still trembling. Others had bright red eyes bloodshot from drinking, as if they were trying to wash away the memories.

But Sophie persisted, "What do you know about what happened in Minsk?"

Fritz shook his head and couldn't answer. His inability to tell her, the one person in the world whom he trusted implicitly, was enough to indict him, to implicate him in the horror that she was guessing at. There were rumors about Hitler's orders for the Eastern Campaign. No soldier or officer in the German Army would be persecuted for harming Russian civilians. He must have seen things far worse than what he had written in his letters. She couldn't take his silence any longer.

"You're lying," she screamed again, lunging at him with a face twisted in an emotion he had never seen before. "You know what happened there, and the truth is too hard to bear and too horrifying to repeat. Isn't it? Isn't it?" Sophie pleaded.

He took hold of her with all of his strength and pulled her close to him until her anger subsided.

When they finally looked at one another, a new expression he dared not name had come across her face. It was not an expression of a twenty-year-old girl but that of a determined woman. It frightened him.

She finally spoke. Goethe had often been to where Fritz was stationed now, waiting for his next assignment. The eighteenth-century Romantic poet wrote one of his best-known poems in Weimar. Sophie recited it by heart.

> Within our inner selves is a universe,
> We need this and it is the best of what we know.
> It is God, or whoever we call God.
> It is with this that we surrender to the sky and the earth.
> To fear. And to love.

Fritz took her into his arms again. Germany was a country of murderers. And he was a part of it. He could no longer deny it. He was leading his men into battle for a cause that could never be justified or even explained. How on earth could he keep his men alive if all of the rumors were true? What about what was happening in that camp in Buchenwald, close to Weimar?

Now Sophie was reminding him of Goethe, one of the best German poets ever. Fritz didn't know what to do or what to feel. Instead he held on to her tighter, unable to say anything until he finally spoke, repeating the poet's lines: "Within ourselves is a universe. It is God, or whoever we call God. It is the best of what we know."

Germany would be changed forever. The world would forever judge his country and his own part in its crimes. Goethe's poetry was only a small consolation. But in that very moment, it was the only prayer he knew.

CHAPTER 5

Nature is my only sustenance, the sky and stars and silent earth

---

BLUMBERG, OCTOBER 1941

SOPHIE SNUCK INTO THE DESERTED chapel and played its dusty organ. She had a half hour break from teaching in the school. She chose her favorite Bach melody but the out-of-tune keys made a broken, almost pointless sound. Capitulating because its effect was the opposite of what she needed, she got down on her knees and prayed. Protestants didn't do this but these were desperate times. News from the Eastern Front was only propaganda. And there were rumors, ones too difficult to acknowledge.

Somehow one Bible remained from the Party's purge to remove books from houses of worship. Sophie found the tattered and torn New Testament under the front pew and sat down. She took a quiet moment alone, flipping through the book. Her fingers rested at Galatians 2:15. The answers to her questions were in here. The conclusion was simple: these Nazi laws weren't ones

Germany could adhere to any longer. She read on and tried to memorize the passage that made this clear.

> *We ourselves are Jews by birth and not Gentile sinners; yet we know that a person is justified not by the works of the law but through faith in Jesus Christ. And we have come to believe in Christ Jesus, so that we might be justified by faith in Christ, and not by doing the works of the law, because no one will be justified by the works of the law.*

Sophie hurried back along the country road. Blumberg was a small village tucked away deep in the Black Forest, but the Party was everywhere. The iron ore buried deep in its only mountain made it a valuable war-supplies destination. Her six-month teaching assignment felt worse than a prison sentence. She knew that the petty criminals forced to mine were less dangerous than the school's fanatic headmistress or even the mayor.

The little church was her only refuge, but essential questions remained. How could she believe in a God who was allowing this? How could she wish for Germany to lose the war when this meant that Fritz, her brothers, and all their friends might have to die? She still could not reconcile these two opposing truths.

At night Sophie wrote as though this was the only action that could help. There were too many rumors she could no longer bear or deny. The pages in her diary filled up quickly, and because of this speed her delicate script was almost undecipherable. In a way this almost relieved her, because what could happen if this diary was seized and read by the censors? She could go to jail.

Sophie had begun to realize that despite everything, believing in God was the only thing that made sense. Then again, His existence didn't make sense. How could this war and Hitler's persecution of Jews and all the others be happening if He existed? Only writing could assuage these thoughts.

Blumberg, November 1941

Sometimes I feel I can forge a path to God in an instant, purely by yearning to do so—by giving up my soul entirely. We should simply entrust God with the worries we so arrogantly cling to, and those we allow to depress us or drive us to despair.

I don't find that easy, because when I try to pray and reflect on whom I'm praying to, I almost go crazy, I feel so infinitely small. I get really scared, so the only emotion that can surface is fear. I feel so powerless in general and doubtless, I am. I can't pray for anything except the ability to pray.

Whenever I think of God, it's as if I'm struck blind. I can't do a thing. I have absolutely no conception of God and no affinity with Him aside from my awareness of the fact. And the only remedy for that is prayer. Prayer.

Fritz seemed to have more time to read than she did. She took care of small children twelve hours a day. He was still waiting to be deployed to Africa and didn't seem have much to do in Weimar. A copy of Kierkegaard's *Either/Or* landed on his desk—he didn't say how—and he quoted often from it. They were grappling with the same questions, and sometimes they argued in their letters. The threads of discussions got lost through time and distance.

ULM, DECEMBER 1941

In the main train station, people no longer greeted one another. Sophie tied her scarf tighter around her neck and buttoned up her threadbare coat. Now it was missing two buttons. The feeling of fear had grown larger and more pervasive with the increasing cold. Hitler issued death orders against anyone caught voicing political opposition. With the United States joining in against them, the main train station was a catacomb of fear. It was everywhere: fear of an air raid, fear of being overheard and reported, fear from neighbors who heard of people randomly disappearing, fear of not enough food, fear of the camps that one could no longer deny the existence of, fear of bad news from the front. It was like a stone wall surrounding the city. It locked everyone inside of a lonely, psychic prison. But Sophie was glad today. She was going to see her family and she had missed them.

As she walked through Ulm, black and white posters screamed at her from the windows of deserted shops and buildings: *Jews Are Our Enemy! Turn Off All Lights at Night! Support the Army's Collections! The Enemy Hears You—Don't Gossip!*

Fritz had to stay up north in Weimar for Christmas. Hans was coming home from Munich with a new girlfriend, Traute. What would this one be like? Inge reserved the ski cabin for all of them on the mountain in Coburg between Christmas and New Year's. That was something.

A pickup truck full of coats and blankets suddenly sped past her, splashing Sophie with mud. The men from the Army's winter collection were even more aggressive this year. She picked up her pace. The truck circled back, slowed.

"What do you have for us," the driver leered out of the window. He leaned forward, pointing to her suitcase, a cigarette dangling from dirty hands.

"Women's clothes don't fit soldiers," Sophie answered and kept walking. They followed her. Her legs weakened.

"Are you refusing to help Germany?" The older man gawked, sitting next to the driver. His eyes ran all over her.

"It looks that way, doesn't it?" She said directly, staring right back at him. She clutched her suitcase even tighter and kept on walking. She had packed Fritz's long underwear. Her mother washed them without asking any questions.

By supporting the war Sophie knew that she was just helping to prolong it. It didn't matter whether German soldiers or Russian soldiers died. Germany had to lose the war. One was either for Hitler or against him. She knew someday she would have to tell this truth to Fritz.

"Traitor," the men in the truck screamed at her in unison. She picked up her pace.

"The police are going to come after you, little lady," the older man threatened and peeled off, splashing her with more mud. Was she committing treason for not contributing to the war effort? Scared, she ran home.

When Sophie burst through the door, she immediately felt her home's absence of festivity.

Candles for the tree were a thing of the past. Her father managed to get an evergreen from the nearby woods, so she and Inge decorated it with what they had from last year, hanging its branches with their mother's wooden carved nutcrackers, apples and nuts. Magdalena tried to liven up the household by putting on Handel's *Messiah*. When Hans came home from Munich, he brought a box of chocolates but refused to say where he had gotten them. Sophie opened only one package on Christmas Eve. Real hoar paint brushes from Inge. If only her sister knew that Sophie wasn't painting anymore. She sent Fritz her sketches only because he asked for them. She didn't tell him that she no longer bothered with art anymore because true expression required freedom.

Everyone was home including Werner. Their father was in a good mood and for once, he turned off his secret radio and instead of brooding about the day's news, he asked Sophie to play a hymn on the piano. When they all returned home from the midnight service, Hans made a speech about this being his first religious Christmas.

Sophie pulled Inge, Elisabeth, and Hans aside and told them how she resisted the war effort.

"Sophie, that's too dangerous," Elisabeth criticized.

"Don't you feel disloyal to Fritz?" Inge asked, shaking her head.

"I'm proud of you," Hans said and patted his sister on the back.

In less than a day, they would all be headed for a few days of skiing, and Hans promised Sophie that they could forget the war on the mountain.

Even though Hans' new girlfriend wasn't from Schwabia, Sophie was pleased that Traute Lafrenz could keep up. Hans led them down the snowy slopes most of the day, and they bellowed and laughed from the fresh air and friendship. At nightfall, when they reached the cabin, they gathered around the fire and read passages out loud from a Dostoevsky novel. Their protest against the war, Hitler, and his insanity, consisted of reading the enemy's finest writer.

Before the clock struck twelve on New Year's Eve, they ran outside and observed the full moon illuminating the stone-blue mountain. The pine trees cast long shadows. Sophie shivered, trying to name the constellations. She was the first to hurry back inside the warm cabin.

As Traute fed the crackling fire with twigs fragrant with sap, she recited a few lines from Novalis' poem "Hymns to the Night."

The light from the fireplace illuminated the sharp lines on Traute's aristocratic face.

"Novalis has cured my hunger," Traute added, trying to break the spell cast by her beauty.

"What hunger?" Hans asked, wrinkling his forehead, and sat down on the ledge of the fireplace beside her, throwing his finished cigarette into the fire.

"Spiritual hunger," she answered.

Hans shook his head in disagreement. Traute said nothing in her defense. Sophie picked up the thread of Traute's idea.

"Art, literature, and music can help us wake from indifference and supply us with food for our soul. For me, if anything can raise passion in my frozen heart, it's music. And that's essential—a prerequisite for everything else. It can distance me a little from this turmoil around me, from the glutinous, hostile mush."

Hans interrupted his little sister and put his finger in the air as if to say, "Yes, but."

He had spent enough hours discussing this with the renowned religious Professors Carl Muth and Theodor Haecker in Munich. Both had been banned from publishing and teaching, but they still held secret student talks. That's all Hans said about them. He continued in an authoritative tone.

"Spiritual hunger can't be satisfied by music or any other art form. Nothing derived from man can. Only God Himself can."

Sophie was unprepared to accept his strict religious opinion. She straightened her back and choosing her words with care, she spoke in a strong and clear voice.

"Music softens my heart, by resolving its confusions and relaxing it. Then it enables my mind, which has previously knocked in vain on the locked portals of the soul, to operate within it. Yes, music quietly and gently unlocks the doors of my soul. Now the doors are open! Now it's receptive. The reward is a liberated and uninhibited heart, a heart that has become receptive to harmony and things harmonious, a heart that has opened its doors to the workings of the mind."

Sophie strung the words together like pearls. She continued.

"While pondering the hunger that exists in mankind, for which music represents neither more nor less than the air that enables a flame to burn more brightly still, I've become aware that we would starve to death if not sustained by God."

When she finished speaking, she looked up at the cabin's wooden ceiling and put her fingers to her mouth as if she might have forgotten something. Satisfied that she had completed her thoughts, she smiled back at the silent group. The months that Sophie had spent isolated at the women's camp and alone in the village strengthened her. The lonely hours had exposed her deepest fears and darkest thoughts. There was an answer to all of this fear. This newfound strength would be what defined her.

"The reward," she repeated, "is a liberated and uninhibited heart."

The fire, left unattended during her elegy to music and a Higher Power, continued to burn down in an orange glow.

Ulm, January 1942

Robert Scholl's accounting practice had grown so much that he had rented a small office close to home and hired an assistant and associate. He had also taken to the strange habit of saving soldiers' obituaries. He was counting the growing number of boys from Ulm who died a "hero's death for *Volk, Vaterland and Führer.*" Often he recognized family names next to the iron cross and swastika. Hitler's promised Final Victory was nowhere near. Robert was worried most for his youngest son. The Army had conscripted Werner to fight in the infantry on the Eastern Front. He knew implicitly what this meant.

Cold winter rain trickled down his office window. Pitter-patter formed its own kind of music. His new secretary, Fraulein Muller, knocked on his door and without his having to ask her, she brought in his afternoon tea.

"Thank you," he said and barely looked up from his paperwork. A warm drink was necessary on days like this one. She smiled and set the tray down on his desk. When she turned to go, Robert stole a glance at her legs.

She wore those new silk stockings with piping. She must have saved her ration cards for months for such luxury, he thought. Or perhaps her boyfriend, who had been part of the French occupation and was now fighting in Russia, had gotten them for her. She turned around abruptly and caught him admiring her youthfulness. Instead of pretending he hadn't stopped to admire her, he complimented Fraulein Muller.

Turning bright red, she rushed out of the door and stumbled. Robert Scholl was bewildered. He had enough experience with his wife and three daughters to know how complicated a species women were. *If I didn't notice her, she'd be upset, and if I do, she's insulted,* he thought.

He shook his head and went back to work.

The next morning it was still raining when Robert watched the truck back up to the Münster Church from his living room window.

"What are they doing now?" he shouted to his wife who was in the kitchen.

"I don't know, Robert, why don't you go down and ask them," Magdalena answered, slightly annoyed by her husband's desire to know everything.

Robert continued watching a large crane position itself in front of massive arched wooden doors. Centuries ago artisans carved thousands of religious figures all over the imposing Gothic monolith. The fourteenth-century door was crowned with statues of the apostles distorted in medieval dimensions. Gargoyles gawked from every corner with contorted expressions. Its ancient stained glass windows had been removed two years before and replaced with regular glass.

A few moments later, the crane extended itself into the air and carefully lifted out one of the church's colossal bells and then deposited it on the makeshift platform.

The war effort was extracting the iron for ammunition. A church without bells seemed as absurd to Robert as a lamp without a light bulb. Even worse than this theft was what it implied: the German Army was so short on supplies that it had to resort to such outrageous measures. The war was going to last much longer than originally anticipated.

The only solution to this madness, Robert Scholl knew absolutely, would be that someone inside the military would have to assassinate their so-called leader.

Later at work the same day, Robert's associate came into his office. They knew one another before things had gotten so dangerous.

Robert had to tell him what he had seen earlier. His colleague shook his head in disbelief. He was also aware of what a country needed in order to win a war. Robert glanced at the pile of obituaries that he kept on the window sill. Suddenly without warning and without regard for anything but the need to speak the truth, he raised his voice and said, "Hitler is the scourge of the earth. He has taken God hostage. If the German Army doesn't retreat right now, by next year, I tell you, the Red Army will be in Berlin."

His employee startled. He got up from the office chair and shut the door.

"Please be careful, Herr Scholl!"

Robert sat down, exasperated. He made a mistake. His friend left a file on his desk and quickly walked out of the office without another word.

At her desk outside, Frau Muller twitched and tucked her hair behind her ear as a way of collecting herself. She heard her employer. He called the Führer the scourge of the earth. The nerve. Just when their leader needed the most support. How dare he say that Germany would have to lose the war against Russia. She grew furious. She hadn't heard from her boyfriend in months and she was starting to get worried.

Scholl's words incensed her. The pervert. She knew what she would have to do. She could become a hero. Maybe there was some kind of reward for reporting traitors. When she got home to her furnished room in the boarding house, she used the phone in the hall to call Ulm's Party Office.

Magdalena called her husband at work before opening the letter from the Gestapo. Robert told her to wait until he got home. "Not to worry," he said sternly. "It is probably nothing."

She put the sealed envelope on the kitchen table but couldn't forget about it all day. She had never forgotten when the Gestapo invaded their home, taking away her children. Fear had its own memory. She got down on her knees and prayed. She felt her heart skip. There had been something wrong with her health for months but she hadn't told anyone.

When Robert got home, he put his briefcase down, and without taking off his rain coat, he opened the letter. His employee, Fraulein Kirsten Muller, had reported him. He read on. They were accusing him of sedition. *Speaking derogatorily about Hitler in public.* A court date was set for August. If found guilty, it meant a year in prison and a revoked license to operate his business.

Magdalena lost her composure. She threw her arms up in the air. "What have you done, Robert? Couldn't you be more careful? What good did it do? What will the children think? What will happen to you now? How will we survive?" The room filled with desperate questions.

He didn't hear her and put the letter back into the envelope, looking back at her blankly. His wife was so agitated that she required instruction.

"Do not tell the children. We don't want to worry them needlessly."

He hung his wet coat up in the closet and told Magdalena that he wouldn't be eating dinner. He had plenty of work still left to do and would be in his office downstairs for the rest of the evening.

Lake Constance, February 1942

Habe Sonntag frei! Fritz tore open the letter and drank its happiest words. Sophie could take Sunday off. He immediately began planning the long train ride and where they could meet. Weimar-Frankfurt-Freiburg-Blumberg-Donaueschingen-Konstanz. They could meet at a train station in some forgotten town and go together to Lake Constance. A twelve hour train ride didn't matter against the chance to spend an evening together at the pacific Swiss border on one of its most magnificent emerald green lakes. Even if it were completely frozen, it was sure to be majestic, surrounded by an Alpen mountain chain. Skaters etched long trails of white lines on the ice.

Sophie was about to complete her war duty once and for all and go to Munich to study with Hans. Fritz doubted whether he would get to serve under his former teacher, Rommel, in Africa, and he worried about being deployed to the Russian Front. But right now he couldn't think of anything beyond Lake Constance and being together with Sophie. He smiled. They both agreed that telling the receptionist they were engaged when they checked into the famous Insel Hotel saved them from being sinners.

The light inside the former Dominican monastery flooded their room in the morning. They explored three floors of painted medieval mysteries told in Gothic frescoes and studied religious history on its pictorial walls. Legends from the Old and New Testament called to them, side by side, in pastel robes, sandals, and bare feet with enigmatic faces and in painted gold halos. In the evening they would seal the promise of their futures with physical closeness, so that in the morning when she boarded the train, their separation would be all the more painful. The tranquility of Lake Constance gave them relief from the growing frightfulness of the nearing war. There in its green peace Sophie returned to the person she was when she first met him.

Munich, May 1942

Sophie turned her head and studied the stone horses leaping out of the empty fountain's basin and imagined what it would look like with flowing water. Two statues of women in togas leaned gracefully into one another. This was the city that King Ludwig designed and built as a monument to Greece. Or was it Rome? Tomorrow she would matriculate at the famous Ludwig-Maximilians university, one of the oldest in all of Europe. She was the one her father had selected from among her sisters to be able to study. It was the biggest honor, even though most of the subjects she wanted to study were now closed to women.

The Bavarian blue sky full of giant white clouds looked exactly as she had seen in so many Baroque paintings. Soon a pastel dust of pinks and blues would descend over the city, illuminating it in tender colors. Together Hans and Sophie sat quietly in the street car that glided around the city's center of Neoclassical buildings, past the majestic statues, fountains and the overpowering five-story Palace of Justice.

Like a visible sign of hope, giant chestnut and linden trees bloomed in rows impervious to the war. Munich inspired some of the best German philosophers, writers, and artists. But now, gazing out of the street car's window, it seemed to Sophie that the only people showing any spirit were marble statues. She caught the inscription of King Ludwig sitting on horseback, leading a charge. She smiled as she read it: *Beharrlichkeit*. Perseverance.

The war showed itself everywhere, mostly in the form of wounded soldiers returning from the front on crutches with missing legs, arms in slings, and faceless men bound in dirty bandages. Storefronts had nothing in their windows. The city felt abandoned, its people in hiding. Swastika banners and cone-shaped speakers hung on every street corner. Men and women in brown uniforms randomly stopped civilians, demanding their identification papers. Sophie hated all the signs forbidding Jews in restaurants, shops, and parks. And all the warnings: *The enemy is everywhere! Turn out the lights at night! Donate to the Party! Community! The Leader knows everything!*

Women huddled around the newspaper shops looking for news about their loved ones, wearing head scarves and heavy stockings buckled at their ankles. This wasn't the city she had imagined. They passed the National Theater. She arched her neck to study the colorful tiled façade of a Greek hunting scene with greyhounds, the ochre and brick tympanum with Ionic columns.

"Will we have a chance to go there?" Sophie asked out loud, breaking the silence. The war hadn't disrupted opera performances. But Hans didn't hear her. She decided not to disturb his thoughts again and continued absorbing the city's architectural splendor in silence.

They got out at Hohenzollernstrasse. The city street was lined with apartment houses painted in dusky hues of pink, green, and blue. Hans carried her suitcase, and she struggled to keep up with his long strides until he stopped at massive wooden doors. He rang the bell and pushed them open. He was going to introduce her to his friends in his pre-med classes, all part of the student-medic company.

Sophie followed her brother inside and up the creaky spiral wooden staircase to a second-floor apartment. A striking blond, blue-eyed man played jazz on a piano. Traute, also studying medicine, welcomed them inside, kissing Hans hello on both cheeks. She reached out her long hand with red nails to Sophie, pushing a wavy bob cut away from wide almond eyes. The piano player got up and introduced himself to Sophie as Willi Graf. Sophie guessed that Willi's shyness hid a thoughtful person. He sat back down on the piano and continued playing. They gathered to celebrate Hans' sister's arrival and her twenty-first birthday, which had been a week ago.

"Congratulations Sophie Scholl and welcome, finally, to Munich," Hans toasted his little sister.

Traute, dressed in a flowing cotton dress tucked tightly at her thin waist, put on a new coat of red lipstick and checked her white teeth in an antique silver compact. Willi struck up another tune on the piano. Traute and Hans started dancing together, and soon the room filled up with smoke and more friends.

When the door opened for the last time, Traute shouted out happily.

"Alex! You're only an hour late!"

When the newly arrived guest laughed, the party lit up by several degrees brighter. His father, a well-known doctor, wanted him to study medicine, but Alex preferred to work in his artist's studio sculpting marble or to ride his horse. Tall and thin, Alex's dark brown hair was slicked back with the right amount of pomade. Joyful eyes engaged the world around him.

Lifting two green bottles of champagne from under a well-tailored tweed jacket, he made his way to Sophie and kissed her hand.

"Why aren't you in uniform, man?" Hans scolded the party's new life force. "You know the new laws. You could cause suspicion."

Sophie had overheard. Why had he used the word "suspicion"? Alex only shrugged his finely shaped shoulders, smiled, and winked. Uncorking the champagne, foam rose up from the bottle, and he sprayed it into the air.

On their way through the city on the street car to Professor Carl Muth's house outside of town, Sophie couldn't stop thinking about the party. She couldn't wait to write Fritz about it. But where would she write to him? All of the time he spent in Weimar for his marching orders to Africa was for nothing. He and his expertise would be needed in Russia. The Eastern campaign was into its second year. She knew, as well as Fritz did, that it would be physically impossible to make Russia a part of the Thousand Year Reich. History had already proven that.

"Alex is part Russian, but he is a typical Bavarian," Hans read his sister's distant thoughts. "You'll meet Christoph too," he continued. "He's stationed in Austria but he's coming to Munich to study with us. You'll like him best of all."

Sophie was excited. At the party they had celebrated imperviousness to the perversity of their world. She couldn't remember when she had felt such freedom. It was late by the time they arrived at Professor Muth's. Hans let them in, bringing Sophie up to her new room.

"In the morning he will have breakfast ready for you," Hans said, closing the French doors which looked out to a balcony and a garden. He shut the curtains, smiled, and left her sitting on the small bed. Hans met Professor Muth through his friend Otl Aicher, and Muth agreed to board Sophie for a few weeks.

Sophie woke to the smell of coffee and toast. She put on her best dress, worn but ironed into newness by her mother. He was waiting for her in his kitchen. Professor Carl Muth sat hunched over his newspaper in a faded three-piece suit with a pearl stud pinned to a wide silk tie and a gold watch tucked inside a vest pocket. He stroked a long trimmed white beard as he read.

When Muth looked up from a newspaper Sophie didn't recognize, he stood up and welcomed his new house guest with a handshake. She hesitated before sitting down. He poured her a cup of hot brown water that was supposed to be coffee. They laughed. She waited for him to speak. They talked about the spring weather for a long time.

Because Professor Muth was a suspected anti-National Socialist, the Nazis forbid him to teach or publish. He hadn't published his Catholic journal for two years. Although he didn't mention it, she knew from Hans that he had a hard time finding enough money to eat. In the afternoon they sat together in his garden under willow trees in wicker lawn chairs.

"Despite being forbidden to write, I still keep a diary, Sophie," Muth confessed, almost suddenly. "There must be some kind of record that not all Germans supported the Antichrist."

Sophie sat upright. It was the first time she had heard an adult besides her father speak out against Hitler. During their long conversation, which eventually turned to religion, the sun changed position, its brilliant rays filtering into the stone patio through willow wisps.

When he excused himself to take a nap, Sophie went back up to her room and re-read Fritz's last letter. He received new orders to lead a communications regiment as part of the assault on Moscow. Sophie took the news calmly but inside a new fear grew inside her. It was a death sentence. No odds in the world could count on him coming back.

Sophie often traveled alone to Hans' apartment in town. Alex was always there, and the threesome stayed up late, talking and drinking too much wine. Munich's street lights turned off at night. The city had suffered bombings for over a year now. Pockets of destruction were increasing everywhere. Sophie wondered what had happened to the people who lived in buildings that were now just rubble. Street cars stopped at dusk. Warning sirens blew all day and intensified at night.

One night, drowsy from drinking too much wine, Sophie fell asleep at Hans' apartment while the boys were discussing politics. She woke up awhile later and could hear them still talking. Disoriented, she strained to hear. Were they arguing? Schurik, Alex's Russian nickname, spoke in an elevated voice. Calling him by that was risky but a lot of fun. Careful not to make a sound, she got out of bed and cursed the creaking bed springs. Schurik's voice was filled with urgency.

"Hans. Who among us has any conception of the dimensions of shame that we will have—and our children—when the most horrible of crimes—crimes that infinitely outdistance every human measure—reach the light of day?" Alex was angry.

"We must write what everyone knows," he spoke in a low but forceful voice. "We must write it in plain German."

What were they talking about? Sophie couldn't make out Hans' response. Her brother had the habit of formulating his responses and picking his words with care. Sometimes she thought that he wasn't even in the conversation, he was so deliberate in his listening. She could imagine her brother's faraway expression.

"Most of the people already know," Hans finally answered. "And they aren't doing anything about it."

"If we tell our people what they already know, then our protest won't be effective. No, we must appeal instead to their intellectual side. Rally them into action by quoting what the best of Germany has been—Goethe and Schiller. Then they can see that the Nazis are wrong."

Hans paused and let his statement rest for greater impact.

"Besides," he added, "don't you remember that Goethe compared the Germans to the Jews and Greeks as a tragic people?"

Sophie thought she heard Alex starting to type. Hans was dictating.

"Therefore every individual, conscious of his responsibility as a member of Christian and Western civilization, must defend himself as best he can at this late hour; he must work against the scourges of mankind, against fascism and any similar system of totalitarianism."

Alex raised his voice, "But we must tell them what they can do." He repeated it again. "They need practical advice. No one knows what they should be doing. How could they?"

Hans reminded him to be quiet, "You will wake Sophie," he warned. Sophie strained to hear Alex's lowered voice.

"Passive resistance and *now*. That is the answer, Hans. We must tell them that they cannot wait for others to do it," Alex argued.

Sophie looked at the clock. It was past 2:00 in the morning. What were they doing? She crawled back into bed and let sleep come over her. When she woke up, Hans and Schurik were sleeping. Hans woke to Sophie washing up and the clamor of plates in the kitchen. She grinned at her older brother, and he smiled back. She admired his quick way of waking as if he hadn't even been sleeping.

After they ate some stale bread—their coupons had run out the day before—the threesome got on bikes and rode through Munich's monumental Siegestor, Germany's homage to France's Arc de Triomphe, and along Leopoldstrasse, past the elegant classical houses that reminded her of pictures of Florence that she had seen in travel books. They cruised along the poplar trees, brought to life by spring. Sophie cycled ahead of them, edging on a race, and Alex pulled the back of her bicycle, gaining the lead.

Sophie matriculated in the natural sciences and philosophy. This semester she was reading Leibniz and botany with Professors Huber and Schmidt. They wouldn't miss her. They lectured into the compliant air in dull monologues, and everything that she needed to know she could learn in textbooks. She didn't think about how angry Hans would be if he caught her snooping through his things. She raced back to Hans' apartment, letting a blustery spring wind push her along. It had brought in clouds, and she looked into the now grey sky and cursed it.

CHAPTER 6

The urge to act

———

MUNICH, MAY 1942

LETTING HERSELF IN WITH HANS' key, Sophie walked over to a pile of books stacked haphazardly in the corner of the living room. She was careful not to disrupt their order. She glanced at their broken spines. Schiller. Goethe. Sitting cross legged on the floor, she opened *The Awakening of Epimenides,* Act II, Scene 4, and flipped to its underlined pages. She read the passage:

> Hope:
> Now I find my good men
> Are gathered in the night,
> To wait in silence, not to sleep.
> And the glorious word of liberty
> They whisper and murmur,
> Till unaccustomed strangeness,
> On the steps of our temple
> Once again in delight they cry
> Freedom! Freedom!

In between the book's yellow pages she uncovered a single sheet of paper. Her hands began to tremble. It was Hans' handwriting. *A spiritless and cowardly people deserve total defeat. Forget not, every people deserve the kind of government that it puts up with.*

This was a written protest against Hitler. What were Hans and Alex intending to do with it? Stunned, she didn't know what to do next. She couldn't confront them. A few days ago she had overheard Alex speaking on the phone to his neighbor, pretending to be an officer. He asked for the use of a typewriter, saying he needed to type up some memos for Berlin. When she called him on it, he told her to mind her own business. This is what he needed the typewriter for. Just then she heard footsteps.

Hans opened the door to find Sophie still sitting on the floor with his books strewn around her. His dark complexion whitened. Unasked questions flooded the room. His eyes grew cold. She had trespassed and it was too late to invent an excuse that might have made the situation less painful.

Sophie said nothing.

"Damn it Sophie, don't you have a higher opinion of yourself?" Grabbing a medical text from his desk, he reprimanded her for skipping class and then without saying another word, slammed the door behind him.

Sophie took a deep breath. The shame and embarrassment of getting caught snooping through Hans' things didn't seem as important as knowing for sure. Hans and Alex were finally doing something. She knew they could use her help.

Throughout this war Fritz had told her about what the Nazis were doing. She knew about the SS shooting Dutch civilians demonstrating in Amsterdam, their plan to kill black POWs in

France, and even "population control" measures on the Eastern Front. These weren't just rumors. She knew and the truth had made her life unlivable. There were mornings when she was paralyzed with guilt. But Hans would never let her help. He would say that it was too dangerous for a woman. They were committing treason and it was punishable by death.

She would wait until the right time to ask him. She was going to ask Hans in front of Alex. Then she had a better thought. She could *prove* that she was strong and smart enough to join them. Her heart started racing. Like nothing else that she ever wanted—she couldn't even compare this to wanting to be with Fritz—she wanted to be a part of this.

Sophie admired the Bavarian skies from the State Library's reading rooms. Since her discovery in Hans' apartment, she tried to study drawings of ancient ferns, but she had too much difficulty concentrating on their Latin names. Her mind wandered to the leaflet's contents and to the name Hans and Alex had given themselves. The name "*The White Rose*" repeated over and over in her mind. What did it mean?

She ran into Traute in front of the State Library.

"Let's get a cup of coffee, Sophie. It looks like you could use one," Traute suggested, tucking dark bobbed hair around her ears. Looking at her pretty friend, Sophie felt her own appearance's neglect. Her hair had gotten too long and she had dark circles under her eyes from not sleeping.

The students at the café outside of the university sat in a stony silence. The days when they could congregate and converse was a thing of the distant past. Traute leaned closer to Sophie.

"Have you noticed anything different about Hans lately? He seems more anxious than usual. He looks tired all the time," Traute's blue eyes bored into her.

She had helped introduce Sophie into the Munich circle of friends, but most of all, Sophie respected the way she challenged her brother. Hans needed someone like Traute, unafraid to question his opinions. She hoped that the two would stay together, especially after the war. Sophie's friend Gisela from the Nazi women's camp in Krauchenweis had just come to Munich, and although Sophie had introduced her to Hans and Alex and all their friends, Gisela wasn't Hans' type. She didn't need to worry about that.

"It's not another woman." Sophie answered so quickly that Traute immediately suspected that it was a lie. She had met long-blond-haired Gisela and didn't like the way she eyed Hans. She was younger too.

"What's going on then?" Traute asked impatiently.

"I don't know, Traute, really, I don't." The first in uncountable lies.

Finished with their coffee, they each put down a coin on the table's counter and left the café, throwing their book bags over their shoulders. As they walked together towards the library, Sophie suggested calling Hans. She stopped at the nearest telephone booth and stepped inside. As she dialed the number, she noticed two pieces of paper stuck in the phone book. She took it out.

"Can I speak to him when you're done?" Traute peered her head inside. They looked just like the one she had seen in her brother's apartment.

"Look, Traute," Sophie pushed a page into her friend's hands. The intensity in her eyes revealed the whole story.

Traute skimmed the sheet of paper and then started to read aloud, dumbfounded.

Anything may be sacrificed to the good of the State except that end for which the State serves as a means. The State is never an end in itself; it is important only as a condition under which the purpose of mankind can be attained. This purpose is none other than the development of all of man's powers, his progress and improvement.

She knew immediately. "Hans wrote this. He quoted Schiller to me only yesterday."

"And I am going to help," Sophie burst out. "Whether Hans likes it or not. I'm going to help them copy and distribute. Just like it says here," Sophie pointed out the line and read it out loud, not bothering to look around first if anyone could hear them, "please make as many copies of this leaflet as you can and distribute them."

"Be careful, Sophie," Traute urged, taking a leaflet out of Sophie's hand and putting it in her bag without realizing that she was also now taking the risk. They couldn't go on speaking like this in public. Students passed by them on their way to class. "Please be careful."

They kissed good-bye on both cheeks. When Sophie reached Professor Muth's house by street car, she tore open her knapsack and began underlining the leaflet's essential points.

Have the Germans sunk so deeply in a sleep of death that they can't wake up? Why are the Germans behaving so apathetically about all of these most horrific and inhuman crimes?

She understood Hans' tactic. And then, finally, she got to its main idea.

It's not only compassion for the victims of these criminals that is lacking. But he will soon feel guilt. He is guilty for allowing this "government" to keep on existing, and he is guilty for even allowing it to exist in the first place! Guilty! Guilty! Guilty! But it's not too late to remove this disgusting misfit of a government from the world. If he acts now, he can stop piling more guilt upon himself. It's the duty of every German, now that he knows what the National Socialists are doing, it's his only and most important duty to exterminate these beasts.

They had struck a nerve. All she could think now, and the thought almost blinded her, was that she had to help. Somehow.

The leaflet ended with some quotes from Lao-tzu, the Chinese Daoist philosopher. What a peculiar selection. Was Werner somehow involved in all of this? Her younger brother was the one who was always interested in Eastern philosophy. For one brief second Sophie remembered that only six years ago she had believed in the Nazi Party and their perverse biological religion.

She made herself some tea, sat down on her bed, and read the leaflet again and again.

Since the conquest of Poland, 300,000 Polish Jews have been murdered in the most bestial form. We are seeing the most horrible crime against the dignity of humankind, a crime that has never been copied in the history of humankind.

The Jews are also human beings—one can ask the Jewish Question as one will—and on these people this question is actually being practiced.

Perhaps some say that the Jews have earned such a fate; this claim is monstrous arrogance.

This was the bravest and most truthful passage of all. She had to tell Fritz about this. They shared one another's secrets for so long now, and she couldn't really imagine not telling him. But it was too dangerous. Could she tell Professor Muth? No. She couldn't tell anyone. Not even Fritz.

Sophie had to prove her courage to Hans. He couldn't stop her from joining them. Besides, her guilt had become almost unbearable. She couldn't stand hearing the rumors any longer. She vowed the next time that she saw Fritz she had to ask him more persuasively what he had seen. He was not protecting her by denying her the truth. Guilt was a force that paralyzed all movement. Sometimes in the morning she could no longer get out of bed. And now Fritz was leaving for Russia. What were the chances of his coming back? And if he did, in what kind of condition would he return?

There was only the present moment. One learned this during wartime. Sophie remembered the last time she heard the high-pitched siren and she ran into the shelter by herself, holding her hands over her head. She wasn't sure which reaction was more terrifying: the old people's stoic silence or the frightened mother's attempt to stop her baby from wailing. She took out her diary and began to write as though this would save her:

June 1942

Many people believe that our age is the last. All the omens are terrible enough to make one think so, but isn't that belief of secondary importance? Mustn't we all, no matter what age we live in, be permanently prepared for God to call us to account from one moment to the next? How am I to know if I shall be alive tomorrow? We could all be wiped out overnight by a bomb, and my guilt would be no less than if I perished in company with the earth and the stars. I know all that, but don't I heedlessly fritter away my life just the same?

I don't understand how "devout" people can fear for God's existence today because mankind is dogging his footsteps with the sword and vile atrocities. As if God didn't have the power (I sense that everything rests in His hand). All we should fear for is the existence of humanity, because it has turned away from Him who is its very life.

She stopped writing for a moment to pray. *O God, take away my frivolity and self-will, which clings to the sweet, ephemeral things of life.*

That night after trying to study, she had a dream that convinced her. God rapped on her shoulder. Calling her into account. She awoke knowing that today was the day that she was going to steal the paper that they needed from the university. She was going to prove to Hans that she was brave enough. They needed more paper. Its supply was so tightly controlled one needed a special coupon to buy it in bulk. She knew where Professor Schmidt kept reams of paper.

Sophie pedaled furiously down Maximilianstrasse towards the university and threw her bike into the stuffed rack. During class, the botany department's hallways were empty and the supply closet wasn't locked. She prepared herself. She had less than five seconds.

Looking to the left and right, Sophie flung the closet door open and stuffed her knapsack full with blank sheets of paper until she could barely shut it. Then she looked around again, and seeing no one, composed herself. Sweeping her fingers through long brown hair, she took a deep breath. Instead of running out, which would have only caused attention, she walked calmly out of the building.

Adrenaline rushed through her. Biking wildly along Leopoldstrasse, she traced the events that had led up to this action. Speaking up at the girls' Hitler Youth meeting, reading the Bible and other banned books at the Nazi camp, silently rejecting the ideological training, arguing with Fritz about his role in Hitler's Army, sneaking in to play the organ in Blumberg's chapel, refusing to donate to the Winter Collection, listening to the radio with her father, talking with Carl Muth.

All of this had led up to this moment.

Sophie crossed the line. Up until now, she resisted the regime in small ways. Finally she was part of something bigger and something that could change the course of the war. She checked behind her to see if the heavy knapsack was still hooked onto her bike. Tomorrow Fritz was coming to Munich to say good-bye before leaving for the Russian Front. She needed to use the afternoon to study so that they could spend the day together. For the first time in their relationship she wouldn't be able to confide in him. Sometimes it was the omission of truth that opened up endless pathways to mistrust.

The biggest worry on her mind wasn't about Hans and Alex's deciding to let her help. Sophie's preoccupying thought was that her boyfriend was about to leave for the Eastern Front.

Fritz and Sophie planned to meet at the Botanical Gardens near King Ludwig's Nymphenburg summer estate, where swans swam in pairs along the canal leading up to the majestic palace that resembled Versailles. Greek mythological statues lined the formal garden's pebbled paths, trimmed neatly by perennials. Sophie cycled over the cobblestone street to the back entrance of the garden. She was excited to see all of the exotic species of plants. Munich had one of the finest botanical gardens in all of Europe.

Once inside, Sophie didn't feel like she was in Germany anymore. This wasn't like anything she had ever experienced. The garden existed as evidence of an international community; trees of the same species co-existed and thrived with one another in perfect peace. She looked at the Latin name tags next to the multitude of conifer trees and studied their differences. Collecting herself, she couldn't resist the impulse to bike faster on the gravel pathway towards the pond where they had agreed to meet. She caught her breath when she saw him.

Fritz was there first, like he always was, wearing his grey but now worn uniform that hung loosely from his too thin frame. He grinned standing by a rhododendron bush where white buds had started to grow. She hopped off her bike and they hugged one another and held one another tightly. Despite everything, not much had changed between them since the first time they met. The impulse to be close had only been strengthened through time and space. Even their constant discussions about the war and his part in it had formed a stronger bond between them.

She kept her promise. She loved Fritz because of the good in him. Because of what made him a human being. It was no longer impossible to her that she loved a soldier whose fate lay in Hitler's detestable plan. The war had to fail. It was clear to both of them that defeat in the war was not the defeat of Germany, but the defeat of National Socialism, and they were two very different things. Fritz was about to join millions of doomed soldiers on both sides. Sophie had trouble letting go of him.

He took her by the hand and without a word, they began walking along the small paths, along the assorted flowers which were in bloom or about to bloom, pausing to read their little white signs. Like always, the things they wanted to say would come easier to them when they walked together.

They passed through the arboretum and admired the white birches from North and South America. Sophie said something whose meaning, he realized, might take a lifetime to discover.

He had long ago accepted and even welcomed these kinds of abstractions. He would take the chance that someday he could understand them. She looked forlornly at a copper beech whose branches grew downwards, touching the ground and said, "I simply yearn to be a piece of tree bark, an odd notion, but it has haunted me for years." She looked away and kept walking. They sat on a bench by a cluster of rocks covered in ancient moss and tiny multicolored wild flowers.

She didn't have the energy to tell him about her courses, professors, or the university. Or even about the evenings with Hans, Schurik, Christoph, Willi, Traute, and drinking too much wine. She didn't tell him even that Gisela, her only friend from the camp, had come to Munich to study too and that Sophie had introduced her to the circle of friends. She didn't tell him that Gisela and Hans were flirting too much when Traute wasn't looking. She didn't tell him about the White Rose leaflet.

She quoted Willi when the conversation turned again to religion. "In reality being Christian is a difficult and uncertain life, one full of difficult stress, and always demands overcoming new challenges."

Fritz listened closely. He loved this type of conversation. In France, he realized that his belief in God, strengthened by his love for Sophie and which also existed through Sophie, were two separate things. Beside them, the garden bloomed in springtime. He hung on to her words as though they were a rope, and he was dangling over a cliff. Rough waters raged under his calm exterior, about to engulf him. He would rely on his faith in God and in both of them to survive.

Sophie suddenly stopped talking as she had a habit of doing, and he turned around to face her. They were both thinking the same thing.

"There is a good chance, isn't there, that we might never see one another again?" Then she quickly apologized. "Forgive me, please. I'm sorry. Of course we will. Let's not make this meeting too serious. Let's not talk about that. Can't we just forget it all, just for a moment, in this place where the trees seem to be the only living things which still embrace peace?"

Fritz smiled and nodded. They entered the white steel-framed greenhouse that sheltered tropical plants, cacti, fruit trees, unusual orchids, and giant water lilies. The humid air smelled sweet. An elderly gardener in blue overalls walked past them with a watering can and greeted them with the old Bavarian greeting *Gruess Gott* and not with Heil Hitler. He smiled at the young lovers and gently watered the bright violet plants.

"Too much water is just as lethal as too little," he said to them and pushed his wheelbarrow down the path. Sophie and Fritz sat in the café in front of the multi-variety rose beds, whose fragrance enveloped them. White statues of chubby angels cornered the rectangular garden, trimmed with boxwoods. This paradise was the result of the co-existence of natural treasures from all over the world. They held hands, listening to the birds and allowed the sunshine to warm them.

Then it was time. His train was leaving for France in forty-five minutes. By night he would be in Le Mans, and in the morning he was leaving for the Don River in Stalin's Soviet Union. Sophie hadn't asked him for a single detail about the supposed progress towards Moscow. He was grateful for that. He would only have to tell her again that his only duty was towards his men—which meant keeping them alive.

He told her to watch over her mother, who wasn't well. He was still trying to get a pardon for Sophie's father. His trial kept being postponed and he had two more months in prison for speaking badly about Hitler in public. Fritz had become a part of the Scholl family and felt an allegiance to them that even he couldn't understand.

Then he took her by the shoulders and faced her squarely. He didn't want her to come to the train station. They had had enough of saying good-bye at train stations all over Germany. He acknowledged that he was tired of seeing her standing alone among the other women—soldiers' wives, children, mothers, sisters, aunts, grandmothers, girlfriends, friends. He preferred for her to stay instead in the garden for a while and to enjoy the fountain and to sit among her favorite flowers.

He asked her to pray for him.

"I'm not going to promise that I'll come home, Sophie."

He kissed her long enough for the promise to linger and then turned abruptly and didn't look back. Sophie watched him until he disappeared from sight. She didn't cry.

When she returned to her new room on Mandlstrasse, she wanted to take every detail of those hours and put them away in a box which she could always open. A place where the memories of the trees and flowers, the gardener, the birds, wouldn't fade. But most of all, she wanted to remember exactly how it felt to be loved and to love like this. But when she tried to recall their last hug and kiss, she couldn't.

A part of her was so frightened by the future that it hurt too much to feel this deeply, this inexplicably, and that although she mustn't think it—she must *never* allow herself to think it—it might have been for the last time.

In the evenings, Hans, Alex, Willi, Christoph, Traute, and Sophie met at their friend's architectural studio on Leopoldstrasse. Tonight they were hosting a reading by a well-known Munich actor. Hans refused to talk about the leaflet that Sophie had discovered in the apartment. He acted as though she didn't know. Hans was busy entertaining both Gisela and Traute. Lately he took less of an interest in Traute. He liked the way Gisela lightly tossed her enviable blond mane, laughing easily with astonishing pale-blue eyes. She smiled a lot more than his girlfriend, who had a tendency to think too much.

Sophie walked around the giant studio, taking in its gigantic library with worn books and broken spines. Blue prints were tacked up on every square inch of wall. The studio belonged to a Manfred Eickemeyer, an architect forced to work in occupied Poland.

Then it struck her. It was he. It had been Herr Eickemeyer who told her brother about the murdered Jews. Everything was starting to fit together. After the actor's reading, Sophie finally pulled Hans over to the side and out of earshot from the others. The real drama was about to unfold.

"I have something for you," she whispered, opening her knapsack, showing him the reams of paper. Hans gasped and reached out to touch it. They had just run out. This was exactly what they needed.

Hans looked back at her with eyes so penetrating they could have opened a safe.

Then, without allowing him to say anything, Sophie took out a recent letter from Fritz. He had been in Russia for less than a month. She started to read out loud: *Yesterday I had to put up with another evening in the officer's canteen. It's really too bad, all the wine that is senselessly wasted so that they all can get in "a good mood" as quickly as possible—all this is converted into filth, loud noise, and broken glass. How poor these people are, that this is the only joy which they are capable.*

Bored, Hans looked past Sophie, searching out either Gisela or Traute. Sophie cleared her throat as she got to the passage that Hans had to hear. Bringing this truth to light wasn't easy. She had been living with these letters for years without sharing their contents with anyone. *It is horrifying with the cynicism and coldbloodedness that my commander speaks about the slaughter of all the Jews in occupied Russia.*

He had underlined the word "all." Sophie repeated it twice.

Hans covered his face with his hands. Sophie continued, *He is also fully convinced of the justification of these actions.*

She slowly folded the letter back up and put it into her dress pocket.

At first Hans didn't know what to say. He looked back at her with intense eyes. Sometimes the most important agreements were made by the contract of two pairs of agreeing eyes.

"I'm so sorry, Sophie," he finally said, recognizing that it must have been hard for her to live with these truths. Hans was sorry for everything. Why had they waited so long? He touched Sophie lightly on arm, took her knapsack off her shoulder and told her to come to the studio tomorrow morning.

Hans and Alex talked between themselves and decided Sophie's responsibilities. They allowed her to sit in on their discussions but they limited her contribution to accounting duties. Alex argued with Hans. He thought that Sophie could help formulate text. She was often smarter than both of them put together, he argued. Hans disagreed. He didn't want her getting too deeply involved. Alex only laughed at the contradiction but didn't insist. Sophie was just glad to have been invited into their meetings.

The next draft was spread out on two large drawing tables next to a typewriter and an outdated, rusty, lever-operated copy machine.

Sophie kept track of the White Rose's expenses in a green book. Her father taught her how to add and subtract in tiny columns. Hans didn't tell her where he got the money for the stamps, ink, and envelopes, and although she was curious, she didn't ask. She sat in on their meetings and listened to her brother and Alex discussing the proposed text, bouncing ideas back and forth. Their goal was to write, produce, and distribute as many copies as they could in a short period of time.

Hans paced and changed the language constantly, referring often to wide-ranging political and religious thinkers. He asked Alex for his opinion more to hear the sound of his voice than anything else. Alex didn't seem to mind. He was more of an artist than a political thinker. Alex made a joke now and then. Sophie howled. Hans, too intent on the leaflet's perfection, didn't even seem to hear them.

Alex smoked out of a skinny pipe, and Hans and Sophie dragged on cigarettes in Eickemeyer's studio. When the work was done, they drank bottles of wine stolen from Alex's father's dwindling collection. Hans often left their meetings abruptly and to which woman he went to he didn't say.

The line at the post office went out the door. Sophie took a swastika pin out of her knapsack from her days in the League and pinned it to the lapel on her Bavarian jacket. Alex looked at her and raised his eyebrow. When they finally arrived at the counter, Alex asked for two sheets of fifty Reichsmark stamps. The postal clerk studied their intelligent and innocent faces.

Alex didn't smile.

"Why do you need fifty stamps?" The clerk asked out of duty, his voice worn thin from having to interrogate people for wanting to send letters.

"My aunt just died," Alex answered plainly, "and I need to send notices to our family and friends."

The clerk seized up his patrons. Noting Alex's elegant clothes and the sad girl wearing the Party's pin, he made a quick deduction that rich people had to send more death notices. Without expressing his sympathy, he tore off an unusual amount of stamps. He was tired of such long lines and asking questions.

Once again, Fritz had sent Sophie some more money. He had specified that it was for books. She handed some bills over to Alex. Once outside of the building, she jumped up and down. Alex hugged her, and then quickly pulled back. She was Fritz's girlfriend. He couldn't get too close. They had just completed finding all of the supplies and were ready to send out the White Rose's leaflet Number Three to postboxes all over Munich.

The Party pasted new black and white signs on almost every street corner: *Care for your gasmasks!* Everyone knew what this meant. The Allied Forces carpet-bombed cities day and night now. The roar of airplanes filled the skies and then, seconds later in the far off distance, she heard the bombs exploding. Sophie could swear they were getting closer and closer. Shelters were familiar. Rumors filled the city about stricter Gestapo measures, especially since Party Leader Wagner, the famous drunk who often fell down during speeches, had a heart attack. Sophie read in the paper about a man who was caught stealing flour from a store after a bombing, looting for food. He had been sentenced to death.

Hans dictated a new leaflet to Sophie, who sat at the typewriter. They needed her help. She typed as fast as she could. The keyboard was missing the "s" key. She begged Hans constantly to slow down. He continued, at the same pace:

Every person has a right to a useful and right State, one that assumes the freedom of the individual and community. After God's will, the person should be independent of the

State, and its natural goal is for the individual to search for self-sufficiency.

Our "State" is a "dictatorship of evil" and we've known this for a long time, but why do we allow it? Why do we allow ourselves to be commandeered by criminals and drunks? Don't we know that it is not only our right, but our moral duty, to remove this system?

Don't hide your cowardice with the coat of intelligence. Every day that you don't act, your guilt grows like a parabolic curve, higher and higher.

Alex and Sophie objected to this line. They thought that it sounded a bit morally high-handed.

Sophie spoke up. "This will alienate the reader. We need them on our side."

"I'm so sick of the indifference." Hans got up, started pacing again.

"But do they need to be reminded of their guilt?" Sophie argued.

"Let's tell them how to resist," Alex wanted the leaflets to give practical advice. "Obviously we don't know how to act against this kind of oppression. How should we? Where should we have learned it?"

Sophie started typing again. Alex continued. Hans listened.

Everyone is in the position of helping to destroy this government. With the united effort of convinced and active people, we can achieve our goal. Our medium: passive resistance.

We must ask ourselves, how can I fight against the present "State"?

All three got excited over Alex's concrete formulations. This was the answer. These leaflets had to *teach* their countrymen how to resist Hitler.

Hans, Alex, and Sophie compiled a list how and where people could passively resist the National Socialist regime:

Sabotage factories.
Sabotage rallies and meetings.
Sabotage propaganda posters.
Sabotage in classrooms.
Sabotage wherever you can.

Finished with writing, they assembled the production line. Hans wanted one thousand copies by morning. The three took turns feeding paper into the antique copy machine, turning its creaky handle. One by one, the sheets rolled off of the press and into a pile. It took all night.

The next day they skipped their classes. The phone rang in the studio, and no one picked it up. Alex stole a public telephone book, and Hans went through every page, hand-selecting names and addresses. Doctors, lawyers, café, restaurant and gallery owners, university professors, writers, museum presidents. He was convinced these people were the ones who still had enough will in them to act. Sophie and Alex took turns addressing the envelopes. They stuffed and licked them, dividing them into three batches.

Hans took out a map of Munich and assigned neighborhoods.

Alex got Nymphenburg, Hans the Altstadt, and Sophie Schwabing. They were to locate three or more mailboxes in each section of the city and unload their batches at each one. Then go home. In case of capture, they didn't even think of a plan.

Sophie looked up into the overcast sky and remembered that it was a new moon. The Americans wouldn't drop their phosphorus bombs without the aid of moonlight. Tonight Munich would be spared the green mist that would engulf the city and, once it cleared, reveal deep pockets of destruction. She hated the familiar sight of lights in the sky forming the pattern of what looked like Christmas trees, the flares that came before the bombs. She got on her bike and headed toward the university, the soul of the student quarter. With her heart pounding, she would finish her first act of active resistance in less than five minutes.

She knew where the mailboxes were located. Sophie stopped her bike at the corner of Tuerkenstrasse. All she had to do was lift the first bunch out of her knapsack, toss them in, get back on her bike and do the same at the next one. Four boxes, four times. The calm, light air embraced her as she rode down empty streets. Schwabing was deserted. Students no longer congregated or spent their nights in bars and cafés. The night policeman on the street turned the corner.

Sweat beaded on her forehead and with her pulse racing, she got off her bike. Sophie looked in both directions down the empty cobblestone street and dropped the next bundle into the mailbox. At the last one, she felt like a professional spy and with her knapsack empty, she biked home slowly to her room. The night air embraced her and she was surprised by a new feeling of confidence. It had been so easy. She wasn't even that scared. It was a mystery. If she had been caught, her life would have been over.

Something essential inside of her changed. No longer guilty of indifference, the burden of guilt had been lifted. She felt weightless and free. She remembered her favorite Psalm. Number 13. It worked—petition, prayer, trust, and praise. This was the rejoicing part. Hans wanted to start the next leaflet tomorrow. They had to keep getting their message out and give people instructions on how to resist. Exhausted, she fell asleep in her clothes. She had to get up early in the morning for her philosophy class.

Professor Kurt Huber dragged his foot across the creaky wooden floor on Tuesdays, Thursdays, and Fridays. The packed lecture hall slowly came to attention as his aid erased the blackboard behind the worn podium. A deep wisdom defined his middle-aged, weathered face. Huber waited for his students to come to attention. Also burdened by a lisp as a result of a childhood epidemic, he refused to have to shout. "Leibniz and His Time" was a secondary lecture.

He won his reputation with his work in musicology, tracing the history of Bavarian folk songs. Due to his physical shortcomings, as the Nazis took over the universities, Huber hadn't been allowed to become a full professor. "We can only use professors that also can become officers" was the reason for his rejection.

Huber was so clever at disguising his lectures that even when the Nazi students monitored them for subversive content, they couldn't identify his teachings as anti-Nazi. Sophie came in late and made her way quietly to the back row. She took out her notebook and began to sketch. As Huber began the lecture, Traute sat down next to her. They greeted one another with just a smile. Sophie switched to taking notes.

"Leibniz wansed to crease new polisical ideas from German myth-sicithm."

Even though it was difficult to discern his words because of the way he blended "s's" and "t's," Huber spoke with such conviction that a hush fell over the classroom. A few students looked around to see if they would be allowed to commit this heresy to paper. Huber was sacrificing his career and perhaps even his life to make these statements. He waited before he continued. These students were Germany's last hope. He still hoped that an inkling of honor and justice existed within some of them. The breeding of Nazi ideology was also due to the failure and cowardice of teachers like him.

He took a deep breath and rested his arms on the podium. His tired tweed suit, frayed shirt, and cumbersome old orthopedic boots no longer made a shabby and sad impression. Students could still recognize the unmistakable light of truth. The beginning of a smile slowly swept across the professor's face. The students rapped on the lecture hall seats with their knuckles to signify that the lecture was over.

Huber's aid wrote the assigned text for next week on the board. Several students gathered around the professor, eagerly asking him questions. The philosophy lecture had made sense to them, although Leibniz's ideas and Huber's interpretation of them were the complete opposite of what they had learned growing up under the Third Reich.

They had all been taught that the individual served the State, and not vice versa. Huber was telling them something different. Leibniz's political treatise— the philosopher had been educated in German law—was based in rationality, but didn't discount the irrational feelings of love for one's neighbor.

Huber remained patient. He knew how systematically these young people had been brainwashed. This was his chance. But the excited group of students by his podium would bring unwanted attention by the daily watch, so he insisted that the questions be asked only during his office hours.

Sophie and Traute filed out of the back row, slinging their heavy knapsacks on their backs. Traute, late for her anatomy class, kissed Sophie lightly on both cheeks. The White Rose, as they called themselves now, were taking a break today after their successful mission, and Sophie, tired from not sleeping two nights in a row, biked home to Mandlstrasse next to the park.

When Sophie returned to her new room in an empty apartment, she collapsed into the overstuffed chair and put the heavy black phone into her lap. The dial spun around slowly. When she heard her mother's voice, she knew immediately that something was wrong. Magdalena stated the facts slowly.

"Your father was heard speaking out against Hitler in his office. His secretary denounced him." She paused for a moment to gain the strength to go on.

"The trial is set for August and we need you to come home. To help out in the office. I'm sorry, Sophie. I know you've waited so long to study. But this is just the way it is."

Sophie promised to take the earliest train in the morning. Without a moment of hesitation, she sat down at her desk, looked at the yellowing pink roses in the blue glass vase, and got out her secret paper. She smoothed it out with her hand and, taking her favorite fountain pen, started a letter to Fritz.

She asked him if he could request a pardon for her father from Ulm's Party Leader. She signed it with "Yours," and sealed it slowly, bringing the envelope close to her lips. She remembered for a moment what it felt like to be together with him. She put the letter on top of her packed bag so she wouldn't forget to post it, and for comfort turned on the radio, hoping for some Bach.

Once again, she fell asleep in her clothes. Munich's new Party Leader recommended sleeping in one's clothes. One could speed up the process of evacuating into a bomb shelter that way. The music on the radio, a Beethoven symphony, infused her dreams, ones in the morning that she wouldn't be able to remember.

When Sophie arrived in Ulm the next day, Magdalena Scholl told her the story about Robert's arrest in a detached voice, choosing her words carefully.

"He was overheard saying that Hitler is the scourge of the earth. Then he predicted that the Red Army would soon make it to Berlin. His new secretary called the Gestapo."

Magdalena shook her head in disbelief. Of course, they all felt this way but he dared to say it out loud. Neither she nor Sophie mentioned the death sentence for those who spoke out. They would revoke his business license and sentence him to prison. She couldn't bear to think what this meant. They were all hungry enough already.

Inge made her sister dinner with a leftover portion of potatoes. They split it into three. Even with their food ration coupons, there hadn't been enough to eat for months. Sophie's mother put on a special dress for her daughter's homecoming. Appearances had always been important to her mother, but now the people in Ulm looked as if they were having trouble with the basic needs of food, shelter, and clothing.

Despite Inge's shabby dress and holes in her heavy stockings, she had a suspicious new glimmer in her dark eyes. Sophie would ask her about it tomorrow. Was she spending more time with their friend, Otl Aicher? She suspected that her older sister had finally fallen in love. They joined hands in prayer before eating.

"Thank you for bringing us together, dear Lord," Magdalena spoke softly. "Please bring Fritz safely home from Russia. Please keep Werner and Hans safe. Please give my husband strength to endure this unjust arrest." She kept her eyes closed for a moment. Sophie thought about Ernst, Hans' school friend who recently died in combat.

She took out a white candle out from the cupboard and lit it. Magdalena wanted to tell her not to. There were so many air raids and candles in short supply, but she decided against it. They could enjoy the candle for half an hour.

Sophie gazed into the candle's flame. Wax dripped down its softened side. It flickered in an invisible wind and then got strong again. Magdalena studied her daughter's face carefully.

Her otherwise calm and gentle eyes couldn't stay focused. She was way too thin. She played with her hands and kept her nails so short her mother wondered if she was biting them again.

She had seen Sophie preoccupied during her days in the League, but this was something different. Her daughter was hiding something. She didn't ask what it was. Magdalena raised her children with the hope that they would come to her if they needed her help or advice. She stroked her youngest daughter's back and smiled gently at her, trying to read her daughter's eyes. Sophie returned the look, but said nothing, getting up from the table and retreating into her bedroom, crawling gratefully into her childhood bed. She missed Elisabeth, who was working as a nanny near Stuttgart, and they hadn't seen one another for months. Sophie wondered if hers and Hans' secret would separate them.

The guilt holding her back was lessening. She was anxious about all of the work they still had to do. What would be their next step after the leaflets? Both Alex and Sophie relied on Hans for leadership. She missed Fritz—his quiet strength and thirst for knowledge and truth. She missed the way he loved her. She missed his low voice and his height. Recently she thought too much about Alex, or even Otl. He was Hans' close friend and maybe even Inge's new crush. She cursed her duplicity. She often felt foolish when she admired Alex's aristocratic mannerisms, the way he drew on his pipe and his patience with women. She felt less of a mystery to him than to Fritz. She asked God to show her the right place and fell into a deep and restful sleep.

The skinny foil bent and then rebounded with a twang. Willi's footwork on the leather mat couldn't save him from Christoph's relentless offense. Tink. Tink. Tink. The foils crossed again and again. Then, finally, Willi drew back and retreated, lifting the mask up from their fencing helmets. Christoph did the same, smiling graciously as he leaned lightly on his foil as it wobbled and then straightened again. They took off their long gloves and shook hands. It had been an equal match and a difficult win. Almost two hours had passed before they heaved themselves out of their white quilted uniforms.

Christoph Probst's stature was outdone only by his down-to-earth good nature. He was the only man in the student medic corps who was married. He was already a father of two young children. Willi knew that Christoph, Hans, and Alex spent a lot of time together outside of the university. He wondered what they talked about. Willi liked the way Christoph outsmarted him in their fencing duel. The women students admired Christoph's dark and handsome looks but he never let on that he noticed.

Willi was from the North and Christoph was Bavarian. The two usually didn't mix. Bavarians were typically loud and funny; Northerners were grave and serious. Willi sang in the choir and kept to himself in the student barracks at night, either writing or reading. But the fencing match had broken pretenses, and Christoph, the winner, invited him to a drink in the student medic lounge.

"I've served on the Eastern Front," Willi said. "There are no heroes in the occupied territories." He lowered his voice and, with what could only be described as shame, looked down on the floor.

Christoph recognized that his new friend was suffering the burden of knowing an unspeakable truth. Alone in the men's locker room, they confessed their mutual hatred. Words got caught in awkward sentences. Christoph waited until the right moment.

"Come to our friend's studio on Leopoldstrasse Friday evening. Several of us meet there weekly to discuss some important things. Have you ever read Muth's *Hochland*?"

Willi's eyes lit up. He had read the Catholic magazine regularly until it had been banned.

When Carl Muth and Theodor Haecker finished reading, they opened up a discussion. Hans, Alex, Christoph, Willi, Sophie, Traute, Gisela, and some others sat in a circle. They were debating again. Was it right to resist tyranny with force?

Willi, new to the group, answered first. "I just don't know if this can apply here. Humanity has never seen these types of crimes before."

They argued for an hour. Neither side would budge but when it was time to go, Professor Muth and Theodor left the studio into the warm summer evening smiling. Since when had they been able to talk like this?

With just Christoph and Willi remaining in their group, Hans sensed that it was time. They would be able to risk what was necessary. He took copies of the leaflets out of his bag and handed them to Willi and Christoph.

"Do you want to join us?" Hans asked after they had a chance to read the first paragraph. Willi shook his head yes. He, too, had been waiting for this chance and it had finally come.

"I know students in Hamburg from our old Catholic fraternity. I can go up there and speak to them. We need to broaden the reach. Unite with other resistance groups."

"Christoph? What do you think we should do?" asked Hans.

He hesitated. He thought about his wife and two children. He had married Herta after getting her pregnant. They were only twenty-two then. And it had been the best thing he had ever done, he ever would do. His own father had committed suicide, consumed by inner demons, and he wanted his children to grow up knowing their father.

"We need two more editions before we go to Poland," Hans continued. He had a captive audience. Willi, Alex, and Hans had just received their marching orders to the Eastern Front. They were to serve in field hospitals through Warsaw, Malkinia, and Vyazma.

Sophie worried about her brother's appearance. He looked tired, overwhelmed, and sometimes, she thought, slightly possessed. Sophie asked him to slow down. To try and sleep. To rest with Traute or Gisela. He took on leadership duties with an openness that she admired. The others respected him and did what he asked without questioning. But Hans' desire to produce and distribute two more leaflets and to double the amount of copies seemed impossible.

Christoph had written a leaflet. Hans, Alex, and Sophie read over the first draft. He wrote with his faith. Sophie envied something that he had naturally, an inner confidence that came from something so unshakeable, something higher. With the faith of this writer, his readers would be convinced to act:

Every word out of Hitler's mouth is a lie. When he says peace, he means war. When he sacrilegiously calls out the name of the Almighty, he means the power of evil, the fallen angel, Satan. His mouth is the stinking revenge of hell, and his power actually has even been rejected.

One must use rational methods to lead the National Socialist terror State. Behind all of the logical and text book considerations exists the irrational, the fight against the demon, the bringer of the message of the Antichrist.

Yes, man is free, but he is defenseless against evil without a true God. He is like a ship without a rudder that has been abandoned in the storm, like a baby without a mother, like a cloud that disappears. Has God not given you the power and courage to fight? We must attack evil where it is most powerful, and it is the most powerful in Hitler's hands.

Christoph used a quote from Novalis, "Only religion can wake Europe again."

Hans and Christoph both agreed that they needed to make it clear that these leaflets were written from inside Germany: *The National Socialist power must be militarily defeated, and we also desire a renewal of the broken German spirit—from within.*

The ability to be born again, Christoph believed, must be encouraged. The Germans had to come to terms with their guilt. Perhaps it was their guilt, he thought, that was paralyzing them. He ended the leaflet with: *We are your angry conscience! We will not leave you in peace!*

Sophie smiled. Christoph wasn't like Hans, preoccupied with inner thoughts. The last time she saw him, she gave him little booties for the baby that she had knitted with wool that Fritz sent to her.

Their imminent departure to the front signaled a celebration. They accomplished so much. Once again, they had written, produced and distributed thousands of leaflets all over Munich. Two new and committed members had joined them and they numbered sixteen. Momentum and confidence fueled the party.

The late July evening's humidity cast a lazy spell over the students. Before coming to the studio, Sophie and Traute went down to the Isar in the English Garden and swam in the river, letting its tide take them along. They allowed the current to sweep them along past willow trees, their long branches dipping into the cold, refreshing water. Alex stole whatever he could find from his father's wine cellar, opened a few bottles, and let them stand on the long table that was normally occupied with the typewriter, the rickety broken down manual copy machine, paper and envelopes.

Tonight they came to say good-bye to Willi, Alex, and Hans. Even Professor Huber had been invited, and strangely enough, he agreed to come. He sat proudly at the front of the room and made the group sing a folksong. Christoph rapped on the glass to get the group's attention. Willi sulked in a corner, unable to rally himself for the toast. His memories of what he had seen in Warsaw in April still haunted him. This was no cause for celebration.

His bad mood was also caused by Sophie's increasing role in their missions. He didn't want Gisela and Traute to help, either.

He worried about their safety. Women were not strong enough for this work. The Gestapo in Munich was looking for them. Ads filled the newspaper offering a 1,000 Reichsmark award for information leading to their capture. He didn't like Sophie's impulsive nature, and he wished that she didn't know so much. She was, after all, just a girl, like his sister, Angelika. He was careful that his sister knew nothing.

Christoph cleared his throat over the din of the party. He would return to his post in Austria after his friends left and wait for their return.

"Live in deep trust, my friends, that everything has a purpose and that there are no coincidences in life," his eyes scanned the room and he smiled. "All worthwhile battles are ultimately fought for good and our life goal is the completion of our person, and not outside achievements. Because life does not begin with birth and does not end with death."

He paused. He knew his friends were about to leave for the Eastern front as medics and therefore be daily confronted with dying. No one spoke.

"Life is the great assignment of a preparation for another existence in another form. Only later a light will shine on all the things of our life that we have not understood. It will allow us to finally be clear. But first we must accept, and even recognize, our lack of knowledge. We found the right way, and now we will experience joy, real joy, something that no one can take away from us." He paused and lifted his glass. "Here's to the White Rose."

The room filled with hoorah's. Tears welled up in Sophie's eyes. Then it was Alex's turn to say something. Everyone knew how excited he was to return to Russia, to see the country where he had been born and where his mother, whom he never knew, came from. He couldn't wait to speak his native language again.

Tipsy from too much wine, Alex's toast took a different tone than Christoph's. He made a vow.

"I will never shoot a Russian or a German." That's all he said. Then he sat back down, taking another gulp from his third glass. Alex's nervous eyes darted and finally fell on the floor. He didn't want to have to carry a gun. Willi looked over at Hans, expecting him to take the lead. Then finally, Kurt Huber cleared his throat and with a lisp that made it difficult to understand, he helped clarify the situation.

"You are brave men. You will have to fix up German soldiers who have been fighting for Hitler and send them back again, but this is your job as medics and so you will do it. Good luck, my friends. I am honored to be among you," choking back too much emotion, he sat back down.

"If I must, I will stand by my fellow soldier," Hans finally spoke, still sitting. This was the principle by which Fritz lived his life. Sophie had heard Fritz say similar things all the time. Everyone in the room knew what this meant. Willi shook his head in agreement. He had had enough experience already to know that this is what soldiers did for one another. Ideology, especially one as senseless, irrational, and demonic as the one the German Army was supposedly fighting for, meant nothing to a man who had the power to protect his brother, his friend. Also, they had to come back home again, and begin again the work they had started.

Siblings Hans and Sophie Scholl and Christoph Probst at a train
station in Munich, July, 1942. Scholl and Probst are in student-
medic uniform, preparing to leave for occupied Poland.
Photo: George Wittenstein/akg-images.
Reprinted here with permission.

CHAPTER 7

A chance to preserve our integrity

––––––––––

MUNICH, JULY 1942

SOPHIE WASHED HER FACE WITH cold water. She pinned a daisy
in her hair from a bouquet of wildflowers on the kitchen table.
Getting on her bike, she pedaled towards the train station. She
said a quick prayer over and over. "Please let them return safely,
please return them safely." Jamming her bike into the rack and
running onto the packed platform, she smiled, waving to Hans,
Alex, and Willi. Christoph had come to say good-bye too.

Sophie's flower made a statement of peace among their green
field uniforms. As usual, Alex joked about it and made her laugh.
About fifteen of them wore felt caps identifying them as medics.
A day earlier, the Jews from Milbertshofen stood on the same platform to be deported to Dachau. The police had carefully hosed it
down. It was perfectly clean now except for newly crushed cigarette butts smoked by nervous men.

They were headed into occupied Poland: Warsaw, then onto
Vyazma in western Russia, and final stop Gshatsk. Someone snapped
their picture. Sophie raised her hands in the air, smiling at the camera.

So did Hans and Alex. They didn't think at that moment, wearing German Army uniforms, that this picture could someday indict or implicate them. Hans didn't realize how much of a contradiction it was that they were smiling with the task that lay before them. The task would be to witness. And then to refuse to deny.

For three days the train veered through Poland, past the plundered and empty fields. They talked, played cards, read, and slept. They laughed and swapped stories about the women they knew and those they hoped to know. Hans was careful not to fall asleep on Alex's shoulder. Finally, the train stopped in Warsaw at the Danziger station. Earlier, as the train neared the city, they saw a railroad sign, "Umschlagplatz Station, Special Operations Only." Hans made a note to investigate.

They headed for the city's center. Observing the cues of daily life, it took only a few seconds for them to realize that they had entered a place paralyzed by terror and fear. The city's humidity hung on to them tightly as they trudged along mysteriously quiet streets. Their enormous back packs filled with supplies weighed nothing compared with the heaviness on their minds.

A street car passed them, ringing its bell, warning them to get out of the tracks. Willi was the first to see that it was headed towards Umschlagplatz. Inside, skeletal figures with black, hollow eyes looked back at them. Hans motioned to the others to follow the train's tracks.

The SS guard at its entrance refused to let them in.

"Go get a drink, *mein Herr*," he said in German, pointing down another street. "There is nothing for you to see in here. These rats don't need your help." Then he looked away from them, indicating that he was done speaking. "Move on." He motioned towards his holster. Alex covered his nose, and held his stomach, retching from the ghetto's stench.

July's hot sun had already set by the time they found the bar. Brown, black, and grey uniformed officers and soldiers filled the blue smoky bar with big wooden booths. Men had carved their initials into the tabletops, and women in short skirts and fishnets sat at the long dark bar and watched for customers in the mirror.

Hans, Alex, and Willi joined the others but didn't drink fast shots of the clear vodka. Instead, they nursed their drinks in slow, small sips. They wouldn't allow their secret to be loosened by alcohol. The White Rose was on a mission to discover and confirm. What they could only guess at burned inside each of them in silence like a slow fire. Willi took out his journal and continued writing his daily notes.

On their way out of the bar, Hans saluted his superior, making his choice from one of the working girls. Late evening claimed the last of summer's light. Temperatures had dropped dramatically. Stars rose and shone brightly in a moonless sky. Suddenly a machine gun's rat-a-tat-tat broke the evening's calm. Did they hear a thud? A scream? Then another rat-a-tat-tat. Hans wasn't sure where it was coming from. Alex pointed to inside the ghetto. Frightened by the sudden orphan gunfire, they rushed back to temporary quarters inside of the hotel.

Once safely inside, Hans started a letter to Professor Huber. He was sure that it would be censored so he chose his words carefully. *The ghetto, the city, and everything else, has made a decisive impression on us.* Decisive. Decision causes action. Action involves a desire for responsibility. Hans finished the letter quickly, asked his friends to sign it as a show of solidarity and opened his own journal, writing furiously, recording the day's experience.

The next day they boarded the train and headed towards Gshatsk. The train ripped through the Russian landscape. This time the quietness among them was caused by the endless beauty of the steppe. An orange afterglow lit its horizon, accompanying the speeding train. In Germany, one sensed the dimensions of fields, forests, and lakes. In contrast, Russia appeared limitless. Alex peered out of the moving train, mesmerized by the steppe's vastness. The fields, hills, and valleys went on forever. He drank the sight with his eyes until, unable to watch the fertile and vibrant scenery any longer, he passed out from tiredness.

When they arrived in Vyazma, Willi sat on a park bench while the others walked through what was left of the city. He saw an onion-domed church through the ruins—untouched by the torch of war—sitting on top of a hill. He closed his eyes and began to pray. He didn't want anything. In this absence of desire, Willi felt God's presence most, even in this devastated city where the odor of death and destruction permeated the air that he needed to breathe.

Munich, July 1942

Because it was the only thing left to do, Sophie cycled to the English Garden, still named after the enemy, sat down on a bench by the lake, and took out her diary. The familiar feeling of hopelessness stalled her movements. Working on the leaflet missions liberated her from guilt that oppressed her for so many years.

With her boyfriend, and now brother and friends at the front, she felt her powerlessness again. God knows what they were seeing. Would they be asked to participate too? And what was she supposed to do now? Wait for their return until she could act again? What if they didn't return? She wrote painfully slow, etching out the words to her Higher Power one at a time.

> *My soul is like an arid wasteland when I try to pray to You, conscious of nothing but its own barrenness.*
>
> *My God, transform the ground into good soil so that Your seed doesn't fall on it in vain. All I know about You is that my salvation resides in You alone.*
>
> *Don't turn away from me if I fail to hear You knock; open my deaf, deaf heart. I am so powerless. Do with me the best You can...*

Had writing the leaflets been enough? Guilt swept inside of her again like poison. She looked up at the quiet lake and swans, and remembered all the times Fritz risked his life to tell her the truth. The terror he had seen first-hand. Now she knew the way Hans, Alex, Willi, Christoph, and the others knew. Eickemeyer had known. Dr. Muth and Professor Huber knew. And her father, in prison. He had always known. She started writing again.

> *The only solution to all of this is more prayer. If only I didn't stand in my own way. I pray for a compassionate heart, for how else could I love?*

I often forget the sufferings that ought to overwhelm me,
the sufferings of mankind. I place my powerless love in Your
hands, that it may become powerful.

She would have to wait for their return. In five months they could start resisting again. When she got home to her room in the villa on the park, a letter waited under her door. It came from the Nazi Party headquarters in Ulm. Knowing that it had to be bad news, she sat down, braced herself and opened it. She was being sent to work in an arms factory for the rest of the summer.

Sophia Magdalena Scholl
August 18 – September 30, 1942
Fervor Ammunitions Factory, Ulm.

For twelve hours a day, she was going to have to work in a factory, making weapons to kill for Hitler. She pounded her fist against the wall and crumpled up the letter, throwing it on the floor. Then Sophie remembered the White Rose's urgent mission. This could be her new assignment. Leaflet Number Two advocated sabotage in the armament factories. That had been Alex's idea. She could secretly—somehow—refuse to comply with procedures for making bullets that killed.

Don River, Soviet Union, August 1942

Fritz pulled on his leather gloves and adjusted his goggles. His driver waited for the signal. Infantry troops had blasted through the dusty steppes of Ukraine and on to the Donets Region two weeks before them. But both men in the communications company knew that any mission through the unchanging territory was still a risk. There wasn't a single reference point from which to orient oneself in the endless monotonous landscape except for the occasional, scorched village. Driving along the dirt road, the dust swirled in their faces making it almost impossible to see. The temperatures began to rise, moving up the thermometer until both men found it hard to breathe. They had to set the communications wire for their next advance.

Starving civilians thronged the side of the road, reaching out emaciated arms as they passed. As Stalin's troops retreated, they burned their own villages. The Russians were trading the clothes on their backs for flour. It occurred to Fritz that they might be liberating the country from a tyrant worse than Hitler. Fritz and his driver kept driving without stopping.

"I've heard, Lieutenant, the Bolsheviks burned down churches and sent the Catholics to work camps in Siberia, starving out whole villages. I heard the story from a farmer whose two sons died of starvation."

"Yes," Fritz answered slowly. "I did hear that." He didn't want to be misunderstood even though they had the same opinion. He hesitated and then because he could barely hold his tongue any longer, came out and said it. "Yes. We might have met with the lesser evil."

They continued in silence through the monotonous steppe.

When they returned to their camp at sundown with communications lines newly set, the temperatures began to plummet as fast as they had risen. Their bodies couldn't get used to the drastic temperature changes. Troops were constantly lining up outside the latrines. During the day they worked without their shirts, carrying cables on their backs and hoisting heavy equipment. At night the men wrapped thick blankets around themselves and shivered. Fritz was worried about the dysentery sweeping through his company, making them weak and tired.

Under clear dark skies, the night broke up with the constant distant sound of shelling, explosions, and roar of machine-gun fire. The horizon lit up with flares. Reconnaissance planes circled, screaming into the night. In the morning a strange mysterious wind brought the monsoons. Fritz cursed the endless steppe and called it a wasteland. He missed the trees that gave form, shadows, and a sense of time to the Black Forest.

During their march through Woroschilograd, they lost twelve of their seventy-three trucks in the mud. Fritz swore at the weather in front of his men. They would have to fall back and return for parts, losing more time. The incessant rain retarded progress towards their new objective—the Volga.

In spite of their fast advance and the Red Army's retreat, unease had descended over Fritz's company. His men knew—and so did the officers in the surrounding regiments—that Hitler wouldn't be satisfied with reaching the Don River. He would order them to push on. Into winter without enough supplies.

Fritz received orders to ration water. The blazing sun returned after the rains finally subsided, bringing with it legions of black flies that harassed and bit him and his men all day and night. Sleep was impossible without a net. Fritz felt like he was abandoning his men when he spent the night in the truck. But without enough sleep, he couldn't think clearly. His men needed him to be able to do at least that.

They continued through the Russian steppe without a single casualty. Laying the lines for communication under random shelling was difficult. Fritz led easily, remembering what he had learned from his teacher. He had heard that Field Marshall Rommel was leading his men to victory in the African campaign. They were also making rapid progress on the Eastern Front. The oil fields in the Caucasus and the Caspian Sea would soon belong to the Third Reich. But the rumors that Hitler was going to set his desires on Stalingrad worried everyone.

"Lieutenant Hartnagel, I have very good news for you." Fritz's superior rapped on the window of his truck in the early morning. The sun was just coming up along the limitless horizon. Captain von Rattinger received many medals during the Great War. He wore his rank in the judgment of his eyes.

Fritz sprung to attention, jumping out of the truck, saluting him. Was he having another nightmare?

"Congratulations. I am promoting you to Captain of the Ninth Company, Communications Regiment of Army Group A. You are now in charge of the destiny of two hundred and fifty soldiers prepared to sacrifice their lives for the Third Reich. You will bring them into Stalingrad and herald the promises of the Führer."

Fritz took a moment to adjust to the news. Since when had Stalingrad become their official objective? There weren't enough men and supplies to carry out two Eastern Fronts in the middle of winter. Logistically, it wouldn't be possible. It was a death sentence.

"Officer Hartnagel, the celebration of your promotion takes place in the officer's canteen at twenty-one-hundred hours. Dress in full uniform." Noticing his subordinate's hesitation, he warned him. "Be prepared to accept this new responsibility with the gratitude and honor it deserves."

Fritz straightened up his stiff and crumpled body and met his officer's black squinty eyes. He was expected to click his heels and salute. Fritz swallowed hard and clenching his teeth, he put the heels of his muddy boots together.

"Heil Hitler!"

"Heil Hitler!" the older officer replied quickly, encouraged. With a hearty gesture, he slapped Fritz on his back.

"Make us proud, Hartnagel. Show us what you learned at Potsdam. Stalingrad will belong to the Thousand Year Reich." He rolled his eyes up and down his subordinate. "And get those boots polished, Captain." Fritz's new rank made him cringe. He shut his eyes in a psychic pain.

Shaking his fist in the air, von Rattinger turned his back and despite his age, walked away with the kind of youthful posture of a man who never lost at anything. Fritz watched him, wondering if he had ever given any thought to what they were fighting for.

He didn't know what to do next. The news hadn't sunk in entirely. It would still be another hour until the morning siren and he would have to announce it to his men. Experience in this war—during the occupation of France and Holland and even waiting in Weimar—proved to him that he wasn't a mathematician. He couldn't calculate sacrifice. After dousing himself with two liters of cold water, he lit a cigarette from the pack that Sophie sent to him and got out a sheet of letter paper.

He blew the smoke upwards, collecting his thoughts. She didn't write much about what she was doing in Munich so he couldn't respond to what might concern her. Without fearing censorship, he started writing. His feelings about this news, as terrifying as it was, would come clearer by telling her.

Don River, August 5, 1942
Dear Sophie,
I prefer not to be promoted up the ranks in a system I'd most likely turn my back on. I'm like a puppet—I show the world something on the outside that I'm not on the inside.

And it was getting worse.

I'm grateful that I can find refuge with you in my thoughts. O dear you, who laid you so deeply in my heart? I pray for you as I pray for myself. I long for the good, the real, and the light.

All of a sudden gunfire exploded around him. He threw himself on the ground. From across the river bank, Fritz could hear the shouts of charging infantry. He loaded his machine gun and began to yell instructions to his men, who started to panic, running in all directions. Aiming his weapon towards the gunfire, he pulled the trigger. The war raged on and within him for what seemed like eternity. But it was only hours.

Once the fighting stopped, German planes flew out one thousand wounded men from the Donets Region. It was only the second time that Fritz actually shot at the enemy.

He walked through the officer's canteen shortly before the ceremony began. In the distance the war raged on, and inside the tent, the roar of exploding grenades and artillery seemed to be coming closer and closer. The clear sky lit up with bursts of light. Stories of survival and a bizarre, corresponding laughter filled the dim smoky tent, with officers sitting on rows of benches at long rectangular tables. Every one of them drank heavily.

Fritz sighed, sitting down at the end of a bench, and cursed his situation.

"The man of the hour," Captain Fischer bellowed, pointing to him. Fischer was Fritz's new equal. His thick nose was already red and his stomach bloated from too many nights of too much alcohol. Two giant permanent sweat rings bled out under his bulbous arms. He needed bigger pants. Fritz always worried about Fischer's inclination to be left behind as they marched through the burning Russian villages.

After the ceremony, officers pushed Fritz into the middle of the table. Urged by the desire to forget, he raised his glass for another shot of vodka. He gulped it down. The room spun and men's faces appeared blurry. He struggled to concentrate on Fischer's diatribe.

"The Führer is history's greatest genius. I am looking forward to the real world order. Germany will be forever thanked for achieving the right population numbers."

Suddenly conversation stopped. The Captain broke the taboo and opened up the officer's canteen to something every man sitting at this table learned years ago not to talk about. "We will use every means necessary!" he started shouting. "I don't care if it means that the German Army has to take part in it. Things need to be evened out!"

Fritz cringed. Did Fischer really not know what the Führer and his men implied by "population control"?

"Soon you will have your own chance to balance things out, Captain. There is no way the SS can do this job by themselves." Another officer next to him grinned fiercely. Fritz was momentarily blinded by intense hatred. If this man gave any consideration to God at all, He had become Hitler.

"With all due respect, Captain, what do you mean?" Fritz asked, downing another shot of vodka to shore up his confidence.

The other men stopped talking and put their drinks down. But the captain didn't act surprised. He expected someone to challenge him and welcomed an opportunity to share his ideas on the forbidden subject. Fischer was impaired by toxic levels of smoke and alcohol. His unfocussed eyes settled on Fritz but he could no longer speak coherently.

Fritz spoke, "Whatever is happening in these camps under the guise of 'population control' is not a viable solution to achieving any balance of power. Germany will be disgraced for all time by our supposed measures for living space and evil ideas about a superior race."

Fritz paused. Who had given him the strength to speak like this? Was it Sophie? Or was it God? Everyone sitting at this table could accuse him of treason for the words he had just spoken out loud or worse, he could be ordered to fight in a penal battalion, the ones sent on certain death missions against the Red Army.

But no one had heard. At that moment, Fischer pounded his round fist on the table and yelled out for more vodka. The others started chanting for more alcohol. The truth was lost in the drunken haze. A warm sense of relief swept over Fritz. How long had it been since he said what he felt?

Just hearing himself speak out loud against Hitler was enough of a victory. He joined in the festivities for an entirely different reason, and when another bottle of vodka arrived, he raised his glass for more.

Returning to his field tent, he found Private U Huebner slumped over outside. Fritz woke Jürgen up by tapping lightly on his shoulder, helping the boy up off the cold ground. Huebner snapped to attention and whispered in a barely audible voice.

"Congratulations, Captain Hartnagel," Huebner managed to say sleepily but didn't look at him. "Here is the Bishop of Münster's sermon." The young man—he couldn't have been more than eighteen—handed him an envelope.

Fritz stepped back. Even in his inebriated state, he remembered to look over his shoulder for anyone who might have heard him. He stuffed it quickly in his jacket pocket and thanked him.

In the morning they drove along the western shore of the Don River in search of areas to set up new communications stations. Fritz read what was inside the envelope. He knew that Sophie had read it too. Hans probably as well. The Bishop of the German

Catholic Church wrote how the National Socialists broke every single one of the Ten Commandments. The sermon, like an underground leaflet, circulated like wildfire throughout the army. Fritz knew that his driver would want to talk about it. It put him in a terrible position, having to lead his men when so many of them already knew instinctively how he felt about whom and what they were supposedly fighting for.

Before they could start talking, Huebner slowed down. Up ahead it looked like a dozen or so more logs had been tossed on the side of the road.

As they approached, both Fritz and Jürgen realized that they weren't tree stumps but bodies. Fritz counted twenty dead Russian POWs. Bones protruded out of what was left of shredded, filthy uniforms. An odor like no other was starting to fill the already heavy air.

Huebner stopped the truck and burst out with a petition to God. Fritz ordered him to keep driving.

"Don't be foolish," he said, angry at his driver's emotionalism. A soldier couldn't stay alive by acknowledging horror. "And don't tell anyone what we've just seen."

As they drove on, Fritz could think of nothing except the indisputable truth: these men had been starved then murdered.

When they returned to the base camp, Fritz wrote Sophie. He had to. His letters to her had become confessions.

Don River, August 18, 1942

There is so much horror, hour by hour. Millions of soldiers on both sides are in constant danger and are only occupied with the thought of killing one another. I saw fif-teen to twenty dead Russians on the road today. A few days earlier, however, they weren't lying there. It could only have been prisoners who were either suffering from exhaustion or starvation and then were shot by guards. How should we bear such misery that is of our own making?

He stopped writing and looked up at the blue summer horizon. He didn't care if the Gestapo censored his letters and came for him. He had to tell her. But this time the words on the paper did little to absolve him of his own guilt. He was implicated in this. He shuddered. The image of the starved dead soldiers on the side of the road would belong forever to his memory. He would never be free of it and it would become a part of him.

His nightmares became more frequent. A real life-and-death spiritual battle had begun. Sophie taught him that his salvation lay in his ability to pray. But what if he looked into her eyes again and saw only images like these? Fritz couldn't afford the luxury of this thought now. Perhaps later. Sophie wouldn't forgive him if he began to question His existence when he needed Him most. She was the one who reminded him that life wasn't worth living if he were to turn his back on God—especially when His presence was impossible to feel.

Sophie had asked him to send money for books. He took 200 Reichsmark from the tin box he kept under his bed and enclosed the bills in an envelope. He didn't think for a second that his girl-friend, who he trusted with his life, would lie about the money's purpose.

Since they began their relationship, Sophie sent Fritz books. One by Martin Deutinger lay in a stack next to his cot. He envied her child-like faith and curiosity in religion. She was being tested too. He worried about her passion. For how long could she, like the rest of the German people, deny the truth about the camps? The disappearance of their own neighbors? And the rumors? They were spreading faster than the German tanks over the steppe. He worried about Sophie's penchant for truth. The absence of any real comment on the worsening situation in her letters concerned him. Throughout the war she managed to communicate how she really thought, even though she couched her feelings in their letters for fear of censorship. Now he read her letters and could only guess at what they didn't say.

ULM, AUGUST 1942

"Cep-zebs," the Russian girl pointed to her earrings and laughed again. She was teaching Sophie her language. They continued to stuff the powder cartridges into the ammunition shells. The conveyer belt rolled on in front of them. The girls could barely hear one another over the loud cranking machines.

"Ceb-zeps," Sophie repeated.

Olga giggled again and wiped her brow, getting grease on her face. It was so hot inside the factory Sophie felt like her insides were boiling.

"No. *Cep-zebs,"* she said one more time, looking into her new friend's curious, eyes.

Sophie nodded. These girls were different than her German friends. Russian girls laughed with one another even when their much older and angry supervisor swore at them. The factory's monotony and loud clanking of machines didn't seem to grate on them either. They worked until the sirens sounded with their faces grey with the lack of oxygen and smudged with oil and grease. Sophie heard that the Russian women were being kept in a camp outside of the city. A bus brought them in and out of the factory every day. Even at nightfall, overwhelmed by the tedium and exhaustion, they giggled among one another, cherishing some kind of a private joke.

Olga looked as though she hadn't eaten in several days and tucked her thinning hair into the long, dirty headscarf. Sophie worried about these girls, and she noticed that sometimes one or two of them even disappeared altogether. No one mentioned them. She looked up from the assembly line. Hundreds of silent women in headscarves, covered in grease, stood next to one another, stuffing gunpowder into aluminum shells.

The supervisor yelled brutally and threatened to sentence Sophie to additional hours if she got caught daydreaming again. Olga gently elbowed her new friend as a way of getting her attention. Sophie smiled back as a way of thanking her. She noticed that they were willing to help one another in ways that the German women couldn't. When she trudged out of the factory, broken from hours of work, her friends were utterly consumed with misery.

Sophie never forgot the message in their second leaflet. *Sabotage wherever you can.* Occasionally, Sophie let a shell pass by on the conveyor belt without filling it with powder. Each time she did it she wondered what if Fritz, Otl or Werner ended up with an empty shell. What if they were being shot at by the Russians and the bullets didn't work? The shame washed over her again.

Robert Scholl clenched his fist and shouted at the Judge in his empty courtroom. Robert was undeterred by the Party's threat to take away his business practice.

"I will use my freedom of speech. Don't you remember this as a sacred right, Judge?"

Herr Scholl's bow tie and mustache trembled from fear and rage. Judge Seligmann tilted his grey head forward. He administered justice in the spirit of National Socialism for nine years and could still look like a man deliberating the cause of right and wrong. Five years ago Seligmann sentenced his eighteen-year-old son Hans to prison for joining a prohibited youth group. He was to be feared. Still, he couldn't back down.

Magdalena sat in the courtroom and prayed. She could barely lift her head to look at her husband. "Six months" was all she heard as Seligmann struck his bench with a worn gavel. The police took Robert away in handcuffs. She caught eyes with her husband. He looked relieved. It had been a light sentence. The Nazis imposed the death sentence for speaking out against Hitler in public. His wife had forgiven him for it. Their marriage worked because they seldom acted out of character. It was each other's person that had attracted one another in the very beginning of their courtship when she was a nurse and he was a Mayor. Magdalena was always proud of him. Everything was going to be all right. Eugen

Grimminger in Stuttgart would help with the business until he got out. They would make the next six months work and once the war was over, they wouldn't be among the guilty ones. Robert Scholl had spoken out and could not be counted as a bystander.

Once inside his cell, Robert remembered his children. He tried to imagine what it must be like to be young without freedom. Everything he taught them was no longer possible in this country. His thoughts turned to his friend Eugen, who had lost his job with a big bank for being married to a Jew. Eugen risked everything to falsify papers so that his wife's family could escape to Switzerland before the war started. Jenny insisted on staying with him and they lived trapped in fear. Robert looked up at the crucifix hanging in his cell and without meaning to, he cursed it.

Sophie heard a man's voice call out from outside the door. She froze. Her mother and Inge were out trying to get food with their coupons. They had been gone for a long time. The cupboards were empty. Constant hunger was a dreaded companion. She sat at her father's desk, trying to reconcile accounts. Inge was much better at it. She started to sketch on the ledger's margin. Fritz kept asking her for one of her drawings. The knock on the door jolted her out of daydreaming.

"Who is it?" she asked, trying not to sound afraid. She braced herself.

Certainly the Gestapo would come again. The time had come. She was all alone. What if they hurt her? What if they took her away without telling anyone?

"Sophie Scholl, is that you?," the voice came kindly from behind the door. "It's Eugen Grimminger, your father's friend from Stuttgart. Please let me in."

Sophie sighed. She remembered Herr Grimminger. He used to bring candy with him when he visited. She unbolted the front door's three locks and opened the door slowly. He didn't look as she remembered him. His face was drawn and he looked too thin. Her father told her that he had lost his job because his wife was Jewish. For a brief second Sophie acknowledged how much worse his worries were from her own.

Eugen still managed a smile. "Fraulein Scholl," he exclaimed, "You look...you look," and then unable to complete his thought, he simply added, "Well, well, well, now I know what your father means when he tells me about the concerns he has about you." He used the formal form of "you" with her for the first time.

"Is your young man on the Eastern Front all right? Your brothers? Hans? Werner?"

Sophie nodded that they were all still alive. As far as she knew.

"Your wife, is she, is she...?" Sophie didn't even know how to form the question.

"Yes, Sophie. Jenny is with me." Eugen's entire face dropped in sadness. Sophie didn't know what to say. Instead of replying, she showed him into her father's office and offered him some tea. Coffee was a thing of the past.

He stayed for what little they had for dinner and came every week after that to help out with the business. They struck up a friendship. Every time he came, Sophie asked about his wife. It comforted the older man that his new friend knew how dangerous and even imminent the situation was, how much he thought about it and couldn't stop forgetting that she could be taken from him. When he came home from his trips to Ulm, Jenny could be gone. In fact, it was no longer even a possibility, but a probability.

"Herr Grimminger," Sophie entered her father's office one day and shut the door. Despite their friendship, she addressed him formally, respecting their age difference and authority.

Eugen looked up from the piles of paperwork that kept growing.

Sophie cleared her throat. She had prepared what she was about to say.

"You won't have to worry much longer. The Germans will be the ones to stop Hitler first."

He wasn't sure what she was saying, so he stayed quiet and allowed her to continue. "We have started an underground movement at the university and we call ourselves 'The White Rose.'"

Eugen didn't know what to say. Maybe for the first time in his life, he couldn't find the appropriate emotion. Did this young woman—his best friend's daughter—know what happened to those who spoke out against the Party? Her father was in prison for it. Did she really think that a few leaflets could save his wife? Sophie, excellent at being able to read the minds of others, answered his thoughts.

"Please, please, don't tell my father," she said quite plainly.

A strange expression of pity and admiration crossed Eugen's face. Her idealism shone like a single ray of light piercing the ground. The kind of light born of faith.

Before he left for the long train ride back to Stuttgart, Eugen poked his head into the kitchen where Sophie was by herself, sketching.

"Thank you for helping with our clients," she said, looking up from the charcoal drawing. "My father won't know how to repay you."

He took out some paper bills from his wallet and laid them on the table. "This, my dear child, is the least I can do for your efforts in Munich. But please, please be careful. You know the consequences."

Sophie jumped up from the kitchen bench and kissed him on the cheek, hugging him with such force he thought he might fall down. She was way too passionate and it embarrassed him. Her father had told him that she was the smartest of his three daughters, the one with a brave heart and clear reason. These kids needed money for supplies and recruiting. Perhaps there was hope for Jenny.

CHAPTER 8

We will not be silent

MUNICH, NOVEMBER 1942

HANS, WILLI, AND ALEX RETURNED from the occupied territories in early November with an even greater sense of purpose. Witnessing the Warsaw Ghetto gave them all the information that they needed. They changed their name from the White Rose to something more purposeful. The German Resistance. Hans wanted to work through nights on more leaflets and start graffiti action. They needed to get a lot more aggressive. Alex read in the paper about Walter Klingenbeck, a nineteen-year-old Munich student executed for transmitting a radio program.

One night they were together straining to listen to the English broadcaster:

"The Gestapo arrested Arvid Harnack last week together with Harro Schulze-Boysen. Both men, from prominent Berlin families, are accused of treason."

The transmission broke up for a moment, and then continued again.

"They have been implicated in disseminating Communist leaflets in a plot to overthrow Hitler."

Alex shot a painful look at Willi.

"British intelligence suggests that Harnack and Schulze-Boysen were working together with high-level military leaders. Ten or more other members of the alleged Red Orchestra group were also arrested. Leaflets termed 'subversive' have been..."

Radio waves crackled and then drifted off into space.

Hans sat back in his armchair and ran his hand though his thick hair. Alex got up and paced back and forth, lighting a skinny wooden pipe. Hans put the news together quickly. He began scribbling in his diary and talking at the same time.

"We must know the timing of a planned assassination. Imagine, Alex, if a revolution erupts? What if Goebbels or Himmler seizes power? Who will take the lead here in Munich? Another lunatic as crazy as Hitler could take over. We have to be the ones responsible for new leadership when it comes to that."

Alex nodded in agreement. His friend was right. Their efforts, after all, were leading to exactly this outcome.

"We must, we absolutely must, get in contact with the military resistance in Berlin. Immediately."

They were well aware of risk. Harnack and Schulze-Boysen were dead men.

Falk Harnack, Arvid's brother, didn't like to be kept waiting. Dressed in a grey officer's uniform, he paced up and down the hotel's tired lobby in Chemnitz. He checked his watch again. Five more minutes and he would have to leave. He looked over his shoulder to see if he had been followed and began to walk towards the once grand hotel's unkempt gardens. An acidic smell of unpruned boxwoods filled the crisp autumn air. Arvid's friend in Munich had set up this meeting. Traute said it was urgent that they meet. He didn't want to be here. Since his brother had been arrested, Falk was sure he was being followed. The situation was way too dangerous.

Hans saw him first. He was exactly as Alex's friend described him. Tall, thin, standing perfectly straight in uniform, holding his arms behind his back, pacing.

"Wait, please," Hans yelled out. At the last minute he had to convince Alex to risk the four-hour trip from Munich. Without proper papers, they could be taken in as deserters. Alex argued that he could take death by execution but not by serving in a penal battalion. Hans laughed at him for being dramatic and convinced him to get on the train. They were dressed in khakis and tweed suit jackets even though it would arouse more suspicion, two fighting-able men not at the front and taking a passenger train in the middle of the day.

They caught up to Falk in the labyrinth of hedges and pebbled walkways. Introducing themselves, and because of their approximate equal ages, decided address one another informally. They found an empty bar and slipped inside, careful not to be noticed. The November sun shone brightly against a pale blue sky and filtered into the dingy room, revealing dust and tired furniture.

The conversation stalled.

"I'm sorry to hear the news about your brother and sister-in-law," Alex expressed his sympathies.

The stress of the previous week left deep lines on Falk's drawn and tired face.

"My brother's wife is an American and a professor at the University in Berlin. They will release Mildred. They have to." His voice cracked, revealing his uncertainty. "I'm not so sure about Arvid. They have found evidence to implicate him. We've heard rumors that he'll be executed after a mock trial. Have you heard about this crazy President of the People's Court, Judge Freisler?"

Alex and Hans nodded. They had heard about the insane judge in Berlin issuing death sentences to anyone even suspected of speaking against Hitler.

Hans couldn't wait any longer. He pulled out the folded papers from his jacket's pocket.

"Will you read these? Last summer we wrote four editions of these leaflets, producing, sending and distributing thousands of copies all over. We reached at least thirteen cities. Now there are at least eight of us willing to do whatever is necessary. More and more students are joining us."

Falk's green eyes lit up for the first time since their meeting.

"Can you get us a meeting with your people in Berlin? We are the ones who will make it happen here in Bavaria."

Falk understood what Hans meant. Underground groups from every city had to unite in order to successfully reclaim Germany for the Germans.

"Yes, I can," Falk answered, folding their leaflet and putting it in his pocket. Even though it would be dangerous for him, he would take the risk and bring it to his people in Berlin. Or at least to the ones who were still living.

Don River, November 1942

General Friedrich Paulus, the Sixth Army's new commander since August, had successfully led them from the Don to the Volga River where Stalingrad stood at its basin. Stuka bombers screamed over the advancing army, clearing the way for the infantry as they blazed through the flat and barren woodlands. Reconnaissance planes picked up the additional flak of Stalin's retreating army.

Swastika flags flew over ninety percent of the burning city. Rumors reached Fritz's troops outside of Stalingrad that tens of thousands of men were dying. Eighty thousand dead Russians, 7,700 dead Germans, 31,000 wounded in hand-to-hand combat, street by street, building by building.

Just outside of the city between the Don and the Volga, Fritz's regiment spent most of October digging bunkers out of the already frozen earth. His biggest challenge wasn't finding shelter from the Russian winter without wood or supplies. It was witnessing the columns of the city's starving civilians or POWs trudging past them in silence. The constant and gnawing hunger was also a problem. They couldn't live on the dwindling rations: one hundred grams of frozen bread a day and watery soup.

Fritz repeated daily to his troops what he had learned at Potsdam. *It is not the strength of the army that matters, but the brain.* It worried him that not a single officer trusted what Hitler wanted to do next.

Sophie's last letter worried him. Why did she need so many envelopes? It seemed as odd as the request for a copier back in June. He dismissed the question without thinking about her reasons for asking. Were they related? He shook the thought out of his mind. He wouldn't allow himself to wonder why she would need a copier or so many envelopes. Surely she wouldn't be doing something as dangerous as it sounded.

He re-read her delicate script:

Ulm, November 1, 1942
Dear Fritz,

We must pray, and pray for each other, and if you were here, I'd fold my hands with yours. O Fritz, I can't write anything else now because of the terrible absurdity about a drowning man, who instead of calling for help, launches into a scientific, philosophical, or theological dissertation while the sinister tentacles of the creatures in the sea bed are encircling his arms and legs and the waves are breaking over him.

Because I'm filled with fear, that and nothing else, and feel an undivided yearning for Him who can relieve me of it. I'm still so remote from God that I don't even sense his presence when I pray. Sometimes when I utter God's name, in fact, I feel like sinking into a void. It isn't a frightening or dizzying sensation, it's nothing at all—and that's more terrible. But prayer is the only remedy for this, and however many devils scurry around inside me, I shall cling to the rope God has thrown me in Jesus Christ, even if my numb hands can longer feel it.

What had changed for her in Munich? What was she involved in? Over the past few weeks, Fritz felt exactly the same way as she did: prayer was the only remedy. He felt like the drowning man described in her letter. How was he going to find shelter for his men in these worsening conditions? For how long could they avoid starving and freezing? The towering smoke plumes of the burning factories and buildings in the distance scared him even more. When would the orders come to advance towards Stalingrad? Without reinforcements or supplies? It was only a matter of time. All of his men knew it.

He remembered Sophie's earlier instruction: *I pray to learn how to pray.* He folded up the letter and began issuing orders again. His men had to dig faster. These earth bunkers would save their lives from the murdering cold. Every night the temperatures sank further and further. It was the cold that would kill them first, then the lack of food.

Later that night with the unrelenting shelling and shooting continuing in the distance, he wrote her a letter. His fingers hurt from the punishing cold and he could barely hold the pen but the words came easily.

Stalingrad, November 9, 1942

Take this letter as if I were beside you as we were together in Freiburg, as our hands will find one another's like they did back then until they lose their grip only in sleep…O love, how glad I am, that you are my you. I say this not only out of habit but because it is true. You are my you. I say this to myself quietly and then I am no longer alone. You, love, is all I need to say and all of these terrible responsibilities of war go away, as if they have no meaning at all. You, love, and then I think only of you and all the joy that fills me, fills me up double knowing we feel the joy together. Can you always feel it, how my heart is with yours?

You are in everything around me, even in what is happening now.

He felt her presence even here in this wasteland, at the end of the earth. She would help him to find a way out. In the darkness the shooting temporarily stopped. He closed the letter with a good night. As he slept he dreamed of Africa. He was reassigned and fought alongside Rommel, now known as the Desert Fox.

MUNICH, DECEMBER 1942

Sophie had one tree to measure the seasons by. She stared out at the courtyard from the little cottage's window and studied the snow covering its branches. She and Hans moved in together into an upstairs apartment tucked behind Franz-Josef Strasse. Hans was never home. Letters from Fritz kept coming so she wasn't too worried, even though the news from the front was getting worse. The meetings were getting larger with Jürgen Wittenstein, a book dealer, their artist friend from Ulm, Wilhelm Geyer, another student medic, Hubert Furtwangler. They all wanted to help. The German Resistance was growing.

They met up in Eickemeyer's studio almost every night. Since returning from Poland, Hans was obsessed with wanting to do more. His next idea involved defacing Party buildings throughout the city. Alex, Willi, Christoph, and Professor Huber agreed. They had to get braver. Without a doubt, the Russians would defeat Paulus' Sixth Army in Stalingrad. The German people would have to finally be ready for drastic measures. Hitler was sacrificing tens of thousands of men in battles that couldn't be won. When Sophie heard them strategizing, she tried to remain calm. They were also fighting for Fritz's life. And Werner's. The war had to stop.

She prayed every day for Fritz to come back. She would finish her studies and they would get married. He wanted to be a farmer. Sophie wasn't so sure about being a farmer's wife. Sometimes she wondered if that wasn't Alex's pull on her. He was an artist too. Their lives during the war would belong to the past. Until then, she had to keep on. With their resistance growing so fast, the delegation of duties was as haphazard as the way they handled authority. But somehow, the absence of organization didn't matter. Their cause was all that mattered. There was something that she knew even more concretely than this. She knew it from being an artist. From all of her painting and drawing. It was something all artists knew. The outcome of their actions was not as important as the tasks themselves.

They were releasing Sophie's father from prison soon but on the condition that he could no longer run his business. All of Fritz's requests to have him pardoned helped with shortening his sentence. The Party declared him "politically unreliable." They would always be watching him. Once again, Sophie had to ask for Fritz's help. He offered many times during the war to help pay for things. The Scholl family couldn't survive without the income from her father's business. She had to write and ask him to send more money.

Stalingrad, Soviet Union, December 1942

Fritz was the only officer left. He had been ordered to create an infantry company out of a remaining 150 men. They were still holding their positions. Fritz thought that they might cut in from the west and go around Kalatsch. There had been so much madness and killing since the Red Army surprised them from the north and the south. They were surrounded. Fritz knew that when he sent his men out on solo missions they probably weren't coming back. He also knew that every letter he wrote to her could be his last.

> *Yesterday, my dear Sophie, as the Russians fired on our position with heavy artillery and the alarm went berserk, a little bird suddenly sat at the edge of my trench and peeped with joy, as if it didn't have a single care. I don't know what moved me in this moment to know with such certainty that it only could have been a greeting from you. Then I felt safe again in my hole in the earth, as if nothing in this world could bring harm to me.*
>
> *Perhaps this letter will reach you in time for Christmas, when I have a chance to send it with the transport plane. It's all I can send you.*

Munich, end of December 1942

Willi couldn't console himself. All the way back to Munich by train, he tried to pray for understanding. *Thy will be done, thy will be done*, he repeated to himself over and over. Bonn. Freiburg.

Saarbruecken. Munster. Cologne. He hid White Rose leaflets in the lining of his suitcase. Only two of his friends from the Christian Grey Order and New Germany, the brothers Bollinger, agreed to join the resistance. The rest had declined.

Willi ran their objections through his head one more time to see if he could have answered them better. "You're insane. You're committing suicide. Catholics don't commit suicide. The Gestapo is everywhere and even our own people are reporting on one another. You will be murdered. For what? Writing a few leaflets? Not worth it. Wait for the military to overthrow Hitler. You'll be needed then. Don't waste your life on a meaningless action when we'll be needed after the war to help reorganize democracy."

Then came the argument that Willi resented the most: "One cannot fight evil with evil. Advocating a revolution or an assassination uses violence exactly as Hitler does. These aren't methods of true Christians. The sword of the spirit is our best defense."

"Be patient," they told him.

Willi pounded his fist against the train window and then put his head in his hands. If he was caught without proper papers and searched, he could be tried for desertion and treason. He held his breath and waited. This time and the others before that, he had been spared a random search on the train. Willi took all of this as a sign. He'd been asked to do this work. He was one of the lucky ones. Willi wasn't going to hide behind indifference, theology, or cowardice. As he stepped off of the train at the Munich Main Station, he remembered what Hans had told them: we've decided to act whatever happens. Whatever doesn't happen.

His supposed friends in the Christian Order wanted to be convinced of the rightness of Willi's actions. That was something he couldn't do. It was unfathomable to him that his friends would need some sort of justification to do the right thing.

ULM, CHRISTMAS 1942

Sophie gasped. She was reading the Nazi newspaper together with her father. The Allied Forces bombed Munich again. The Party wasn't hiding the bombings anymore. Instead, civilian coffins were paraded through town, meant up to stir up anger against the enemy. Magdalena looked up at the ceiling and thanked God that almost all of her children were home for Christmas. She hadn't much to offer them but Handel's *Messiah* again and a barely decorated evergreen. Robert was out of prison. Her only fear now was for Werner. He'd been sent to the front in Russia. Magdalena hid the fact that her heart beat skipped erratically. She was thinking of asking Sophie to stay home this upcoming semester, but she couldn't bring herself to disappoint her youngest daughter.

She wished Hans would sit down and talk with her but he couldn't be still. What was he doing again over at the Hirzels? Magdalena wondered where he was at all hours of the night. Should she try and talk with him? Or just let him go? She wondered if she should ask Robert to talk with him. Since Fritz had been sending the family money while Robert was in prison, her husband felt like a man without the right to an opinion. All of her children would go skiing after Christmas like they usually did. She knew it was there, on the mountain, that it was possible for them to forget the war. With this thought, her heart stopped aching.

MUNICH, JANUARY 1943

"What are so many women doing in this audience? You should be at home, raising children for the Thousand Year Reich. And if you don't have children, you should be home making them, at least!"

Munich's Party Leader Giesler yelled at the female students sitting in the red velvet rows of the German Theater on the Isar River. A wave of unrest swept through the packed crowd. It was the celebration of the University of Munich's 470th birthday. The Party mandated attendance.

"If you can't find a partner, I can get you one; there are plenty of not so attractive willing men in the German Army," Giesler continued with smug and smiling Party functionaries standing to attention next to him. The eighteenth-century Baroque building had never been the host of such crazy, outlandish speech. Its ornate, gold moldings shone in the kind light cast by an enormous crystal chandelier.

Gisela sat with her male friends from class. They looked at one another in horror. Was he joking? They weren't sure. Hans discouraged Sophie and Traute from going. Alex thought that he was just being paranoid.

"No," Hans had insisted. "I have a feeling that they are close. The Gestapo is closing in on us."

The Party Leader harassed the women students in the audience again.

"Do your job for the Reich!" he shouted with a raised fist.

A student sitting in the row in front of Gisela started to hiss. Then another. Suddenly the men started in. Together the students stomped their feet and started clapping. Someone started to heckle Giesler. Dean Wust took the microphone from him and ordered the students to quiet down.

They refused to obey and started chanting. The police shut the doors in a vain attempt to contain them but they were pushed open by the angry audience. Gisela fled out the side door. She jumped on a passing street car and took it to Hans and Sophie's apartment. She couldn't wait to tell them the news. For the first time, the students at the university publically revolted against the Party. But the morning's newspaper didn't report the incident. Rumors circulated around the university that 22 protestors had been arrested.

STALINGRAD, JANUARY 1943

Fritz couldn't feel his hands or feet anymore. Delirious and stumbling over to his men in the improvised lean-to outside of the encircled city, he fell into their huddled circle. Only eight of them were left. They held on to their empty guns like Bibles, and each one of them now believed in redemption, salvation, and the afterlife. Unable to sleep from hunger, they waited for death either from the cold, starvation, or the encroaching Red Army. There was no wood for burning. They had given up on the promised planes to airlift them out. Covered in torn blankets filled with lice, none of the men had strength to look at their leader from their sunken, blood-shot, and blackened eyes. Life was draining out of them. Icicles dangled from their overgrown beards.

"I need you to help me to write a letter, Jürgen. I can no longer feel my hands." Fritz's fingers were black and bloated beyond recognition. The sound of artillery began again. Was it day light or twilight? Fritz knew that the tanks were rolling closer and closer. It was a matter of days before the Red Army would be firing at them at close range. A plane suddenly screamed over them, dropping a single bomb, exploding only 100 feet from them. Instinctually, Jürgen threw himself on top of his superior.

"What's the use of writing a letter, Captain? We're certain to die today," Jürgen's voice didn't even tremble. Fritz remembered this boy's first shave. For how long did death have no meaning? He was no longer giving orders or receiving them. They weren't soldiers anymore. Or even recognizable as human.

"You said that yesterday, Jürgen," Fritz replied. Any emotion had been frozen inside of him. "And we haven't. We're still here."

"I am dead, Captain. Even if we survive this, I am dead," he repeated. "The city is surrounded. Hitler is refusing to surrender and no plane is coming to save us."

"Please help me, Jürgen. I can no longer use my hands," Fritz repeated his request. He had to be able to say good-bye.

Jürgen pulled out a water-stained roll of paper from under his blanket. For six years Fritz wrote Sophie only the essentials because he worried that she would use the information in a way that could hurt her. Sometimes he regretted telling her what he had seen. But he made her promise not to keep secrets. Fritz could no longer trust himself to think clearly. His thoughts were confused. He was drifting in and out of consciousness.

Jürgen looked at Fritz to signal that he was ready. They were losing light and the freezing temperatures and vicious winds would soon make it completely impossible to complete the letter.

January 13, 1943
My dear Sophie!

We've have some very bad days behind us. For eight days we've been steadily retreating from Stalingrad. For eight days we lay outside in -30°C, without the possibility of getting warm. My hands are completely frozen. I was on the way to the main field hospital to get treated, but they are only taking the severely wounded.

I don't know how everything is going to work out here. The situation is pretty hopeless. When another fate doesn't befall me, with God's help and a miracle I am spared, then perhaps I will become a prisoner in Russian captivity. But I haven't given up completely. And if we don't hope for this life, what then can be taken from us? I will pray and pray again in the next few days, and you and all your loved ones are included. What can I do for you but ask God for your protection?

From my heart and in closest love, I send you my greetings, my dear, good Sophie. Tell your parents and your brothers and sisters hello, and also my parents and sister, should I be unable to do so.

I remain, your Fritz.

Artillery fire stopped in the darkness. Fritz wavered and passed out, falling into Jürgen, who folded the finished letter and put it in Fritz's chest pocket. It was dark when Fritz came to again. Two of the eight men died the quiet death of starvation. Remaining green and grey colored faces peered out at Fritz. They couldn't expend their last energy on burying their friends. None of the men wanted to live anymore. They were more comfortable dying out in this forgotten frozen landscape, covered with lice, consumed with typhus, and delusional from hunger. Life would never mean the same thing as it did before, now that they knew this.

"Help me to the airstrip, Jürgen. It's near here," Fritz begged.

Fewer and fewer planes flew overhead. He couldn't remember the last time he heard one. Even the artillery fire was getting less. Survival was a thought greater than hunger or freezing to death. At the very least, he had to get the letter to Sophie out of Russia.

For two days they trudged along the freezing steppe towards the sound of approaching gunfire until like a mirage, they saw it. Thousands of soldiers surrounded a field hospital and what was left of the landing strip. They stood still like ghouls. The only sign of life was a thin strip of smoke billowing from the remains of a canvas tent. Fritz managed to get through the silent crowd of enlisted men and peeked into the ravaged tent. He announced himself as Captain Hartnagel. Rank still had meaning in this last place on earth.

"Captain Hess," the tent's only occupant replied. "Come in." Hess had somehow managed to find a cot, stove, and wood. The warmth from the little fire embraced Fritz and made him faint. The captain reached out to help him. With a torn grey uniform falling off of a skeletal frame, his face darkened by charcoal and black eyes deeply buried in his face, Fritz could barely tell if he was still human.

"Please. I have a letter in my jacket pocket. Can you take it out and make sure it gets posted?" Fritz collapsed onto the cot and lost consciousness.

When he woke, Hess had cut the boots off his feet and wrapped both his hands in a dirty cloth. His left hand ached like nothing he had known before. A moldy frozen piece of bread lay next to him. Fritz stuffed it into his mouth like a starving animal. The letter was missing from his pocket.

He was still alive.

"A plane finally came in while you were sleeping, Hartnagel. And rumor is that it leaves tonight. Only officers and the severely wounded are allowed on it. I'll be on it. You can stay here and take your chances." Captain Hess' eyes glistened with madness as he toyed with a hand gun. Fritz nodded. Outside they could hear shooting and the distant rumble of tanks. They were coming closer.

At dusk, the zombie-like men began to shuffle towards the white bird that sat perched with its beak pointed into a lifeless pale grey sky. Hundreds of what was left of men slowly pushed toward the plane. Some fell down from the strain. Fritz watched from the tent. The captain was standing inside of the plane's exit door, pointing the gun at the crowd, protecting his position. Rolling off of the cot, Fritz stumbled toward the plane. No one spoke.

The strongest officers hoisted themselves up into the plane, pushing the weaker and more wounded ones down. In between the chaos, medics hoisted the wounded on stretchers. Others squeezed and pushed their way in. The propellers stalled. Faltered. The pilot attempted to start them again and again. The engine sputtered. The pushing intensified. Some men started shouting. Fritz thought for a moment that he was being trampled. The plane couldn't get off of the ground. The propellers were frozen.

It couldn't start with all of the weight. Some men were trying to hold on to it as it attempted to taxi. This was a question of survival. All of a sudden the propellers began to spin. Then with great force and spinning like giant razors, the plane's propellers pushed away the throngs of clamoring men.

Fritz heard shots. The officers positioned in the doorway of the plane began firing into the desperate crowd. Fritz got close enough to see that the shooter was Captain Hess. He shouted his name. Recognizing Fritz, he hoisted him up and into the plane. For the second time in two days, this madman had saved his life.

The last plane to airlift survivors out of Stalingrad began to taxi down what was left of the airstrip. It would still have to escape the baptism of fire from Russian anti-aircraft fire.

MUNICH, JANUARY 7, 1942

The fifth leaflet began in clear, political language. Hans deleted intellectual phrases in favor of persuasive statements. Hans, Alex, Sophie, Willi, and Gisela sat around the architect's drawing table. Willi began to read aloud from it in perfect German characteristic of Northerners.

Are we to be forever the nation which is hated and rejected by all mankind? No. Dissociate yourselves from National Socialist gangsterism. Prove by your actions that you think otherwise. A new war of liberation is about to begin. The better part of the nation will fight on our side. Make the decision before it is too late! A criminal regime cannot achieve a German victory.

Sophie brought in some more wine on a wooden tray.

"Who is going to read all of this, anyway?" Gisela finally interjected, her bow-and-arrow lips stained red. Sophie had liked her at the women's camp in Sigmaringen when they had been forced to ingest Nazi propaganda all day long. Together the two women had silently rejected it and made fun of the others who gullibly drank it all in. Sophie had been grateful to Gisela for that. Now she was no longer sure who she was.

Alex flung a rubber band at her. Willi got up, looked around blankly as though he had forgotten his wallet, and excused himself. Women shouldn't be allowed in on their conversations. Gisela had just proven his point.

Hans hadn't even heard her.

"Let's get started then. Let's see if we can make 6,000 copies of the German Resistance's fifth leaflet for every major German southern city. Falk will get it to Berlin too."

"And Austria," Alex chimed in. "Linz. Vienna. Graz. Salzburg." He got up and closed the curtains.

Averse to rolling up her sleeves, Gisela said something about having to study for a literature test and left abruptly. Since Gisela's presence, Traute attended fewer and fewer meetings. They all missed her.

By the time Sophie ran out of paper, Alex had fallen asleep on the table. Hans was still addressing envelopes on the type-writer. Tat-a-tat-tat, all throughout the night. The "t" key had broken and cracked every time Hans pressed it. Willi was still turning the handle on the ancient machine, oiling it gently as Sophie slowly fed it pieces of paper, sheet by sheet. Its handle fell off every few turns. Willi stopped and patiently screwed it back on, picking splinters out of his hand.

By the time they were done, they had two piles: 4,000 for mailings, 2,000 for distribution by hand. The hands on the clock had spun around and the moon was replaced by another grey morning winter sky.

AUGSBURG, JANUARY 22, 1943

On most days she was absolutely certain that all this work was going to make the difference. The student body at the university would revolt. They were going to be the ones to show Germany. To show the world. Today was different. On the way to the train station she slipped on a sheet of black ice, dropping the heavy knapsack filled with 200 hand addressed leaflets in envelopes. Fear bored into her from all sides.

Would this be worth it? If she got caught, surely they would kill her. As she picked herself up she remembered asking: for this she wouldn't be able to have children? Or paint? Never see her mother or Fritz again? Or run in the fields? Listen to Bach? At this point Sophie turned her thoughts to God, remembering what Professor Muth had taught her.

Every thought was a conversation with God. Then, like the professor had instructed her, she stopped walking, closed her eyes for a moment and listened. What was it that specifically brought her mind to the hereafter? She knew for sure. There, she wouldn't have to worry about these kinds of things. She remembered when she and Fritz went skiing together before her graduation from school and how the mountain air felt like something she could imagine of heaven. They were so happy and free even when her binding came loose and she fell laughing. This memory propelled her forward to Munich's main train station to do what had been asked of her to do. For certain it was a Higher Power giving her the strength to do this work.

Sophie passed the first-class compartment, nodded her head to the well-dressed passengers until she found one empty. Entering it, she hoisted the green canvas knapsack—the kind the soldiers used—above onto the luggage rack. She noted the cabin number, 0175. Catching her breath and reminding herself to be calm, she walked to her reserved seat in second class. Her pulse thundered. She repeated to herself over and over until her pulse returned to normal: *Thy will be done. Thy will be done.*

Sophie's heart sank. She wanted to be alone with her thoughts. Travelers took up every seat in her assigned compartment. A young soldier in uniform. An elderly couple. A mother and a sleeping child.

"Excuse me," Sophie said, pushing by them, wondering if they thought it unusual that she didn't have any luggage. Probably not.

Augsburg was only an hour south with the fast train. Hans assigned her to this city because she visited Fritz once before the war and together they snuck into his barracks.

The young soldier wanted to talk. He couldn't have been more than eighteen. His grey uniform and the heaviness of it hung on him as if he were just a boy playing a game of war. But his face revealed something different. His eyes possessed the knowledge that he was being sent to a battle that had no right to be fought and had no chance of being won. He looked again anxiously over at Sophie, wishing for her to start a conversation.

The soldier cleared his voice. Perhaps it would be his last chance ever to speak to a pretty, young girl. Rumors were spreading all over Munich about the fate of Paulus' Sixth Army. Sophie hadn't heard from Fritz in over three weeks. Although for a long time now she knew the war couldn't be won, shouldn't be won, she couldn't bring herself to believe that Fritz wouldn't be all right. He would find a way out.

"Have you been to Augsburg before?" he began.

"Yes, once," she answered. She didn't add that she'd been to the Prince Heinz barracks. She smiled to herself remembering how mad Fritz was when she and her friend Lisa got stuck in his room and he had to sneak them back out without the guard noticing. "And you?"

His grandparents lived outside of the Bavarian city and he wanted to see them again. He could have said "one more time" but he didn't. They continued on instead with an easy conversation, avoiding talking about the war, the subject that was deciding their lives.

When they ran out of things to say, the soldier closed his eyes, and Sophie stared outside at the frozen landscape. She tried to imagine the trees in spring. She began to pray. She was going to act like an undercover spy whose cause was freedom.

Sophie went over the entire campaign in her mind, visualizing every step and each of the necessary most dangerous actions: collecting the knapsack in first class, buying stamps, posting the letters in various mailboxes, and finally boarding the 8:15 p.m. train with an empty knapsack. She was going to be very careful, and when she was finished with informing Augsburg's citizens about resistance, she would go on to Stuttgart. Suze Hirzel, her friend from the seminary, was at the university there and she wanted to recruit her. The German Resistance needed a few more women. They needed Stuttgart too.

Two days later, Sophie boarded the 4:30 p.m. train from Munich with a second knapsack full of leaflets. She proved Hans right. There was less of a chance that the police would search a young woman's bag than a man's. All men were supposed to be fighting on the Eastern Front now.

When the train arrived, Sophie looked up warily into the black, starless sky. Stuttgart, city of steel factories, received its share of Allied bombings. Because of the blackout measures, she couldn't make out the damage, and for a second it occurred to her that she hadn't contemplated the possibility of an attack. She thought of what she would do. She would throw the knapsack away and find a bomb shelter. Just like everyone else. As a way of dispelling her fear, she recited some of the leaflet's passages to herself as she walked through the station, filled with commuters and passengers coming and going, arrivals and departures.

"Freedom of speech, freedom of religion, the protection of individual citizens from the arbitrary will of criminal regimes of violence—these will be the bases of the New Europe," she repeated the line that she and Alex had written.

Almost effortlessly, she tossed batches of letters into different mailboxes, walking city streets confidently and assured. The devastated city was like a ghost town. Only shells of municipal buildings remained. Most shops were closed and boarded up. A gaunt man with a yellow star on his torn lapel passed her. They didn't dare look at one another. No one in the streets of this city took the chance of looking someone directly in the eyes.

"Young lady. Stop." A voice called out from the darkness. Sophie froze and clenched the knapsack.

A black-uniformed man approached her in a side street near the train station.

She had just finished emptying the knapsack's contents into the last mailbox and was headed to Suze's apartment near the university. Had he seen her put the batch of letters into the mailbox? He would ask her why she was sending so many letters. And to whom. She had already prepared her answer: her grandmother just died and she was posting the announcements. Then why was she in Stuttgart if her identification papers said she was from Ulm. She hadn't prepared an answer for that question. Fear ran through her and with terrified eyes she looked at her accuser.

"Identification papers." The policeman looked her up and down.

"What was in that knapsack?" he pointed to the empty canvas bag.

Sophie hadn't prepared for this particular question. Then, a lie came out, fluidly, unexpectedly, and perfectly. "I'm getting clothes from a friend who lives in Stuttgart. I'm on the way there now. She grew out of her wardrobe and is giving them to me." It could have easily been the truth. She thrust out her papers.

The man scanned her identification documents. She wasn't much interest to him. He knew by their cover that she was Aryan. This girl seemed a bit frightened and his intuition told him to pry further but his mission tonight involved looking for Jews. His orders were to make sure that they were no longer walking the streets of his city.

"Do you know the way to Lindenstrasse?" Sophie inquired in the tone she used when she wanted something. She wanted desperately for him to start thinking about something else. It worked. He gave her directions and told her to get off the streets as soon as possible. It was no longer safe from bombings, even at night.

When Suze Hirzel opened the door to her apartment, Sophie immediately noticed that her friend had changed. There was little that remained of the fresh-faced girl from the seminary. Suze looked tired and frustrated. The two hugged, and Suze rushed her through the door. The girls talked until late into the night. Suze brought Sophie some fresh clothes and rubbed her feet until they were warm. The war had forced them to be mistrustful of others. But this friendship brought back the selves that they had been before the war took over. Suze played some Mozart on her flute.

When it was time for Sophie to go, she told Suze about what they were doing in Munich.

"I'm no longer guilty, Suze. I will not be guilty. We have stood up for what we always believed in. For our natural rights. For the things that were taken from us."

"And if you are caught, Sophie? What then? What about Fritz? What does he have to live for, if you die?" Her friend pleaded.

"I won't get caught, Suze," Sophie answered.

"Then why haven't others tried? They are watching us, Sophie. They're watching us very closely. And with your father's arrest, they'll be watching your family most of all. Please don't do this, Sophie. I have a bad feeling." Suze got on her knees and begged.

"I'm absolutely convinced of what I'm doing. Even if I get caught, the war will be over soon. 'Enemies of the State' get ninety-nine days before an execution. The Americans have joined the war. They'll free us. The war will be over soon." Sophie glowed and continued.

"Either we'll bring an end to this madness, or the Allied powers will. Soon. Don't worry, Suze. Please. Then we will be free again. I don't even remember what that feels like."

"Sophie, leaflets will do nothing to change anything. And you're risking your life because of it." Suze was pleading with her friend to come to her senses.

Sophie's tied up the laces of her worn leather boots.

"I have to go, Suze." Sophie couldn't hide her disappointment. She put on her coat. "I can't rationally explain what I've chosen to do. Perhaps I don't even fully understand its consequences. I don't even think about it much anymore. Or I try not to. I think about those who are suffering—those who are powerless to do anything."

Suze started to cry.

"I think about Fritz, Otl, and Werner fighting in Russia under impossible conditions for impossible reasons. And then there is so much I don't know. Do those camps really exist? What do we really know for sure? But I will not be guilty. Everything else—and I'm sorry, Suze—is cowardice."

"Sophie…" Suze trailed off. "I don't possess the faith you have. I'm not as strong as you are."

Sophie smiled and hugged her friend. She couldn't judge a friend who was always more fragile than she was. She kissed her, shutting the door behind her. A razor-blade wind cut into her, causing her to buckle. She cursed the cold. The 11:25 p.m. train would take her back to Munich. She didn't worry about arriving at three in the morning. Sophie slept on the train and woke up as it pulled into Munich in the dead of night. She imagined her life at the end of the war. She thought about graduating from the university. The first woman in her family. Would she be a botanist? A horticulturist? Would she help to rebuild the woods, fields, forests, and gardens? She thought about marrying Fritz. He wanted to be a farmer. She wasn't sure she wanted to be a farmer's wife. But what she knew for sure is, like her mother, she wanted many children. Six. Or seven.

She walked through the silent and deserted city towards Schwabing. As Alex said, he was ready to carpet bomb the city with truth. That's how she saw it. The Germans wouldn't be able to deny what they had written. She prayed for Alex's and Hans' safety. She worried about them. Would they be as careful and meticulous and slow as she'd been? Or would they be impulsive and reckless? Sometimes she wondered if her brother calculated the dangers as closely as he should.

Hans and Alex distributed leaflets all over Munich until four in the morning. When they completed their mission, they had left 2,000 leaflets. Hans walked the north of the city in the night's freezing cold, and Alex covered the south. They were getting to be experts at working underground.

Walking her favorite city in those desolate hours, she admired the Neoclassical and Baroque columns and detailed façades. King Ludwig once hoped that Munich would be the next Greece or Rome. She chuckled. For them, it was. The German Resistance was carrying on the democratic traditions of Plato and Aristotle. Tomorrow the city would celebrate the ten-year anniversary of Nazism. Red, white, and black banners draped over the city's fine architecture, contaminating them.

Sophie thought again about freedom and God. She thought about all of their late-night discussions and debates, all the books she read to find the answers. The fifth leaflet summed it up best: *Where there is no individual responsibility, there is no freedom. Freedom only exists when one can articulate and express it. The State can guarantee freedom, but freedom is always a question of the individual citizen.* These leaflets were a culmination of everything she had learned. And now, everything that she was actually doing. The recipients of the leaflets would know what to do. They would break out of their denial. They would help return Germany to the Germans.

CHAPTER 9

The last rays of the sun

―――――

MUNICH, JANUARY 23, 1943

"THEY BOTH MADE IT. HERTA and the baby are going to be all right," Hans hollered down their short hallway. Sophie rushed into the kitchen. He hung up the phone, hugging her so hard she lost her breath. Fever consumed Christoph's wife for the last month of her difficult pregnancy. They had all been told not to expect any miracles.

"Can you believe it? Christoph has *three* children," Sophie gushed and started dancing around the kitchen. She turned on the radio hoping for some music. With the constant bomb scares, explosions, reports of death, and the lack of food, it was almost impossible to feel anything but fear and slow hunger. This news was the ray of hope that they needed.

"I can't imagine if anything ever happened to them," Hans replied distractedly. "Christoph couldn't survive it. He and his father-in-law are coming up to Munich next week. Herr Dohrn is involved in a Christian resistance group in Murnau, and Christoph has been working on a new leaflet."

At first Sophie couldn't believe she heard correctly.

"You suggested that Christoph write a leaflet?" The smile on Sophie's face disappeared. "He's already in too deep, Hans. His only real responsibility is to his family."

But Hans was no longer on the topic of his best friend. He was already thinking of something else.

"Hans? Hans??" Sophie insisted with her voice continuing to rise.

Sophie studied her brother closely. Hans only came alive when they discussed how to get their message out. Voicing his opinions, writing them, and getting others to read them was like an aphrodisiac to him. People like Hans could only live when free.

She tried to reel him back into the present, "Please tell Christoph to forget it. I really don't want him to get so closely involved. Not now. His place is with his family."

"Sophie, I know." He sounded irritated. "But Christoph sees the urgency. We just don't have much time left anymore."

Hans packed his book bag and left the apartment without saying where he was going. Every time he left Sophie worried. Alex told her that he was actually looking for a publisher for the leaflets. He was forgetting about danger. Sometimes he even seemed artificially high. She wondered if he was keeping himself up at night with pills from the student infirmary.

When Hans returned, he found Sophie in the bathroom, combing her long brown hair. It had grown past her shoulders. They had both heard the news. Sophie's face was stained with tears and her usually bright eyes were lifeless, staring into the mirror.

The Russians wouldn't let go of Stalingrad. General Paulus' Sixth Army had to be defeated by now. Even the Nazi newspaper was reporting possible defeat. Men who survived the -20°C and below freezing temperatures, lack of food and ammunition, and fierce fighting would die in the gulags.

Hans didn't know what to say so he took his younger sister into his arms and hugged her. He waited until she was ready to let go.

"I won't stop writing to him," Sophie finally spoke. Her voice gathered more strength as she continued. "Our letters worked to keep us both alive for this long, and they shall work now. In fact, I have to write him today." Her hands trembled. Then she changed the subject abruptly, as if this would make the idea of Fritz's surviving more possible.

"And I need a haircut. Elisabeth is coming tomorrow and she can do it."

She tugged at her long, straggly hair. Hans still didn't say anything. Over the past few weeks he could rally all of the members of the German Resistance with eloquence. They numbered eighteen in total. But he could barely find a single word to comfort his sister. Sophie turned off the bathroom light and found a satchel of Fritz's letters, tied up neatly with twine. Before she wrote to him, she curled up in her bed and read them again.

Elisabeth let herself into her brother's and sister's new apartment on Franz-Josef Strasse. At first she thought she was in the wrong apartment. Clothes were strewn everywhere. Garbage spilled out of cans. Empty bottles of wine lined the walls. She opened the kitchen windows. Dirty dishes lined the sink. Filled ashtrays and the smell of stale smoke stank up the three little rooms. Strewn books lining every square centimeter of space didn't strike her as being unusual. The Scholl siblings were notorious readers. Elisabeth took a moment to read some of their titles. She shook her head. They were still reading banned books.

While she waited for Hans and Sophie to return, she cleaned up the apartment. If she didn't know better, she would think that they were drinking too much. A student apartment was one thing. This was something else. Elisabeth had come up to Munich from her job as a governess to comfort Sophie. Although the defeat of the Sixth Army had not yet been officially announced, people in Munich and Ulm knew. Robert Scholl, let out of the prison in Ulm early for good behavior, was still listening to banned radio stations. He heard an estimated 300,000 German soldiers and one million Russians died at Stalingrad. Fritz's troops were caught right in the middle. Although no one could say it out loud, they said it to themselves. Fritz wasn't coming back.

Almost everyone could no longer deny what the implications of Paulus' capitulation meant. But the Minister of Propaganda still launched into a daily tirade on the radio: *Don't give up. White flags of surrender are treasonous. The home front must keep fighting. If the Allies win, they will destroy Germany.* Although Elisabeth had come to be with Sophie, her sister refused any discussion about Fritz or Stalingrad.

"If we think this way, it will come true, Elisabeth. Don't you know?" Sophie had said.

Sophie wanted to show Elisabeth the city. They borrowed Traute's bike and despite the cold, they rode all over. They passed the museums in the famous Koeningsplatz that Hitler built to look like a Roman square. They biked along the Isar River, past the naked elm, poplar, and chestnut trees. They touched the lion's nose on the brass statues for good luck on Odeonsplatz. They cruised by the grand opera square and saluted Ludwig on the eighteenth-century statute set in the middle of broken cobblestones. They walked along the formerly fancy Maximilianstrasse with its elegant shops closed and no longer filled with heritage clothes. They marveled at the brick red color inside the neoclassical anterior court and painted murals of Romans and Greeks in togas and chariots. They watched the old men in black berets still playing boule on the frozen sands of the Residenz Park and walked their bikes under the gazebo made of ocean shells and adorned with mermaids and fountains.

"So many churches, Sophie, and in such strange colors," Elisabeth pointed to the Theatiner Church, painted in ochre. The bells of the church clanged loudly, striking 18:00. Sophie raised her arms up and started shouting.

"I believe, I believe, I believe!"

Ghost-like passersby hurrying to their next destination stared at her.

"The lion is the symbol of Munich!" Sophie pointed to the reclining stone cats in the temple-like rostrum protecting a statue of an old Bavarian king. Elisabeth ran up its grand staircase and pretended to pet one of them.

She didn't suspect for one moment that her own sister and brother were risking their lives to save the Jews, Germany and its soldiers.

MUNICH, FEBRUARY 2, 1943

The phone rang and jolted Elisabeth and Sophie out of their beds. Sophie stumbled to it, her heart pounding and hands trembling.

"Scholl," Sophie answered. There was a delay in the connection.

"Hallo, Sophie. It's your mother." She could barely hear her.

"Sophie, it's all right. He is alive, Sophie. Fritz survived. He was one of the last to leave by transport plane. He's all right."

Sophie sat down.

"How do you know?" she whispered. She could hear her mother struggle for breath.

"Frau Hartnagel just called me. He made it to a hospital in L'vov in Ukraine."

"Is he badly injured?"

"We don't know for sure, Sophie. I'm not sure he's even conscious yet. We must be prepared. We can't even imagine what he suffered. We must give thanks and keep praying."

Sophie gripped the black phone tighter. At first she could not respond. She had never believed that he was dead.

"Sophie, are you there?" Her mother's weak voice came again.

"What is wrong, mother? I can barely hear you."

"Nothing. Nothing is wrong," Magdalena answered, and for the first time in her life she lied to her daughter. The worry had almost been too much. Fritz had become a son to her, and she loved him like one.

After they hung up, she took Elisabeth's hands and shared with her sister the great news. Their joy only lasted for a moment when Sophie remembered the sound of her mother's weakened voice.

"Mom is sick, Elisabeth, isn't she?"

Her sister nodded. Joy vanished from the room like a too-suddenly-departed friend.

The next day when Sophie and Elisabeth went out to find some bread, they saw people clustered around the newsstand, shaking their heads in disbelief. Women were sobbing. Sophie pushed through the crowd and bought the paper. "A Faithful Ending for the Homeland; The Fight for Stalingrad Has Ended," read the headlines. Holding her breath, she read slowly:

> *From all sides the enemy tanks pushed themselves into the already destroyed city, and then came the Soviet artillery. Hour after hour our men fired upon them from the ruins. Despite this, wave after wave of Bolshevik infantry men fired back. The southern divisions used their last ammunition, and they still fought back heroically in hand-to-hand combat...nearly weaponless men...with their last heartbeat, they dedicated themselves to the Fatherland.*

Sophie couldn't bear it anymore. A small ad beneath the copy caught her eye. Her heart skipped. It offered a 1,000 Reichsmark reward for any information leading to the capture of person or persons responsible for distributing the leaflets of the German Resistance in Munich. Was she being naïve to think they weren't looking for them? She hadn't really thought about this. She quickly folded the paper up to bring it home to Hans.

That evening, the student symphony was performing a concert at the university auditorium. Elisabeth and Sophie first listened to jazz on a banned radio station. Sophie helped Elisabeth put some make up on. Her sister seldom cared for her appearance. When she looked into the mirror, she blushed and wiped off the lipstick.

"I can't be as bold as you, Sophie. It just isn't me." They put their heads together, laughed. Walking arm and arm down Leopoldstrasse, Elisabeth stopped suddenly.

"Sophie, what is it going to take to end this?"

"Someone is going to have to assassinate Hitler. And if a man won't do it, a woman will have to." Sophie answered, staring straight ahead until they got to the school.

Elisabeth glanced at her sister suspiciously. The university's atrium was alive with concert-goers who also needed to forget the daily horror of war. The music of Germany's great composers could heal them if only for a little while.

Hans waited for his sisters to leave the apartment. He checked his handgun to make sure it was loaded and started to fill up a knapsack with tar and paintbrushes. The conditions were perfect. It wasn't that cold and the moon was enveloped behind a layer of stagnant grey clouds. Together Hans, Alex, and Willi walked to the Bavarian State Legislature carrying their suspicious heavy loads. They crept through the Residenz Park past the Palace, whose rooftop was decorated with a multitude of Greek mythological statutes holding harps and flutes.

"Look, they are watching over us. That one," Alex whispered and pointed to a woman wearing a toga and playing a harp. "She's encouraging us."

Hans went first. With giant handmade stencils, he brushed the letters "F-R-E" on the side of the State Legislature, designed after a Greek pantheon. Willi and Alex took their positions at each corner of the portico. Out of nervousness, Alex took a swig out of his father's silver flask and murmured something in Russian. Despite the cold, Willi wiped sweat off of his forehead.

"Hurry up, Hans. It doesn't have to be perfect. Forget the stencils. It's taking up too much time." Alex, the artist, edged Hans on, who was meticulously continuing with the letters "-E-D-O-M."

"Shhh, Alex." Willi could hear Hans from across the porch.

At that moment, the green paint can tipped over and bounced down the Legislature's long steps, clanking loudly on its way down. They all froze at the same time. But nothing happened. Packing up their things, they moved on quickly. On the front of their favorite bookstore, Alex painted "Down with Hitler," this time without stencils, embellishing the letters. Munich, quiet from an evening of no bombings, was deserted. Neglecting the danger of being caught and fueled by the feeling of freedom, they continued to paint the city with calls to resistance until a sliver of light came up on the horizon beyond the Alps. By the time they were finished, they had painted twenty-two buildings. In the morning, the people of Munich would be shocked. The February air even gave a tiny hint of spring.

Hans was absolutely sure that these messages would incite them. Willi argued that it had been too dangerous, too bold. Alex agreed with Hans. They had to step up their measures.

"People have forgotten how to use their freedom of speech. They have forgotten, like us, how good it feels to speak your own minds. We have to remind them. They will be encouraged by what they see—and they will dare to join us."

"We must at least make a start," Hans repeated what Sophie was known for saying during their meetings. "If that's all we are capable of doing, at least it's that." Since Hitler's surrender at Stalingrad, the Germans lost all hope. This was the message that they needed now.

In the morning Elisabeth and Sophie left for the train station. Elisabeth was the first to see the graffiti on the tall cement wall outside of a private home on Leopoldstrasse. Russian women in head scarves were scrubbing off the stubborn giant letters. But both sisters could still see what it said. *Freedom.*

"Whoever did that has a death wish," Elisabeth spoke softly, pretending as though she hadn't even noticed it. They kept walking. Gestapo agents were gathered around, taking notes, looking for clues. Passersby hurried past, pretending that they hadn't seen it. Sophie tried to hide a smile. She knew. This had been the work of the German Resistance. Hans, Alex, and Willi's artistry.

"They should have used tar, not regular paint," she said to Elisabeth. Sophie knew where they had gotten the paint—from Eickemeyer's studio. "The night is the friend of the free."

Elisabeth was puzzled. Sometimes her sister said the most confusing things. All of the Scholl siblings had learned a long time ago not to try and figure them out.

They hugged for a long time beside the platform at the main train station. Elisabeth couldn't let her sister go. Throughout her visit she barely saw Hans. He was always agitated and nervous, and could no longer sit still. Although the news of Fritz's survival was possibly the best news that they could hope for, Elisabeth was worried sick about Hans. He just wasn't himself. But there wasn't time for any more of these discussions. The conductor blew his whistle.

"You must rest more, Sophie. Don't get so overtired like Hans, o.k.?" Elisabeth boarded the train. Sophie lifted up her baggage.

"Summon all the powers that be," Sophie reminded her sister. Their father had taught them this rallying cry from Goethe. It was the family creed.

"Summon all the powers that be," Elisabeth repeated.

They continued waving to one another long after the train pulled out of sight.

UKRAINE, SOVIET UNION, FEBRUARY 7, 1943

The cold rain leaked into the cattle car on the moving train. Lying on the floor, wedged in between the dying and the already dead, Fritz tried to shut off his senses. He had no idea what time of day it was, how long it had been raining, and when their journey would end. He could no longer feel his blackened hands and feet. They were going to have to amputate. For the first time since the war started, he tried not to think about Sophie. He wouldn't want her to be with a cripple. A lieutenant lying next to him struggled for breath. He started choking. Fritz couldn't see his wounds under the filthy blanket but he knew that it was bad. Because he could no longer feel his hands, he started shouting for help. No one could hear him.

All of a sudden, the train stopped. Fritz closed his eyes and prayed. If the Red Army slid the door to the cattle car open, they would be killed. Then he heard a medic shouting in German. They carried out the bloody stretchers, lifting the men out, one by one. Spotting Fritz's officer epaulets, Fritz was put at the front of the line. Gagging from the stench and pain, Fritz passed out.

When he regained consciousness, the operation was over. His arms and legs didn't end in stumps, like so many of the wounded. He looked over at the other men lying still in rows of beds. One of them was in a body cast, and the other's face was completely covered in bandages. It was his twenty-sixth birthday.

"I'm sorry," the young doctor came over to Fritz's bedside, speaking softly so the men next to him couldn't hear. "We couldn't save two fingers on your left hand, Officer Hartnagel. The lost too much circulation for too long. You are very, very lucky. So many others have had severe amputations."

Fritz looked again at the men lying next to him. He felt a pang of guilt and understood the phantom ache now. He wouldn't be allowed to mourn the loss of his fingers. The gift had been his survival. Soon he would be even be able to write Sophie again.

MUNICH, FEBRUARY 8, 1943

Falk Harnack paused at the door of the studio on Leopoldstrasse and looked up. Most of Munich's windows were now either dark or boarded up, so it wasn't unusual that the entire second floor looked unoccupied. Like in Berlin, any light at all aroused suspicion. It could attract either a direct assault from above or a knock from the police. The skies were quiet and clear. Falk blew into his hands to keep his fingers from freezing and rang the bell to the second floor. He ran up the studio's stairs and as they had agreed, knocked three times.

An attractive blond woman opened the door and pointed to the light at the end of the hallway where he could hear the murmur of voices. He clutched his leather suitcase and made his way down the darkened corridor that smelled of turpentine and paint.

Hans was still covering their equipment—the copier and the typewriter—with a white sheet, wondering to himself, at the same time, why. If they were caught, they could never save themselves. He didn't really care. Death was living like this, without freedom. Lately Hans felt his mind's clarity slipping, and instead of taking care of himself as Sophie and Elisabeth pleaded, he desired only more. They weren't trying hard enough. Tomorrow night they would take more action. Something more overt.

Falk entered the room and lifted his suitcase on the table with a heavy thud.

"Gentlemen, *Guten Abend.*"

They nodded to one another.

"Tonight the Munich and Berlin resistance groups begin their partnership to overthrow Hitler."

Alex poured three glasses of wine and handed them out.

"Long live democracy," they toasted.

"Let's get to work," Hans was the first to sit down, spreading out papers and books. They had a long night ahead of them.

Falk spoke quietly but forcibly. His brother-in-law and wife had been sentenced to death for treason. Judge Roland Freisler of the People's Court ordered their immediate executions after the so-called trial. There were rumors that Berlin's military leaders were acting to overthrow Hitler. Falk reported that Dietrich Bonhoeffer, the leader of Germany's Confessing Church, was acting as their double agent.

"An end is finally in sight," Falk said, "perhaps by the end of February. Our military leaders can no longer support Hitler. They know about the camps. They know what's happening."

"We saw the ghetto ourselves," Hans reminded Falk of their tour of duty in Poland and Russia.

"Conditions in them have worsened...," he trailed off, shaking his head.

The men talked late into the night, but instead of the darkness enfolding them, their ideas empowered them. Hans gave Falk a copy of the fifth leaflet. He smiled. They were ready. The time had come.

"When can you make it to Berlin?" he asked, beaming with optimism.

Hans made some calculations in his head. Herr Grimminger was coming soon to Munich to give them more money. Maybe Fritz's money would come through, too.

"We can be there on February 22," he answered definitively.

Falk nodded. "I will set up the meeting with Dietrich Bonhoeffer."

It was settled. The German Resistance in Munich and Berlin were finally joining forces. Together they would be stronger.

"Now tell me," Falk cleared his throat, and both Hans and Alex looked over at their new friend mysteriously, "who is it that answered the door and where did she go?"

Stacks of leaflets surrounded them on the long table, waiting for envelopes and addresses. When Hans, Willi, and Alex woke, the new day brought exhaustion and hunger. They needed a break. Sophie was returning from Ulm, and she could help with addressing the envelopes. Willi reminded them that Professor Huber promised to steal a student address book from the university.

Returning to the city, Sophie went directly to the studio. She wanted to tell Hans not to worry, that their mother was feeling better despite her heart condition. Sophie cringed when she thought about the possible consequences if Magdalena ever found out. She might not be able to handle it. Having their father in prison was bad enough.

Sophie let herself in to the studio and saw stacks and stacks of leaflets lining the hallway. They were thousands and thousands of copies. She sighed. Hans and the others must have been too tired to hide them. Since she hadn't taken part in their recent debates, she didn't know that Hans, Alex, and Willi decided that they no longer could support the German Army. Sophie had decided differently. Her boyfriend was an officer but she loved him "because of the good in him" and that feeling had remained.

Then, she had promised love and not friendship. These were too different things. Sophie closed her eyes and said a prayer for his homecoming.

Sophie glanced at a hand-drawn map of the city posted on the wall. Hans had marked the streets for the next mission. She looked at her territory and traced the passages with her finger: Schellingstrasse, Theresienstrasse, Maximilianstrasse, Kaufinger, Marienplatz, Sendlinger Gate, and The Victory Gate. Another surge of hope cursed through her and she smiled.

As she turned to go, her eye caught some oil paintings pointed towards the wall. This world had become foreign to her. Wilhelm Geyer, Hans and Sophie's friend from Ulm, had come to Munich to paint Professor Muth's portrait and was staying at the studio. One by one, she began to hang them. Geyer was an abstract painter, who could not work openly any longer. His landscapes represented nature's beauty with subdued colors. When she finished, she stood back and studied them. Art served as a constant reminder that life consisted of more than politics and war. It was life.

Sophie heard voices in the hallway. Alex's was the loudest. The leaflets had to be addressed and stuffed into envelopes, with the leftovers distributed again throughout the city. Hans burst through the studio as if he was already aware that there was an intruder. When he saw Sophie, he laughed.

"And if I were the Gestapo? Would you really have pounced on me like that? And how could you just leave this all out in the open? What's with you?" Sophie burst out, forgetting that this kind of chastising did little to affect her brother, who felt himself impervious to rules. He barely responded, peering back at her with lost eyes and dark circles around them as though he had been boxing with Max Schmeling.

Hans answered by hugging his sister so tightly that she lost her breath.

"I missed you," he said and asked about their mother.

"She's going to be all right." Sophie wasn't so sure. "Dad is getting out of prison soon."

Hans chuckled. "We took after him all right."

Sophie laughed. "Not as much, though, as our mother." She was referring to her mother's dedication to the knowing the truth.

"Hey you two, let's get going," Alex encouraged to start on the work.

He handed Sophie a stack of leaflets and empty envelopes. Willi was busy setting up an assembly line with leaflets, envelopes, and typewriters. The broken copy machine sat in a corner, waiting for its replacement. Two more days and Grimminger's secretary promised to arrive with money and a new copier.

The mood in the studio changed. Perhaps it was Wilhelm Geyer's paintings that lightened the mood. Kurt Huber's earlier delivery of the student address book had ignited new purpose. Stealing the book from the registrar's office had been a dangerous mission and significant contribution. Hans, Alex, Sophie, and Willi worked throughout the day. When they were finally finished, they had stuffed almost all of the leaflets into stamped envelopes addressed to students and university administrators. Geyer, the painter, picked up Hans and Sophie, and they went out to dinner to celebrate in Theatinerstrasse.

When Sophie finally fell into bed, she drifted off into a deep sleep, feeling exhausted but strengthened by their purpose. Her last thoughts were about her mother's love and all the amazing things she could do with the confidence created from it.

CHAPTER 10

Be conscious of the time

———

POLAND, FEBRUARY 17, 1943

FRITZ STILL FELT UNCOMFORTABLE AROUND food. The rotting feeling of starvation bore a hole deeper in him than the freezing temperatures had. Nurses came by constantly with warm food, giving him small portions until his stomach adjusted. He waited until they left the room because he couldn't trust himself not to grab it with his hands. They would think he was an animal. Towards the end there hadn't even been the moldy, icy bread. His body still felt like an empty cavern. It seemed like no amount of food or liquid could fill it. A month had gone by since they had been rescued by the last transport plane, and he was only now slowly beginning to recover sensation in some of his body. The screaming pain in his left hand was finally subsiding.

Twice a day a nurse bathed Fritz's amputated fingers and frost-bitten feet. His skin was beginning to heal, but only yesterday he thought he smelled an infection. The ache was persistent. He wanted to scratch it with his bandaged right hand but the place where it ached didn't occupy physical space. The doctor didn't want to operate again. He might lose the entire hand. Or even worse, he wouldn't wake up from the stress of the operation with a body so weakened from starvation.

When the nurse came in again, Fritz closed his book from the hospital library, smiling through the pain. Men were dying all over the hospital, and some were so injured that they no longer possessed the will to live. He didn't want to waste the nurse's time, so he insisted she leave the tub of salt solution. She didn't insist and handed him some extra sheets of paper, promising to be back later so she could post his daily letter. She still hadn't brought him any mail from Sophie. He was worried.

Even though Fritz's left hand was completely bandaged, and he wrote with his right, pain subsumed both. He still shuddered when he remembered how black they were. Most of his men had frozen to death out there. It took several minutes to write Sophie the following words: *The amputations are already half way grown over. The wounds don't hurt so much as the two fingers that aren't there anymore. The nerves go round and round inside both fingers as though they are squeezed into a vice.*

He paused for a moment, holding his wounded left hand with his bandaged right one. He closed his eyes and saw the men on the tarmac who couldn't get on the last plane out of the surrounded city. The ones they left to die. The image of their faces flashed before him all the time.

Fritz shook his head and started to write Sophie again. *Otherwise, I lie in bed like a healthy man.*

When he finished the letter, he put it on his bedside table and shut his eyes, although he didn't want to fall asleep. All of his dreams turned into nightmares. Stalingrad was the place where an essential part of him had died, and he wasn't certain yet what parts of him would return. There was no way that he could have survived when so many didn't and not have to pay some kind of incalculable price. A psychic price way beyond two missing fingers.

MUNICH, FEBRUARY 17, 1943

Upon awakening, Sophie called out Hans' name. He stayed over at Gisela's again. She sighed and, still in her pajamas, sat down at her desk near the window that looked out to the courtyard. During the last few days, she could feel the promise of spring. She smoothed out a sheet of paper and began writing:

February 17, 1943
My dear Fritz,
Yesterday I bought a wonderful blooming bouquet and put it by my writing table near the window, its graceful, charming tendrils occupied through and through with tender purple blooms. They suspend and hang in the balance before and over me. A definite joy for my eyes and heart.

She studied the flowers. It was a long time since she felt inspired to draw their long green stems. Hans would be angry at her for spending money. But when she saw the street vendor actually selling this precious sign of life, she had to have them. Fritz and Sophie had not seen one another in over half a year. He had no idea how life in the resistance had changed her. She was so tired. He had to come soon.

Sophie lifted her pen and stared out of the window into the courtyard. The weeks waiting anxiously for news from Stalingrad had weakened her.

I only wish that you can come before the bouquet peaks. When will you come?

Finishing the short letter, she sealed it and ran to the post office where she mailed it to the hospital in Poland.

Secret Police Chief Inspector Robert Mohr sat in the center of town in his office at the Wittelsbacher Palace and cursed his bad luck. He unburied his silver cigarette case from under the paperwork on his desk and lit up. Grey smoke curled in the sunlight, suspending in midair. It filled up the room, reminding him of the case he had worked on full time since June. They were in a similar fog. Berlin was getting anxious. His job as the head inspector of Munich's Gestapo was in danger. They were very close to finding the perpetrators, these traitors spreading lies. The entire Munich police force was concentrated on apprehending them. How dare these criminals try and undermine the Fatherland when it needed its people the most.

He was so lost in thought that he didn't hear the knock on the door. As his secretary walked in, he didn't have the time to adjust his slumped and defeated posture. Mohr was a short man, well below six feet with a stout physique. His full mustache and two tufts of hair between his shiny bald spot lent an almost comic appearance. His poorly tied bow tie didn't help this pitiable impression either.

"The report from the lab as you requested, Inspector Mohr." Secretary Ratzinger, afraid of his superior's unpredictable outbursts, laid the file on the flooded desk.

Mohr looked up at him, still distracted.

Ratzinger, mistaking the absent-mindedness as disapproval, quickly added the salute.

"Heil Hitler!"

Mohr only smirked in response. He doubted Ratzinger's sincerity.

"The report analyzes the handwriting and the content of the last leaflet, Chief Inspector," his secretary reminded him in a voice so filled with duty Mohr knew that Ratzinger hadn't bothered to read it himself.

Mohr nodded that that was all. He skipped the pages to Professor Harder's analysis. He was a linguistic expert at the university and an active member of the Party.

The authors of the June leaflets are the same as the February ones. The paper and envelopes were purchased in Marienplatz. The author is German and has thought out his opposition to the last detail and with complete clarity. He knows exactly what he wants, and he has detailed knowledge at his disposal.

Mohr paused. Detailed knowledge? Could these men be in the military? He shuddered. This could be worse than imagined. Mohr took out his fountain pen and began to take notes: *The author is a talented intellectual who elevates his propaganda to an academic audience, specifically targeted to students.*

Then it hit him—they were students. Mohr knew this as well as he knew anything that he had ever known. Of course they were students. They were fighting to end National Socialism with psychological tactics, planning to usurp the Party's power by taking away the people's cooperation and obedience.

They were just students. Too young to be responsible to anything or anyone. Too young to realize the risks and their consequences. Mohr grabbed the heavy black receiver and began barking orders.

"Twenty-four hour surveillance," he started shouting. "I want a twenty-four hour surveillance team at the university. Get in touch with the Student Party and patrol the halls. Put spies into the classrooms. Penetrate that damned university. Immediately. Hurry up!" Then he slammed down the phone. He picked it up again to check if he had broken it.

Mohr continued reading. A smile revealing brown and broken teeth swept over his full face. He suddenly felt better. He adjusted his bow tie and wondered if, when he caught them, he'd get a promotion. Mohr himself hadn't been afforded an education and this was his chance to prove that in the end, it didn't matter.

He re-read Harder's report:

The author's spiritual pronouncements are a desk product. And although the tone is not bitter, he is definitely supported by a clique. But it is not a powerful, active group. For that the language is too abstract. They cannot and will not have a wide response among soldiers or workers.

Mohr folded his hands together. A bunch of amateurs. They posed no real threat. No match for him, a trained Gestapo investigator.

He closed his angry eyes and made a vow. He wouldn't sleep until he caught them. No rest until he found these ungrateful traitors. How dare these spoiled students desert the Fatherland when Hitler gave them everything. He opened his eyes and started barking orders again into the phone.

Hans called another meeting at the studio, and although Sophie wanted to stay home and read, she put on her tired brown coat now missing buttons and wrapped a hand-knitted scarf around her long neck. The studio was a short walk from the apartment. Walking refreshed her, gave her purpose again.

All she could really think about now was Fritz's homecoming. Hope rose up inside her and it carried her down the street. Perhaps she and Fritz were going to get married after all. She started to hum.

As she turned down Leopoldstrasse, she caught sight of Gisela's blond hair tucked underneath her cap. Sophie whistled. Her friend picked up her pace, thinking it was a catcall from a passing soldier. Then, too curious, she turned around. Sophie could see that her face, normally as quiet as a doll's, was contorted and twisted. Gisela ran back towards her.

"Hans is in one of his moods, I just can't take it." The cold stung with her words. "I just can't take the pressure tonight, Sophie. I'm going home to read to forget all about this for a while." Gisela looked like she was about to cry.

"Let's meet tomorrow for lunch, Gissie." Sophie stroked her friend's back.

"Come with me, Sophie. We really shouldn't go there at all. It's too dangerous for us."

"I have to go, Gisela. This is my life's duty, and I won't stop now."

"What about Fritz? What will happen to him if you get caught? Have you thought about that?" Gisela tugged at her friend's coat. She didn't want to be the only one guilty of deserting their group of friends.

"Gisela." Sophie's thoughts were lost in a web of tangled emotion. "Tomorrow. Let's meet at the Lake House at the English Garden."

Gisela's blue eyes brightened. The Lake House was such a strange building, designed as a Chinese tea house. They both loved it.

"Götz von Berlichingen?" Sophie replied, reminding her friend of earlier days when they used to sneak a cigarette on top of haystacks in the fields outside of the Nazi women's camp.

"Kiss my ass!" Gisela echoed Goethe's slang and hugged Sophie. Everything was going to be all right. As her friend turned, she saw Sophie rushing to the studio. The frown returned to Gisela's angelic face.

Sophie burst inside with an attempt at humor. *"Führer, wir danken Dir*, we thank you," she yelled out, mimicking the sarcasm in their latest leaflet. No one laughed. Eight tall piles of leaflets stood up against the wall. Willi, Alex, and Hans said nothing.

"Two thousand leaflets. And we don't have enough envelopes to send them out." Willi shook his head. He was the practical one. How could they measure whether or not they were making any progress? Hans was certain that the student protest at the theater indicated that they made a difference. They read the leaflets, they learned, and they would be more and more curious and eventually daring. "We'll distribute them tomorrow in the university's atrium," Hans finally proposed a solution.

"Are you crazy?" Willi stood up angrily, raising his voice.

The graffiti actions were bold enough.

"And when do you suppose this will be a good idea? While the students are leaving their classrooms?" Alex added, sarcastically. The idea of distributing leaflets at the university during the day was too bold even to contemplate.

"While classes are in session," Hans continued with confidence, "the atrium is all but deserted."

He had no intentions of letting up.

"I won't take part in this kind of suicide," Willi had had enough. This was the last straw. Hans' ideas were getting out of control. The graffiti actions were crazy enough. They were lucky to have gotten away with that. Now their leader was asking them to commit suicide.

Alex didn't speak. He lit his pipe and the comforting sweet smell of tobacco filled the room. Hans turned to look at his best friend. Growing desperate, he grabbed Alex by both shoulders. "You're in, right?" Alex had always been able to stand up to Hans.

"I don't think we should take this kind of chance, Hans. It is way too risky. You know that. Our first order of business is Berlin. We're going in a couple of days. Let's take our orders from them. They'll tell us how we should best proceed. Let's first unite Berlin and Munich. We'll be stronger that way."

Hans wouldn't let up. Sophie hated the way her brother looked as if he hadn't showered in days, even if there was only cold water. He persisted.

"You know as I do that the hallways are abandoned when classes are in session. It will be fast. In and out. Simple. Easy."

Alex interrupted, "Hans, the Gestapo is paroling the hallways now. They're looking for us like mad dogs since the buildings. They are obsessed with finding us."

Emboldened by the men's refusal, Sophie cleared her throat. Sometimes it seemed as though in their most intense moments they forgot she even existed.

"I will go. I can do it." Her voice was steady.

Willi, completely exasperated, sat down on the table.

"Sophie, you can't. You just can't. Please. You may be willing to risk your life, but you have to think of us now. You get caught, we get caught." Willi knew that this reason would appeal to her and no other.

Hans stayed silent.

Sophie faced them all squarely.

"Hans, you cannot and will not let Sophie go with you." Alex was angry now.

Hans looked over at Sophie. She, like Alex, had helped start this movement. She had gone to Augsburg and Stuttgart to distribute the leaflets by herself. She had even recruited Gisela. They were eighteen strong now and working on their sixth leaflet. They were even going to meet up with the military resistance in Berlin. Things were beginning to happen.

"We have to act boldly. Now. We have to take advantage of the momentum. People are ready. This is the first step to overthrowing a dictatorship. The Nazis can't continue ruling Germany without the people behind them. It's decided then. Sophie and I are going tomorrow."

Hans shut the conversation down. Alex and Willi left the studio without saying good night to either of them. For one brief moment, Alex held Sophie's eyes in desperation. They pleaded with her. Sophie only smiled back reassuringly.

As they walked home in the darkness, two soldiers passed without a word. "Heil Hitler" was a greeting of the past. Sophie reached out and clutched her brother's coat for no apparent reason. She remembered a long time ago she had written to Fritz what she was feeling now, *It dawned on me that the other side cannot win. I will try and take the victor's side.*

The cold robbed them of the ability to converse. Brother and sister were also accustomed to speaking without words that the silence between them signaled understanding and even peace. Hans was convinced that there was readiness. The students were ready to use their freedom of speech. By bold action at the university, they were showing the students how to resist. Challenging the regime had to be proven by example.

Hans and Sophie's renewed sense of solidarity reminded them of the days before the war. She remembered when Hans' rejected Nazism at the rally. Sophie wasn't sure why Alex and Willi objected to the plan so vehemently. They would be in and out of the university's atrium in half an hour. Easy.

Munich, February 18, 1943

Sophie woke without remembering her dreams. Hans had already stuffed hundreds of leaflets into two separate suitcases. She wondered briefly if he had even slept. Sitting down at the kitchen table, she wiped the sleep from her eyes. Still in her nightclothes, Hans asked her to get dressed. They were to be at the university before eleven a.m., and it was a little after ten.

"We must eat breakfast first," he said as a way of saying good morning. Sophie nodded. She thought of dressing up and wearing her traditional boiled wool jacket with old coin buttons. She quietly paired it with a long pleated skirt and laced up her only pair of boots. They had a giant hole in the bottom. She still looked so *schwabisch*—she was Schwabian after all and not Bavarian. A woman could have worn the same outfit two hundred years ago. She smiled at the irony, got down on her knees, and prayed.

"You don't have to do this, Sophie." Hans said, not looking up from his textbook.

"I know, Hans," Sophie said and bit into the stale bread that they had split between the two of them. Butter and jam were memories from another life.

"I mean it. Don't come with me unless you absolutely feel convinced and right about it. I'm sure we will achieve the desired outcome. We'll motivate them. They'll act now. They're ready."

"I want to, Hans. I do." It had been weeks since he had spoken to her with such tenderness. The kindness had the effect of doubling her desire to please him.

Sophie planned her day—distribute the leaflets and then meet Gisela for lunch in the English Garden café for some girl talk.

As if reading her mind, Hans looked up from his medical textbook and warned her again. "Ten minutes. That's all it should take. We have to be out of there before the classes let out. I timed the student patrol yesterday."

She didn't want to tell Hans about her meeting with Gisela afterwards. It reminded her too much of when she met with Traute back in July and had to tell her that her brother was no longer interested. He broke hearts with abandon. Gisela's was next. She wished that he'd left Gisela alone. She wasn't just for conquest. Women weren't as important to Hans as his ambition.

He shut his book and looked up from the table again. Sophie got up, cleared the plates, and put them in the sink. She remembered Elisabeth's shock when she came and the place was so filthy. As if a woman's only job was to clean dishes and dust. She smiled for the second time that morning. She had more important things to do and didn't even bother to sweep the crumbs off the table.

As they walked through the courtyard, she paused for a moment and allowed her face to soak up the bright sun. Hans looked over his shoulder and told her to hurry. The red leather suitcase was so heavy. Sophie lugged it all the way down Leopoldstrasse with it bumping against her leg.

Hans fed Sophie directions as they headed towards the university.

"Time, Sophie, be most conscious of the time. Go up the main staircase to the second floor. Put the suitcase down in a corner, take handfuls of leaflets and lay them down on the floor in front of all the classrooms' closed doors. I'll make the rounds of the first floor. Meet me at 10:55 a.m. at the entrance. Look at the clock for the time."

Sophie listened. As they entered the university's classical entrance through the wrought-iron doors, she was distracted by his repeated directions. She understood the first time he warned her. *Be conscious of the time.*

They were just about to go on their separate missions when Willi and Traute came rushing down the stone staircase. Traute was flustered.

It was Willi who spoke first. "Hans? We have a lecture at the women's clinic in twenty minutes. Where are you ...?" he trailed off as he spoke, noticing their heavy suitcases.

But Traute didn't see the heavy suitcases they were both carrying. Willi pushed her along, keeping her moving. If she didn't see them, she couldn't be held accountable.

"Let's go, Traute, we'll be late." Traute looked behind her. But it wasn't for Hans. Hers and Sophie's eyes met and in this glance they assured one another of their friendship.

Sophie turned and ran up the foyer's grand staircase and set the suitcase on the marble floor and opened it. Grabbing a handful of leaflets, she bent down and dropped them on the side of a closed classroom door. She could hear a professor lecturing inside. Sophie moved on to the next door. Then another batch. Another corner. Sweat trickled down her face and her heart pounded.

Soon the entire rectangular balcony was covered with leaflets. She looked at the massive clock with Roman numerals. It read

10:55. She contemplated another batch. It was too late. She ran down the stairs. Hans was waiting for her behind the interior Greek columns. He smiled. He reached back his hand and she grabbed it. Together they ran outside.

"Did you get rid of them all?" He asked breathlessly.

"No. I still have about two handfuls left," Sophie answered, disappointed that she hadn't completed the job. She looked at the not quite empty suitcase. "We can go back. We still have five minutes until the bell rings."

"No, we best not, Sophie, let's go. Let's get out of here. We want to be far away from here when classes end and the commotion starts."

"Please, Hans, please." Sophie insisted. She wanted to finish the job. Then, without getting his permission, Sophie suddenly let go of his hand and ran back through the doors and up the staircase. Hans frowned, looked around, and seeing no one, followed her reluctantly back inside.

Sophie set the last stack of leaflets on the top of the marble balustrade. Fueled with adrenaline and motivated by the line "shed the veil of indifference," she pushed them over.

CHAPTER 11

The law that never changes

MUNICH, FEBRUARY 18, 1943

As THE LEAFLETS CASCADED DOWN into the university's foyer, a flickering ray of sunlight blinded Sophie as it reflected off of a Nazi pin. It belonged to the school's custodian. Jakob Schmied, dressed in blue overalls, emerged slowly from behind the Greek columns. He saw the sheets falling from the balcony and the girl and the young man roaming the hallways.

"*Stehen bleiben!* Stand still!" Schmied ordered. Hans and Sophie froze in their tracks.

Then with a loud single shrill, the bell sounded, signaling the end of class and releasing the students into the atrium. Hans and Sophie stood perfectly still. Young men and women gathered on the massive stairwell and downstairs in the foyer, reading the leaflets that they picked up off the floor. Hans appeared fearless. He regained his regal and natural posture.

A few students ran to inform the dean. Someone in the crowd called out for the Gestapo. Sophie retained her detached composure. Her dark and serious eyes stared straight ahead. That morning she had pinned her shoulder-length hair to the side, opening up her face. Taking in the agitation caused by the students reading the leaflets, a warm wave swept through her, and for one brief moment she knew that they had succeeded. It had been worth it.

Minutes later, men in tan uniforms clamored through the crowd. University Dean Wust pointed to the suspects. The Gestapo handcuffed Hans and Sophie and pushed them into separate black trucks.

The caravan sped past Karolinenplatz and the black obelisk commemorating Bavarian soldiers who had died in Napoleon's invasion of Russia. Now Hitler's fight for Stalingrad had just been lost. Looking outside of the speeding window, Sophie realized where they were headed. Her eyes grew wide with terror. Briennerstrasse 50. Gestapo Headquarters. People disappeared without a trace after being brought there. Her heart started racing. For the first time in her life it crossed her mind that she might never see Fritz again.

The Party had converted Wittelsbacher Palace into Munich's secret police headquarters. The former home of a noble family during the Baroque Era, it was filled with gilded ornamentation, marble floors, silk-covered furniture, and crystal chandeliers. The endless hallways and rooms were occupied by black- and tan-uniformed personnel. Agents rushed Hans and Sophie into separate rooms in the basement where they had set up prison cells out of the wine cellar.

The Gestapo found an envelope on Hans. He was carrying a draft of what looked like another leaflet written by a Christoph

Probst. This Probst signed his name to it. The envelope came from Innsbruck. Chief Inspector Mohr ordered his secretary to call Gestapo Headquarters in Austria. At once.

Mohr read an excerpt from the new leaflet found at the university and shuddered. He read it again to check to see if he had read it right, repeated it to himself, and crumbled the paper in his fist. The words found a way to form the sentence again in his mind: *Germany will be dishonored for all time if its youth does not finally rise, take revenge, and atone. It must smash its tormentors!*

He ran a bloated finger around his neck in a vain attempt to loosen his collar. These disgusting traitors, Mohr sneered. They all deserved death.

Sophie sat handcuffed outside of Mohr's interrogation room, flanked by two Gestapo agents to her left and right. Typewriters clacked, phones rang continuously, doors opened and closed, and personnel walked back and forth. Her heart began to pound. They weren't prepared for this. They hadn't thought up synchronized stories. The irony of being in a magnificent building significant in German history and arrested for crimes against the State confused Sophie. Crimes of freedom. She thought about her mother and father. Would her mother be able to stand this stress? Her father would be proud of them. She hoped her mother wouldn't blame her father for setting the example.

Just then the red light outside of the room switched on. The agents grabbed her arm, opened the door, and pushed her inside. Chief Inspector Mohr wore a red, white, and black swastika armband. If it weren't for that, with his two greying tufts of hair and bow tie, duties But this man was a dangerous one possessed by an evil ideology.

Mohr stood up as she entered his office—a requirement of any gentleman when a female entered a room. This wasn't a situation that demanded these kinds of manners, but Mohr was also a simple man. He stood up because this is what men did and for no other reason. This is what he had been taught to do. He motioned for Sophie to sit in a brown leather chair opposite his massive dark wooden desk and took her handcuffs off.

Sophie rubbed her chaffed and bruised skin. She didn't look at him. Mohr sniffed at her cowardice and started his work.

"Scholl, Sophia Magdalena, from Ulm, born on May 9, 1921, in Forchtenberg. Protestant. Correct?"

Sophie nodded.

"Your father?"

She answered quietly. "Robert Scholl, he was once the Mayor of Forchtenberg."

"Your education as school teacher completed?"

"Yes."

"Student at the University of Munich, studying botany and philosophy since summer semester, 1942."

"Yes," Sophie answered, growing more and more afraid.

"Currently still living in Munich, Franz-Joseph Strasse 13?"

"Yes," she could barely speak.

Mohr took out another file. She could see from across the table that it contained their leaflets. Her palms began to sweat. Her mouth was dry. She needed water. As a way of buying time, she thought of asking for some water, then refrained. He would know what she was trying to do. Mohr started taking notes. Sophie started to guess at the questions and formulate their answers. If she could stay one step ahead of Mohr, maybe she could win this game. He was only a Party functionary. They were not trained to think for themselves. Perhaps she could outsmart him.

But Chief Inspector Mohr was good at his job. Before the war he was only a policeman from a small provincial town. He was an expert by the single qualification of being a convinced believer. This man could also smell out a lie. These particular mistruths had been slowly destroying his reputation in his city and he was angry. He was furious because Germany didn't deserve traitors in its hour of need. It needed loyalty. He finally looked up from his notepad.

Sophie sat very still. She smoothed out her wrinkled skirt. Mohr continued to scribble words on his pad. *Middle class. Student. Intellectual.* She fit Harder's description. He looked up.

"Your father's political affiliation?" Mohr inquired with eyes that he tried to disguise as friendly. She answered with a smugness he was unable to dismiss.

"He is inclined towards being a democrat."

He hid his wince. So self-righteous. So superior. He checked himself. He must make her feel safe.

The girl's brown eyes were so soft and she seemed naïve with a kind of inner innocence—or was it some kind of belief? Did she have any idea at all that her life was at stake? And what about her calmness? How did she account for that? But he couldn't let her see his inner deliberations. She mustn't see his difficulty at assessing her personality. This wasn't the first woman he had interrogated but perhaps the prettiest. Perhaps the youngest.

If she were involved—if she had been the one to push those ridiculous leaflets off the balcony—she must be accustomed to this level of intensity and fear. Gestapo Headquarters in Augsburg, Stuttgart, Ulm, Vienna, and Salzburg also reported that these leaflets were littered about in their cities. He picked up the phone and called in the stenographer. She could take down her history. Perhaps she would feel more comfortable confessing to another female.

He abruptly filed his papers together. He was getting nowhere. Although Mohr didn't have a daughter of his own and didn't feel the loss of not having one, he had a son fighting for the Fatherland on the Russian Front. She was betraying him too. He spoke to her in a tone of voice that presumed her guilt. She didn't lower her head or even plead with her eyes. He left the room wishing that she had. This would have indicated remorse or perhaps even shame. How on earth could she compose herself so well under these circumstances and still be guilty?

After about two hours, the stenographer brought him the completed interrogation form. He read through it quickly. He was looking for a clue, anything to indicate rebellion. To his disappointment, he found the opposite. She was a group leader in the League of German Girls. She had worked as a kindergarten teacher for wayward children of the Reich in the Black Forest, performing her duties as required.

Had they apprehended the wrong suspects? Mohr was getting nervous. He drummed his fat fingers on his desk. *What if she hadn't done it? Were the resistors still out there?*

Reading further, he found the clue he needed.

"My father is opposed to National Socialism," she told the stenographer. Mohr picked up the phone again to call the Party

Leader in Ulm. He confirmed it. Robert Scholl had served time recently in prison for publicly speaking out against Hitler. Hans Scholl was also arrested back in 1937 for subversive activities.

This girl's entire family was rotten.

Down the hallway in another interrogation room, Jakob Schmied, the custodian, testified to what he had seen. He imagined himself a hero. He looked eagerly around the room, waiting for recognition. Chief Inspector Mohr grinned as he read his witness statement and shook Schmied's greasy and calloused hands. It pleased Mohr to see such faithfulness. He was loyal, obedient, and true. A real man didn't defect when his country needed him most.

Schmied's interrogation was shorter than he wished. After 48 years of working at the university sweeping its floors and emptying the garbage, he could finally get a promotion. But after they took his statement, he was asked to go. Stunned, he looked around the busy office in disbelief. He had never been so important in his whole life. This was anti-climactic. He put on his ratty scarf and cap and walked through the cold night. He hoped that they would need him for the trial. He heard the words treason and execution. By the time he arrived at home, his gums were aching and he took out his yellow false teeth and dropped them into a dirty glass.

Mohr closed his eyes for a moment, deciding that it was late and that he should return home and get some sleep. He would need his strength for tomorrow. Berlin would be calling with orders. Walking through the palace's cobblestoned courtyard with his black leather briefcase, past the waterless fountain—he had long forgotten which king was sitting atop the equine statute—Mohr didn't feel any differently. He was bothered by this. He didn't feel vindicated. He felt nothing. This was the greatest moment of his career as Munich's chief inspector and he should feel victorious. Instead a strange numbness enveloped his entire mind.

Down the hall at Wittelsbacher Palace, Hans' interrogator was more experienced in instilling terror. It was a calculated risk. Inspector Mahler knew that this student was the one. He was probably even their leader. A traitor smelled differently. They didn't belong to the same blood community. Traitors, like this one, didn't get nervous because they were the masters of their own deceptions. Mahler already had played this game. He didn't care that this young man was over thirty years younger than him. Too young to know the price of death and the pain of dying. He was just some punk playing games. Mahler was going to put him in his place. Show him who was smarter.

Hans felt weak, tired, and cold. The pills he had been taking to stay awake—the ones he stole from the university's clinic—were beginning to wear off and he was crashing. Since they found Christoph's leaflet, Hans had lost all his confidence. He betrayed his best friend. He didn't remember putting the draft in his jacket pocket. How long had it been there? Why did he leave the house with it? And Sophie. Why did she have to run back inside? And then the opposite feeling, why did he have to take her? It wasn't fair. He felt himself slipping, unable to concentrate or stay awake.

Gisela had seen the student commotion from outside Professor Huber's lecture-hall doors. Hans had called out to her, "Tell Alex I won't be home for dinner." It was the one secret code that they had set up. She had to warn Alex. The police were already putting up road blocks and checking identification papers. Gisela still belonged to the Party—or at least it said so on her papers. Her parents insisted she keep her Party status for her protection. Gisela checked that she had them on her and biked to the wealthiest side of the city as fast she could.

When she got to Alex's house in Bogenhausen, she flung her bike against the cement wall and rang the bell. Alex's brother peered out of the window and, recognizing her from his brother's group of friends, he came outside to open the wrought-iron gate.

"Where's Alex?" she pleaded, breathless and frozen from the piercing cold.

"And who are you?" Erich demanded, annoyed that his brother, the artist, had friends who still didn't know their manners.

Alex paused briefly at the top of the winding stairwell. He nodded to Gisela to show her that he had understood and then turned and ran into his room, throwing some clothes into a knapsack. He would hitchhike through the mountains, and once in Tirol he knew some Russian house servants who could help him. He cursed Hans. Then he remembered Sophie. *Oh my God, Sophie. She must have been caught too.* Alex could not bear the thought for a single second, pushing it out of his mind. He took his Bible and then he opened a map of the Alps and planned his escape.

Erich watched this strange scene from the entranceway, and imagining Gisela to be just another of his brother's desperate admirers, asked her if she would like some tea. He had no idea that his brother planned to flee from the Gestapo for acts of treason.

Erich read one of the leaflets that came directly into their mailbox, but he didn't for a single second suspect that his brother would be so crazy to have had anything to do with it. Not a political person, he barely finished reading it. He just wanted the war to be over. The pretty girl didn't feel like tea and she left in as much a hurry as she arrived. From the window, Erich watched her rush off. So enraptured by Gisela's ethereal beauty, he didn't hear his younger brother leave their family home by the kitchen door. Alex was in such a rush he didn't even say good-bye.

MUNICH, FEBRUARY 19, 1943

Mohr and Mahler sifted through the evidence they had found in the suspects' apartment and went through the boxes slowly, taking out each item and writing an inventory. They looked at one another and smiled. Mohr dangled the used brushes covered in paint and threw them back into the box. He lifted up the portable Remington typewriter and inspected it. It was missing the "k" key. "K's" had been penciled into the leaflets. Mahler counted sheets of stamps. Mohr tried on the gloves smeared with paint. He handled the hand gun and pointed it out the window. The stencils with the letters "F-R-E-E-D-O-M" cut out of them sat at the bottom of the box.

"Those dirty liars," Mohr paced back and forth in his office while Mahler sat back and lit a cigarette. "I heard that Judge Freisler, President of the People's Court, appointed by the Führer himself, is coming from Berlin to try them. That will be their reward for lying to us. I almost believed that pathetic girl."

Mahler only shook his head. Women were the worst.

"Berlin wants the trial over as quickly as possible. He has his orders. Martyrs are to be avoided."

Freisler knew the law and wasn't afraid to administer it. Mohr drifted off for a moment and thought about the girl. He could sense her silent derision. He didn't want her in his office or interrogation room again. Why was such an innocent-looking girl involved in all of this? He had even taken out the law books from the Republic and asked her to read the punishment for treason during Germany's brief experiment with democracy. Convicted traitors were sentenced to death.

Sophie hadn't even flinched. He could usually read his suspects. Find their breaking points. Get to their weakness immediately. But this Scholl girl appeared unperturbed by the prospect of being sent to Dachau or even death. After uncovering the evidence in their apartment, getting a confession was going to be easy. Then they would wait for instructions from Berlin.

Sophie glanced at her crossed hands on her lap. If this was going to be the end, then it was God's will. She wouldn't plead for mercy. Sophie never doubted their actions. She remembered when she stood up for Heine at the League of German Girls meeting or when she read the Bible in secret at the Nazi labor camps. A life of lies and denial was not worth living. Fritz, fighting in a war under an insane dictator, knew this better than anyone. He would understand. If he hadn't felt so responsible to his men, he never would have fought in Hitler's Army. It had always been that simple, and she loved him for this sense of duty. He had been trained at the best military academy and he was dedicated to saving as many of his men as possible.

Mohr entered the room with an expression of victory painted on his round face. He walked over to his desk, sat down, and adjusted his bow tie. Sophie barely moved.

"Why did you do it?" Mohr asked.

Sophie looked back at him as though he had made a comment about the weather.

"Fraulein Scholl. We found all we needed in your apartment. The game is over. You know, you are obliged to speak the whole truth. You've been lying, playing with me."

He tapped his fingers on the desk once more, waiting for her confession.

It was finally over. She cleared her throat and spoke forcibly.

"It was our conviction, Chief Inspector Mohr, that Germany had lost the war a long time ago. That every life sacrificed to this lost war was for nothing. We were especially motivated by the victims of Stalingrad. We had to do something against this meaningless blood bath."

Sophie wouldn't mention all the things Fritz told her about arguments with his superiors or what he saw in Amsterdam. Or recently in Russia. A person like Mohr would think she was making it up. She also didn't want to get Fritz in trouble.

Mohr hadn't expected this. He thought she was going to confess that she was sympathetic to the persecution of the Jews and Communists, or that she was going to wax poetic about her rights. He waited for a moment, collected his thoughts. *Of course this had been her motivation. Her boyfriend was fighting in Russia.* He made a note to check on this Fritz Hartnagel. Was he somehow involved in all this? Now he was getting into murky territory. Survivors of Stalingrad were Hitler's and Germany's heroes.

He suddenly had the urge to spit. This girl had resisted out of the simplest of reasons: love. She was trying to save her boyfriend from war.

Mohr needed her full confession.

"Tell me everything you've done. And tell me who else is out there spreading these lies and weakening the fight for the Fatherland."

Sophie waited for a brief moment and then gave him her best friend's name as though it had been a part of a plan. She didn't know why Alex's name slipped so easily out of her mouth. She bit her lip.

Mohr leaned forward. This was finally getting interesting. The girl was breaking.

"Alexander Schmorell was my friend since June of last year and his mother was Russian," she stated. "He helped us." She paused. Why was she saying this? Her face flushed and her heart started racing. If she gave him one name, she wouldn't have to give him the others.

Mohr scribbled the name down and underlined it.

Sophie confessed to everything. She took care of the group's finances, securing supplies like paper, stamps, and envelopes, finding addresses. On the missions, she went by herself at night to Ulm, Stuttgart, and Augsburg and distributed as many leaflets as possible. As many as she could carry.

She spoke fluidly, quickly, not leaving out a single detail. It was all over now. She confessed her leadership as though their activities weren't illegal and punishable by death. She mentioned specific times and exact numbers.

She gave away one of her best friends.

Mohr could hardly keep up taking notes. He ordered his stenographer to come in and help. He needed to get started on catching this other traitor, Schmorell.

Sophie continued, "I was completely clear that our actions were geared towards overcoming the present government, and that the goal of our propaganda was to reach broad levels of the population. Our intention was to continue this work. We never, though, had the goal of pulling more people into our trust and to win them over for active participation. This appeared too dangerous."

Mohr doubted that. This girl was lying again. There was no way that they had perpetrated these crimes alone, and he was going to get all of them. This Alex character would do for now.

"If the question were posed to me whether or not I'm still of the opinion that I acted properly, I would answer 'yes.'"

This Sophie Scholl knew the consequences. Mohr shut his notebook. He reached under his desk and switched on the light signaling it was time to take her down to the prison. Then, he screamed for someone to come in and organize a new arrest.

After her capture, trial, and year's imprisonment for speaking badly about Hitler in public, Else Gebel was ordered to work another year at the prison's admissions desk. Else was in her late twenties and not married. The year in political prison showed on her tired face. She kept her thinning hair, once her prettiest feature, in a tight bun and her black uniform hung awkwardly on a thin and petite frame. Else was accused of telling a joke about the Führer in public. Her sentence for that was two years. Today they were bringing another young female back to her cell. She finished stamping piles of papers, and once back inside her cell, fell asleep waiting for the new prisoner.

Sophie could barely keep her eyes open by the time the guards pushed her inside. Else, accustomed to prison life, slept soundly. Suddenly the city's warning sirens began to wail. Allied war planes roared overhead and the city lit up in flashes of light and phosphorous green. Awakened by the noise, Else grabbed Sophie and putting a cot's mattress over their heads, they huddled in a corner. Allied intelligence knew about this building's purpose and it was a target for destruction.

A bomb went off again outside, followed by more screams and shouting. In order to calm themselves, Else and Sophie needed to start talking. They shared how they refused to give up their freedoms.

"Please tell me, Sophie, everything that you did. I've been hoping, while locked up in here, that there were people like you."

A loud burst shattered the windows above them. Sophie wondered for a moment if this was going to be way she died.

"Tell me what the leaflets said, Sophie," Else tried to keep her new friend talking. "My boyfriend, Fritz, is an officer. He wrote to me almost daily from the front. He told me everything, including the murder of all the Jews in Russia." Sophie put her face in her hands.

Else gasped. She had heard the rumors.

"This is what we wrote about in the leaflets."

Sophie continued on about the old copy machine and how it kept breaking, and about their father's friend who gave them money because his wife was Jewish. She talked until the sirens and explosions stopped.

It was 3 a.m. when they helped one another up off of the cold floor. Sophie asked for a favor.

"Please, tell my parents everything I just told you."

"No, Sophie. You will be able to tell them yourself."

She was no longer sure. How much more of this could she take?

"Tell them I wasn't afraid," she insisted. "Please. Please don't forget that."

Tears swelled up in Else's eyes. She took Sophie's hand.

"Sleep now. God bless you. You will be able to tell your parents yourself." Else spoke with so much conviction that she believed it herself.

Sophie didn't hear her. Sleep had already released her while the city of Munich burned.

Munich, February 20, 1943

They must be brought to justice, thought Mohr. He didn't know how many innocent civilians perished in the night's attack—1,000, maybe 2,000. Towers of smoke tunneled into the cold morning's air, and from every packed bomb shelter people emerged covered in dust and consumed with fear, many of them returning to their homes absent of doors, walls, electricity, food, and running water.

Mohr's contempt blew up his face and neck so much that he had to loosen his bow tie. He adjusted his grey suit jacket and dusted off its shoulders. It had been a rough night in the bomb shelter. He prepared himself for what he was about to do next. This was the biggest day in his career.

Sophie was brought into his office. She sat down in Mohr's chair and sat up straight, folding her hands in her lap. Her eyes kept shutting. She was so tired. Agent Mohr was angry about last night's bombing and he couldn't believe that this traitor was sitting right in front of him—someone who supported the enemies trying to destroy his city.

He cleared his throat.

Mohr studied the expression on the girl's face. Today she looked back at him with disdain. She faced him squarely.

"Do you know the true meaning of National Socialism, Fraulein Scholl? Or have you forgotten?" he asked her, hoping she would wipe the smugness off her face and replace it with fear.

"Yes, Herr Mohr, I do," Sophie answered quickly.

"No, I don't think you do. Then you wouldn't have acted against it. So allow me to tell you. The Führer is our King. He has been appointed by God and leads with His mandate. The Germans are His chosen people."

Sophie shook her head.

"I don't believe that is possible, sir. Respectfully, I disagree. Our Kaisers and Kings in Germany's past may have led with God's mandate, but our Führer is no such thing."

Mohr lost his composure.

"Shut up! Damn it! Shut up! I am speaking and not asking your opinion." He slammed his fist on the table. He had in fact asked.

Rage reared up inside of him, and he started ranting about what the Party had given him. Prestige. A good, powerful position.

"Have you no German honor whatsoever?"

Sophie waited for Mohr to answer for her, but this time he waited for her response.

"Yes, Herr Mohr. This is why we did this. For Germany. For everything that it used to be. I want Germany returned to the Germans."

"Aren't I German?" Chief Mohr was attempting to trick her.

"Are you German?" Sophie asked, looking straight into dark flat eyes.

"I am more German than you will ever be, dear girl. You compromised our security and even your young man, Officer Hartnagel. I know all about you and him." He shook his thick finger at her. "You betrayed him as he fought the bravest of all battles in Stalingrad."

Sophie swallowed hard. For the first time it occurred to her that people would think this.

Mohr crossed his arms across his small chest and walked towards the ceiling-to-floor windows and opened the heavy silk curtains. Rays of late winter sunlight flooded the room. Sophie blinked and adjusted her eyes.

Mohr repeated himself, digging in even more. "Did you or did you not compromise his safety?"

"He will understand. He'll know why we acted as we did. You, all of you, turned Germany into a freedomless state and invaded innocent countries and raped and robbed and murdered. And if that wasn't enough, set up your camps…" Sophie shook her head. "Our German name will be destroyed for all time."

"Don't be ridiculous," Mohr shouted, this time throwing his arms up in the air. "None of that is even true. If the Führer even knew what you were accusing him of…" Mohr scribbled down something on his notes and continued.

"I'm not indulging in these rumors. Let's stick to the point, shall we? I was talking about German men—your boyfriend— sacrificing their lives for spoilt intellectuals like yourself who think it right to subvert Germany in its greatest time of need."

Mohr took a deep breath. He paused after ranting and looked over at her. But Sophie was no longer listening. She was staring out of the window as if she could hear music. Mohr closed her file.

"Fraulein Scholl." Sophie returned her gaze to her interrogator with eyes no longer wet with sorrow but filled with contempt and anger. *Did he really think that Germany was still Germany?*

"We can offer back your life, you know," he continued. "A compromise. If you can admit that you made an error, I will call in my secretary immediately to record it—that you made an error, a grievous error, you can apologize and recant. Tell us that you really do believe in the Führer's promises, in the idea of a Thousand Year Reich, that you believe in Germany's ultimate superiority."

Mohr's eyes grew wide. Not only did he have the power to convert this girl gone astray, he also would be able to save her life by converting her back to the truth. He continued.

"During this entire interrogation, hasn't it once occurred to you that your behavior and actions, especially during this critical phase of the war, are a crime against your very own community, your countrymen, your soldiers?"

Sophie thought carefully before answering. After some time, she spoke.

"The crimes you speak of—you mean the right to freedom of speech? And all of the other freedoms that were possible in Germany before your Führer came to power?"

"No, Fraulein Scholl. I am speaking of the law. You broke the law."

"Laws always change, Herr Mohr. You know that. I obeyed the law of my conscience. The law that never changes. The law that must be obeyed when political law breaks all moral authority."

Mohr smiled thinly. He answered back with conviction, "Not every conscience can determine what's right and what's wrong. That would result in absolute chaos."

"No one has the right to take innocent lives because he alone decides what is right. Only God is allowed to do that."

"And, what if, what if, Fraulein Scholl, there is no God?"

"Well, Herr Mohr, every argument that we will ever have will end exactly here. I'm as convinced as ever that I did the best that I could for my country. I don't regret my behavior, and I will take the consequences for what I have done."

Mohr rose from his desk. She was impossible. Her argument made no sense. He flipped on the switch indicating that they were finished and that his prisoner could be collected. The interrogation was over.

CHAPTER 12

Our idea will prevail despite all of this madness

MUNICH, FEBRUARY 21, 1943

THE SHOUTING BEGAN AT EARLY dawn. Too scared to move, Else and Sophie lay paralyzed in their cots straining to make out the muffled voices outside of the cell. Keys rattled and doors opened and slammed shut. Sophie put her head in her hands. The Gestapo had found Alex. They caught him. It was her fault. Why had she informed on Alex? It was the weakest moment of her life. The betrayal left her unable to breathe. She turned on one of her best friends. She tried not to cry and closed her eyes in regret.

Else rapped again on the cell's small window inside the door. As though he were waiting—listening to their every word—the guard slid it open and peered through the bars.

"What's going on, Kessler?," Else whispered.

"We found him at the student medic post in Innsbruck."

Sophie lost her balance and fell back on the cot. Then, as if she had been kicked in the stomach, she doubled over.

"It can't be. No," She gasped. "No."

The guard slid the window shut.

"Not Christoph, not Christoph!" Sophie lost control, sobbing and banging her fists against the grey cement wall. A wooden crucifix hung over the tiny window tilted. She began yelling at it. God couldn't have let this happen.

Else attempted to comfort her but Sophie pushed her away. Then she doubled over, holding her sides.

She struggled for breath, "It can't be. He and his wife just had another baby. They have three small children."

Else didn't know what to do. Sophie's whole body began to shake. Tears flooded down her face. She fell back, rocking back and forth.

"Christoph is the best of us, Else."

Else didn't know what else to say so she said nothing. The trial was tomorrow. She sat down next to her friend and gently took her in her arms. Giant silent tears rolled down Sophie's tired face.

Chief Inspector Mohr carried the apple, cookies, and cigarettes down to his prisoners without caring who saw him. It didn't make a difference to him one way or another. Neither did this girl's impending death. She admitted to everything. Death was the only true and right justice for those who spoke out against Hitler.

This conviction gave him control and direction over his life. He needed this ideology as much as it needed him. Not for a second could he allow the thought that he would be responsible for the death of a girl whose only crime was using her freedom of speech. If he did, Mohr's entire world would collapse around him.

Mohr jangled the keys on their ring before he got to her cell. He always did this as a way for his prisoners to gain composure. Else and Sophie remained sitting and didn't look at him as he set the tray down on the table. He misinterpreted their silence as a sign of respect. Both women were refusing to speak to him as a sign of protest. Later he would wonder why they didn't salute him with "Heil Hitler." Or why they hadn't thanked him for his generous offering. He had, after all, sacrificed his reputation for this random act of kindness.

As soon as he left and locked the cell door behind him, both women lunged at the tray. Sophie and Else smoked together, inhaling their cigarettes as though they were taking in life itself. The sound of keys came again a lot faster than either one expected. This time it wasn't Mohr's round, indistinctive face.

"It's 3:00 p.m. Prisoner Scholl, are you ready?" Sophie looked over blankly at Kessler who spoke without emotion.

"Get up. Face your indictment," he looked at her in disgust.

Sophie glanced at Else in terror and stretched out her arms to be handcuffed. He led her upstairs without speaking. She prayed silently. She thought of Fritz and wondered what he would do in this situation. He would remain completely quiet.

Sophie returned half an hour later. Numbly, she held the piece of paper in her hand as Else helped her to the cot. During the proceedings, she had turned it over and had slowly began to sketch letters in her best script. An "f" then an "r," "e," "e," "d," "o," and "m."

In all of their missions, arguments with one another, research, and even in the early days when they were looking for answers in Thomas Aquinas, the Bible, and St. Augustine, this was the one word that defined everything for them. *Freiheit.* Freedom. This was all they were asking for.

"Please read it out loud, Else. I want to hear it from you. In front of all these men with their harsh tones and uniforms, I felt I had actually committed a crime," Sophie asked with a slight smile. Tiredness had robbed her of the ability to think clearly.

Else looked back at her friend and began to read in the small voice that matched her frame.

Hans Fritz Scholl of Munich, born on September 22, 1918, in Ingersheim, single, no previous convictions, taken into investigative custody on February 18, 1943;

Sophia Magdalena Scholl of Munich, born on May 9, 1921, in Forchtenberg, single, no previous convictions, taken into investigative custody on February 18, 1943; and

Christoph Hermann Probst of Aldrans by Innsbruck, born on November 9, 1919, in Murnau, married, no previous convictions, taken into investigative custody, February 20, 1943;

All present in the jail of the headquarters, State Police, Munich;

All at present not represented by counsel;

Are accused:

In 1942 and 1943 in Munich, Augsburg, Salzburg, Vienna, Stuttgart, and Linz, committing together the same acts:

Sophie interrupted softly. "They forgot Hans was arrested before and they forgot to list Ulm, our hometown and all the other towns."

Else smiled at the irony and continued:

I. *Attempted high treason, namely by force, to change the constitution of the Reich, and acting with intent:*

    1. to organize a conspiracy for the preparation of high treason,

    2. to render the armed forces unfit for their performance of their duty of protecting the German Reich against internal and external attack,

    3. to influence the masses through the preparation and distribution of writings; and

II. *With having attempted, inside of the Reich, during the time of war, to give aid to the enemy against the Reich, injuring the war potential of the Empire; and*

III. *With having attempted to cripple and weaken the will of the German people to take measures toward their defense and self-determination.*

    The accused Sophie Scholl participated in the preparation and distribution of the seditious materials. In 1942, the so-called leaflets were distributed through the mail. These seditious pamphlets contain attacks on National Socialism and on its cultural-political policies in particular; and on the alleged murder of the Jews and the alleged forced deportation of the Poles.

    At the end of January 1943, the accused Hans Scholl, at the suggestion of an Alex Schmorell, decided to paint

> *defamatory slogans on city walls and buildings. Schmorell*
> *prepared a stencil for him with the text, "Down with Hitler,"*
> *and with a crossed out swastika. In early February 1943,*
> *Hans Scholl, together with Schmorell, painted such slogans*
> *in white paint on several houses in Munich, on the columns*
> *in front of the University, on the buildings of the National*
> *Theater and the Ministry of Economics, and elsewhere.*

Else gasped and then she smiled widely. She had heard about this inside prison. They were the ones responsible. Sophie put her head in her hands and began to cry. The reality of naming Alex became real again.

> *As early as the summer of 1942, Sophia Scholl took part*
> *in political discussions, in which she and her brother, Hans*
> *Scholl, came to the conclusion that Germany had lost the*
> *war. Thus she shared with her brother the view that agita-*
> *tion against the war should be carried out through leaflets.*
> *She admits to having taken part in preparing and distrib-*
> *uting the leaflets in 1943. Together with her brother she*
> *drafted the text of the seditious "Leaflets of the Resistance in*
> *Germany." In addition, she had a part in the purchasing of*
> *paper, envelopes, and stencils, and together with her brother*
> *she actually prepared letters to be sent in various mailboxes*
> *and took part in the distribution of leaflets in Munich by de-*
> *positing them in telephone booths and parked automobiles.*

Else paused for a second to take a breath and then, with an increasing speed, she read on:

The accused Sophia Scholl was not involved in the act of defacement of buildings, though when she learned about it, she offered to assist on future occasions. She even expressed the view to her brother that it might be a good form of concealment to have a woman taking part in this activity.

"And men smart enough to know this, use us," Else said and continued.

The accused Sophia Scholl knew that her brother spent considerable sums of money in the preparation of seditious papers. In fact, she took charge of her brother's finances, since he was concerned about money matters; she kept financial records and issued to him the sums he needed for these purposes.

The accused were willing to admit to their acts.

With that, Else paused. Her voice began to crack.

Exhibits include confiscated typewriters, an antique copier, paint, brushes, stencils, and the leaflets.

She was having trouble continuing. Both women knew what all of these charges meant.

With the concordance of the Chief of Staff of the Supreme Command of the Armed Services and the Reich's Minister of Justice, the case is transferred to the People's Court for action and decision.

"I will never regret what we did," Sophie finally spoke. Her words seemed at odds with her bent-over frame and tear-stained cheeks. "My conscience is free. I will personally not be held accountable for the insanity that took over my country."

Else began to cry softly, trying hard not to let Sophie hear her. The People's Court was a sick instrument of the Nazi Party. Everyone knew that Judge Freisler was demonic.

A hard knock came suddenly on the cell door. A handsome young man in his mid-thirties, of medium height but terrible posture, entered their cell, thanking the prison guard.

"Attorney Thomas Lang. May I?" he asked softly and motioned to the table and chair for permission to sit down, as if manners mattered.

Sophie and Else exchanged glances nervously.

"I've been appointed by the State to defend you," he stated in an unsure voice. He hung his head and spoke so quietly Sophie had to ask him to repeat himself.

Else rolled her eyes.

Sophie took control of the conversation. She spoke with clarity and forcefulness.

"As a member of the German Army my brother has a right to a firing squad, correct, Herr Lang?"

Lang didn't expect this. He hadn't calculated such foresight or forcefulness from a woman. Why was this woman concerned with the manner of execution? He had expected her to think that he could create some line of defense. He didn't have the stomach for this.

"No, Fraulein Scholl. He isn't entitled to death by shooting. He's been stripped of all military privileges. Your brother is no longer considered a part of the German Army. Yours and his will not be a military tribunal. You are both being tried in the People's Court. Judge Roland Freisler from Berlin, presiding."

This meeting was supposed to be about strategy and law.

"This isn't my decision, Fraulein Scholl. I have come here to discuss your defense, not your punishment."

"You know as well as I do that there will be no opportunity for defense, Herr Lang. You know as well as I do that I will probably not even be given the opportunity of speaking at my own trial. My brother and Christoph Probst either."

Lang shuffled nervously. This was his first court appearance. True, the evidence and her confession were sufficient to convict this young lady. Death was the usual sentence for treason even under the laws of the Weimar Republic. But she would be given ninety-nine days after they found her guilty before they carried out the sentence. He wasn't worried that he was face-to-face with a person about to die.

"Your sentence isn't my decision, Fraulein Scholl. Judge Freisler will decide on that."

Lang got up, rapped on the cell door, signaling that the meeting was over. He hadn't even opened up her file. Before the war, he had been educated in the principles of law at the university. It was that clear. As a member of the Party, Thomas Lang would do whatever was asked of him. The Nazis in Munich wanted him as a People's Court attorney. Under no circumstances whatsoever did he want to join the Army on the Eastern Front. Administering law for the Nazi Party and the Court was the safest way out of the war.

When he finally left, Sophie turned to Else.

"My father will understand why we've done this. But my mother will suffer the most. With all her faith and trust, she will still suffer." Sophie bit her lip to stop from crying.

Else held on to her new friend.

"You will be the one to tell her that I didn't suffer," Sophie finally spoke. That I was calm and believing and that I didn't fear death. You will tell her all of this. Yes, Else?"

All Else could do was nod her head "yes."

MUNICH, FEBRUARY 22, 1943

When Sophie woke, she looked over at Else's cot to see her already awake, staring up at the ceiling. The months of being unjustly imprisoned had worn on her small face. Her lips were moving. Sophie thought twice before interrupting her. When she was done, Sophie called out to her cellmate.

"I had the most magnificent dream."

Else turned her face and smiled. "Tell me."

"The sun was out. It was bright and beautiful. I held a baby dressed in a long white dress, and brought her up a steep mountain to a church to be christened."

Sophie paused, got up on her tip toes, straining to look outside the window through the bars. It was going to be a sunny day. Even in this tiny grey cell, she could feel that spring was coming.

"Suddenly a crevice opened up in the mountain. I had just enough time to lay the child down to the side, to safety. Then I plunged downwards into a dark, bottomless pit. I know exactly what the dream means. The child in the white dress is our idea.

And it will prevail despite all of this madness and every obstacle. We were allowed to be its champions but now we will die for the sake of it."

"Ninety-nine days, Sophie," Else reminded her. "You, Hans and Christoph will have ninety-nine days after the trial. It will be enough time. The war has to be over by then," Else spoke with conviction.

"I thought so too, Else," Sophie replied also assuredly. "But now I feel as though the end of my life is coming and I have to be prepared for it."

Sophie began to dress. Her clothes were visibly dirty now, but when she put on her traditional boiled-wool jacket with coin buttons, a surge of pride went through her again. She had five minutes to pray before Kessler would come and take her. Today was the trial. They would face Judge Freisler. She thought again about Fritz. Throughout this war he faced all kinds of terror. How had he prepared himself for battles far worse than with a lunatic judge?

They handcuffed her again and led her through the long corridors and outside where three black cars waited to take them to the monumental Palace of Justice. It was impossible to catch a glimpse of her brother or Christoph. This time the car stopped at the ornate iron gates at the Palace. The guard's tall black boots tapped loudly on the grey and brown striped marbled entrance. The Palace's imposing architecture of stairwells and ornate iron railings was supported by Doric columns, six floors all the way up to a circular glass cupola. Sophie had a moment to read one of the many gilded Latin phrases embedded inside the flights of stairs: *Fiat Justitia, peveat mundus.* Justice must prevail even if the world must perish over it. This building had housed courts during both the monarchy and briefly in the Republic. Now it belonged to the Nazis' People's Court. Today the magnificent building was filled with nervous energy. Judge Freisler was expected shortly from Berlin.

Heavy handcuffs pinched and bruised Sophie's skin. Maintaining her balance without assistance, Sophie pitied the men working in this system, more than bystanders but actual functionaries. The day had long passed since they were capable of making their own decisions.

Policemen brought her up the marble staircase to the first floor and along the corridor lined with closed doors marked by brass numbers. Finally stopping at Number 312, one of them checked his clipboard and then nodded to the second one who threw open the door, pushing her inside.

The smallish, wood-paneled courtroom with wall-to-wall windows was packed with prosecuting attorneys, defense lawyers, stenographers, mandated German Army officers, and onlookers, sitting in rows in a scared silence. The notorious President of the People's Court, Judge Roland Freisler, would be arriving in any minute. A morning sun streamed generously into the room but Freisler's imminent appearance cast an ominous spell. Everyone knew what kind of a man he was. As crazy as Hitler himself.

Sophie was led to the defendants' bench and seated next to two policemen dressed in World War I uniforms. Christoph and Hans sat to her left. If only she could see them, then she might be able to gain some strength. Suddenly the door burst open. The red-robed Freisler followed into the courtroom with six other judges also wearing red fez hats. Freisler stopped at his chair in the middle of the room and cleared his skinny throat. He scanned the packed courtroom, abruptly stopping his crazed eyes on the defendants' bench.

"The federal prosecutor of the Great German Empire…," Freisler started speaking almost incoherently and, then, in the habit of not completing sentences, pointed at a nondescript older man dressed in wilted civilian clothing, "has just informed us that the State is indicting these three… these three grievous, disgusting transgressors."

Freisler's tinny voice choked with rage. He sneered, revealing brown and rotted teeth, and sat back down, impatiently tapping bony fingers on the long judge's bench. Elderly and wounded young officers in decorated grey military uniforms shifted nervously in their chairs. Eight jurists dressed in dark suits sat at a rectangular table, forming a wall in front of the judges. Not a single person had the courage to speak.

Sophie sat perfectly still. Her body stiffened at the sound of his voice and her heart pounded. She began to sweat. Rumor had it Freisler picked out court members randomly and threw them in prison if they didn't respond quickly to his demands. Two guards helped her stand, steadied her, and held her up. Her pulse quickened and for a moment she lost her balance. She focused on the pitcher of water on the table in front of her. She couldn't look at her accusers.

"You are Sophia Magdalena Scholl?" The chief prosecutor took over now, speaking as if playing a role in a movie he no longer wanted a part in. Barely audible, he read out loud from his notes. "When and where were you born?"

"May 9, 1921," Sophie responded quietly. "Forchtenburg."

This procedure only bored Freisler.

"Stop, stop, stop!" he shouted, flailing bony arms hysterically in the air, motioning to the timid attorney. Freisler's red robe hung on his skeletal frame, and his fez cap tilted off to the side. Hitler himself had created this "judicial" branch and appointed Freisler its "president." It was widely known the People's Court had nothing to do with fairness, innocence or guilt, or the kind of justice that had been administered during the Republic or even in monarchical times.

Sophie summoned the courage to look over at the pale and meek judges flanking the rail-thin Freisler. They were like ghosts. He had gone off on an almost undecipherable rant, growing incoherent with rage, clenching his fists and shaking uncontrollably as if possessed by an unseen force. His left eye, much larger than the right eye, rolled around wildly without focus. The angrier he got the more confused the left eye became, like a pin ball ricocheting around in a giant eye socket. The dead right eye looked out into nothing.

Suddenly a calm came over the frenzied man. He was coaching himself into composure. He began to speak in an exaggerated, modulated voice.

"I will now read the following official command from Herr Martin Bormann, head of the Nazi Party Headquarters in Berlin." Then, changing his mind again, he shook his head and laying it aside, spoke officiously, "We must proceed as expeditiously as possible. We must act quickly to rid Germany of this sickness."

Sophie felt like she could pass out.

He turned abruptly to the chief prosecutor.

"Enough with procedure," Freisler continued, shouting again. Taking part in the Wannsee Conference a year ago was his career's greatest achievement, but he wasn't allowed to publicly mention the plans implemented there. This irritated him. The Final Solution was confidential. Freisler rested in the knowledge that the Führer trusted him implicitly to deal with all sorts of traitors. This fueled him with confidence. Nothing in his past, his experience as an attorney, could compare with the glory he felt administering National Socialist justice. He had already sentenced over 1,800 Germans to death for not believing in Hitler and everyone in this courtroom knew it.

"Being accused of treason is the worst possible allegation in the history of the German people. The chief prosecutor," Freisler pointed to the attorney sitting in the first row of chairs, "claims to have evidence that you three have attempted one of the worst treasonous actions that our German people have ever known. Our mission today is to determine what you have done and then according to German law, find a sentence appropriate for these crimes."

Sophie's whole body collapsed. She closed her eyes, thought of Fritz. He had survived hell. She knew Stalingrad must have been beyond earthly description. Perhaps nothing would make sense to him ever again. She asked God one more time for help.

CHAPTER 13

What we said and thought, so did you, only we were capable of saying it

―――――

MUNICH, FEBRUARY 22, 1943

JUDGE FREISLER'S LAZY EYE BULGED OUT of his drawn and ghoulish face as he addressed the courtroom with his intentions. His emphasis on the word "I" made Sophie shudder. Her body slid down the tall wooden back of the defendants' bench, collapsing under the strain.

"The German people have given me the sovereign power to determine what the law is and what it isn't!" Freisler shook his fist in the air. "I am the law! I am the People's Court!"

He could do whatever he wanted with the accused. The audience of officers forced to attend this trial shifted uncomfortably in their seats.

Sophie wished again that she could see her brother and Christoph. She began to pray without closing her eyes. She clasped her hands and held them together tightly on her lap. She searched her mind for a biblical passage or a psalm. Nothing came to her.

Then a memory. She and Elisabeth and Inge lay on the same bed. It was so many years ago. They were still school girls in the nightclothes that their mother had sewn for them. Looking up at the ceiling, she could still hear their praying, "Our Father, who art in heaven, hallowed be Thy name. Thy kingdom come, Thy will be done, on earth as it is in heaven. Give us this day our daily bread…" She continued whispering to herself without moving her lips, and when she was done, she recited it again, blocking out the judge's terror. "Forgive our trespasses as we forgive…"

Once again, his screeching voice rocketed through the court-room, ricocheting off of the walls as though it were machine gun fire.

"I shall proceed as follows." Freisler created his own judicial procedures. Pleased with his senseless rhetoric and intoxicated with power, he enjoyed the spellbound audience that hung on his every word, mistaking their rapt attention for respect and admiration.

"As we begin today's session of the People's Court," he paused here and hunched his shoulders so that his long neck disappeared, "of the Great German Empire…" He trailed off. He wasn't ca-pable of continuing this line of thinking. He slammed his fist on the table, gesturing wildly, and began ranting about the oath that all Germans had to swear to the Great German Empire.

Sophie cringed as he repeated himself. Most of her life she had tried to avoid people like this, the ones whose minds had been warped and destroyed by the sickness. Another memory flashed in front of her so quickly that she hardly had the time to fasten on to it.

What about her days in the Hitler Youth? She swooned forward. The guard next to her helped her up. Sophie once believed. And if she reminded the judge now that she once even taught their ideology to others, could she save herself?

Freisler pontificated on and on with his scratchy, unintelligible voice. It worsened as he continued, almost screaming now. He was speaking so rapidly he had to stop to catch his breath. His left eye struggled to catch up to the dead one. Finally it steadied itself and once again he circled back to the beginning.

"As I mentioned earlier, a brief biological sketch of each of the defendants is necessary."

He looked over at the defendants' bench for a second time. It was now 10:00 a.m. Freisler's tirade had lasted an hour. One of the courtroom guards went over to the tall window and opened it. A gust of cold air swept into the courtroom. A red, black, and white banner rippled behind the judges' bench. The audience of military men shifted in their seats. They had just witnessed one of Freisler's notorious mental breakdowns, and it made them all uncomfortable. This man was one of Hitler's favorites.

Sophie stared back at the sea of grey, black, and brown uniforms, and as if gazing upon the ocean horizon and for one brief second, she felt revived. Her faith had taught her how to safely freeze out a dangerous present. It was a tool she used often at the Nazi Women's Labor Camp. She knew how to meditate—how to drown out the present completely—to disallow a single sound by praying quietly to herself.

When she came to, Freisler was shouting again. Sophie couldn't understand a single word. The court stenographer, the only other woman present, struggled to record him, fumbling furiously with her machine.

Terror swept over Sophie as she realized that she would have to speak for herself, and then right after this wave, the next one came. She felt herself drowning, slipping down, unable to breathe. Then suddenly her body was still again. She relaxed and she felt the supreme and wonderful feeling of being cared for. So far life had shown to her that she could count on Him to guide her, and He wouldn't abandon her now if she didn't abandon Him.

She closed her eyes and began to pray again.

"Here there is only one thing that counts! National Socialist belief! The Führer and his people are always one!" Freisler leaned back in his chair and said, as if he was speaking to himself, "To be able to obey, to win, and to die. Those are the things that are right. The only things."

Freisler's whole body shook, and he tried to pause for a drink of water but couldn't hold the glass without shaking.

"You're all *schlapp schwanz* of defeatists! Just whom do you think you get your orders from? From us or from the beyond? No, no, don't tell me you're all those types! Not those!" As if in the presence of a believer he would melt, Freisler began to recoil.

Sophie closed her eyes and this time, her prayer was of complete desperation and supplication. *Lieber Gott, Hilfe.* Dear God, help me.

Freisler stopped for a moment to take a sip of water. After a few moments of silence, he turned again to the defendants' bench and pointed to Sophie, motioning for her to stand. She had been steeling herself for this moment. The guards hoisted her up by the elbows one more time and walked her to Freisler's bench and the single chair in front of it. She didn't sit in the chair. She barely remained standing, stabilizing herself by leaning on the chair's back.

Freisler pretended to leaf through the binder of his evidence, and frustrated by his inability to read, he slammed it shut.

"Aha. This time a female traitor. How unusual. How utterly disgusting and unusual."

He peered down his long nose and rolled his wild eyes up and down. The judge's ability to shame wasn't an unpracticed skill. Not everyone could perform this kind of pure, intelligent entertainment. Every uniformed man had also been purposely and calculatingly invited to witness his judicial powers. He was here to teach and warn. Now with a female criminal before him, he was faced with a new challenge, one that he didn't want to avoid. He had to be careful. He mustn't lose the respect of the decorated military officers who had come here to learn. He mustn't be too hard on her. Females were so unpredictable. What if she started to get hysterical and beg for her life? What if she was the feisty type and would start to contradict him?

He looked down at the file again. Sophia Magdalena Scholl, sister to Hans Scholl. Traitors were married or siblings. That was the only way resistance could form, through familial or marital relations.

"Sophia Magdalena Scholl?" he demanded in a voice that could have caused a small animal to seek cover. The courtroom shifted. The atmosphere grew even denser and more uncomfortable. Perhaps men could suffer Freisler's humiliations and insults but could a woman?

The court's chief clerk sat among the prosecutors and public defenders on a bench parallel to the defendants' bench and visibly terrified, he began to twitch. This didn't deter the mad judge.

"A student of botany and philosophy at the University of Munich—is that correct?"

Terrified and her voice suffocated by fear, Sophie could only nod yes.

Freisler lifted his eyebrows and shrilled, "Speak up, you nasty little creature."

"A philosophy student, Herr President Freisler," Sophie used his official title.

"A former leader of the League of German Girls in Ulm. Is this also correct?"

"Yes, Herr President."

"A kindergarten teacher for the Great German Empire." He enunciated with so much force that the entire room held its breath, fearing another outbreak. Sophie temporarily lost her balance. Her legs began to give out.

"And now you stand here before the Empire's People's Court accused of high treason—writing and distributing leaflets and assisting and inciting the enemy. How could such a change in thinking happen?"

At that moment the doors of the courtroom flung open, and Robert and Magdalena Scholl broke in.

"I'm their father, I'm their father!" Robert Scholl shouted. "I'm here to defend them! I have the right!" Werner followed the stumbling policemen, who had failed in their duty to guard the proceedings. He was wearing his grey enlisted military uniform.

A thin, perverse smile parted the lips of the lunatic judge. He swirled his tongue over his teeth, enjoying the sudden intrusion in his courtroom.

Freisler took immediate control of the situation.

"You will not defend these traitors. These cowards, these disgusting, spoiled brats. So-called intellectuals," he screamed.

Robert stopped yelling. He too became paralyzed by Freisler's voice and moved forward as if in a trance. The policemen grabbed Magdalena and held her back. Werner stayed behind, trying to protect his mother from their strong-arming her.

But Robert couldn't say anything else because Freisler started to scream again.

"Get out of here! You have not been invited. Who asked you to come? These proceedings are by invitation only. Get out! I didn't ask you here." Freisler's voice ripped apart from its volume.

"Get them out of here!" Freisler raged.

The policemen, desperate to stop him from screaming, rushed over to Robert and began to push him towards the door. Scholl wouldn't move. A SS guard joined in and together three men picked up Sophie and Hans' father and attempted to carry him out. But they couldn't silence him.

"What is going on here? What on God's good earth is happening here? You, you there," Robert Scholl singled out an elderly man in a gray uniform with metals and ribbons pinned to his breast pockets and pointed to him.

"You! How are you allowing this? By sitting here at this circus you are condoning this farce. You're participating in the persecution of innocents." The officer pretended he didn't hear him and stared vacantly ahead.

"Shut him up! Get him out of here!" Freisler was screaming again at the top of his lungs.

"My God! My daughter is only twenty-one years old!" The courtroom door slammed behind him.

Guards returned Sophie back to the defendants' bench.

Freisler was beside himself with rage. His anger seemed to have blinded him, shutting off all of his senses, constricting his throat so much he had trouble breathing. Rage coursed through him like a poison until it finally subsided and he was able to stand up. Then, like a demon had left his body, he spoke calmly.

"We have reached the end of the search for truth in this trial. I ask now if the chief prosecutor desires a break or if he is prepared to read the indictment."

"Ja wohl," The prosecutor answered obediently. Attorney Lang hadn't said a single thing throughout the entire proceedings.

"As we have seen, the accused has not only confessed, but all of the evidence indicates that they are guilty of high treason against the Great German Empire. The question of punishment shall be answered by the laws of March 29, 1933."

Freisler interrupted. "I don't doubt that the court, when it reads the conviction of the guilt of the accused, the guilt that so freely asserts itself, will find this point is very important. This speck of shame on the history of the German people must be eliminated immediately."

The chief prosecutor bowed politely to Freisler and quickly sat down.

"We've determined here what we've always known. There's no doubt. We've determined their absolute guilt. This guilt has been proven by every single measure. The accused themselves feel no shame at all for their actions. We are the ones that have to feel their shame. We can't even put it into words."

Sophie thought she might pass out.

"These cowards betrayed our cause when we needed them most. These useless slobs want to rob our way of life—our National Socialism. This is the greatest insult against us."

One of the uniformed and decorated men in the audience coughed uncomfortably. It was the only sign of resistance throughout the whole proceeding.

"Their treason means death. We will someday march after the Führer into the world of freedom. Everything we are is contained in this universe. It is incomprehensible that they've even been able to think what they thought, never mind attempted to realize it. They have committed treason against the German people!"

Freisler paused for a moment and caught his breath. Captivated by his speech, the courtroom was now completely spellbound. This time the words hadn't vomited out of him, each one assaulting his listeners like arrows piercing the flesh. They came out as though they made perfect sense, as though this was the philosophy of the ages, as though there were never words uttered so profound and applicable. The words had flowed together and in their fluidity, they gathered momentum and speed.

He continued now in a peaceful tone.

"It is treason against the dead of this war. It is treason against the dead of the National Socialist movement. It is treason against all those who died from all other wars in the last 2,000 years, and also those who have died so that their young German sons could not be born. It is also treason against those who will follow, who haven't been born yet. It is treason against our children and our children's children. It is treason against everything that we have, that we are, for what we are living for, for what we are fighting for. It is the most complete treason that we have ever witnessed in our history."

He paused, looked around at the crowd and totally satisfied, breathed deeply and sat back in his chair.

"I have studied the leaflets over the last few days and can only marvel at the pure stupidity of them. Did they really think that the German people would be stupid enough to believe their lies?"

Hans was the first of them to interrupt the mad judge.

"Herr President, they did listen to us, and they would have acted very soon as we instructed them if we hadn't been caught by your henchmen," Hans spoke in a less than convinced voice. He was scared too. "You will all pay the price for not standing up to men like him," Hans continued, pointing to the crowd of onlookers. "Your conscience will never leave you alone, long after the war is over."

Hans had always been the bravest. Taking his cue, Christoph stood up.

"Your honor," he managed to speak loudly above the disruption that had just broken out, caused by Hans' refusal to cower in front of the court's madman. "May you please consider mercy and spare my life for my wife and three children. My infant son has only just been born."

Freisler kept talking as if he hadn't heard him. He shook his head. He was winding down his last offensive and his crazed eyes, with the lazy one following far behind the wild one, began to settle down.

"The punishment for treason by the March 29, 1933, law is death by hanging. There is no more suitable death than this—that and the absolute stripping of their German citizenship."

"Yes, you traitors! Your German citizenship is completely, now and forever, taken from you. You are no longer German!" He began to scream again, pointing at the defendants' bench.

"They will not be hanged! You don't even deserve a German death your wife and children don't deserve a traitor, either. By the order of all the National Socialists in this room, you are to be beheaded!"

The audience of jurists, soldiers, and SS suddenly shifted and turned in their seats. Still, no one spoke. No one offered protest.

Sophie closed her eyes for one last time and kept them shut. Guards rushed over to her, Hans, and Christoph, trying to get them out of the courtroom as quickly as possible.

"Heil Hitler!" Freisler stood up and saluted.

Except for the three defendants, the entire courtroom responded. "Heil Hitler!"

"This session of the People's Court is over," he screamed one last time.

As the guards grabbed Sophie and started to push her out of the courtroom, she finally spoke. With everything that was left in her, she shouted proudly, "What we wrote and said is what you all think too! Only you don't have the courage to say it out loud! Someone had to make a start."

She looked at the silent men in uniform and the lawyers, not at the man who had just sentenced her to death.

They didn't seem to hear her. The only person who responded was Hans. He finally lifted his face up, and, as though remembering for the first time that she was on trial too, he smiled.

Executions weren't carried out until a full ninety-nine days after a death sentence. There would be time for Fritz to send a request for mercy to Berlin. Sophie felt as sure as she felt anything before that he would save them. As an officer from Potsdam and a soldier who fought in Stalingrad, his appeal would be taken seriously. Their death by guillotine was impossible. She had survived the interrogation and now this insane judge and ridiculous persecution called a trial, and she would be all right. God would keep her.

SS and military men began to shuffle out of the courtroom. These decorated and uniformed men, with no voices, still did not utter a word.

CHAPTER 14

No one has a greater love than she who sacrifices it for her friends

---

MUNICH, FEBRUARY 22, 1943

THE RIDE TO STADELHEIM PRISON was short. It was early in the afternoon but by the time they brought Sophie to the tiny, dank cement cell, she could no longer keep her eyes open. The walls were recently white-washed, and the cot, table, and chair barely fit into the small, windowless room. A crucifix hung over the doorway. She was barely asleep when she heard the familiar sound of the jangling of keys.

"Your parents will see you now," a female prison guard yelled from outside the cell.

As she was being taken down the hall past doors and occupied cells, she glanced at the other prisoners, wondering if they would go before Freisler. When she realized that in seconds she would see her mother and father, her knees buckled and the guard caught her before she stumbled against the door.

How could she have done this to her mother? Her father had already caused so much worry. Fritz would see to their mercy period of ninety-nine days. Or Harnack's contacts in Berlin would be successful in overthrowing Hitler. Or the war would soon be over. They weren't going to die, she had to be convinced of this. Not at the hands of Freisler.

"Five minutes," the guard shouted as she suddenly stopped short and, opening the door, shoved Sophie inside.

Her mother sat at the plain table and her father stood next to her. They hugged her as she stumbled into the room.

"Werner has already gone back to Ulm in order to get in touch with Fritz," her mother whispered into Sophie's ear. Weak from hunger and exhaustion, Sophie fell into her mother arms.

"We're proud of you both," Robert stepped towards them and put his hand on his daughter's frail back. Sophie's turned to face him.

"Thank you, father," she said and smiled.

"You will go down in history as the best of Germany. I know it." Robert began to shake. It was the first time in Sophie's life that she had ever seen her father unable to control himself.

"Here, Sophie, I made you some sandwiches and cookies." Magdalena thrust a basket towards her. "Your brother refused them." She didn't say more about Hans' condition. Sophie knew that he must be doing badly. Forgetting Christoph's leaflet in his pocket was a terrible mistake. Sophie didn't say anything about informing on Alex. She didn't ask if they had heard anything about another capture.

"Thank you," she answered. "I haven't eaten since this morning's bread."

It was almost 3:30 p.m. Sophie opened up one of the neatly wrapped sandwiches. She took a bite and closed her eyes, chewing slowly.

"We're going back to Ulm on the next train, Sophie. We need to start a petition from all of the people we know for your pardon."

"Don't worry," Sophie answered calmly. "We still have ninety-nine days and the war is almost over. Fritz will be able to get us pardoned," she assured her mother. But she was no longer sure of anything. She was weak from Freisler's spectacle.

"I know, Sophie. Werner will have already been in contact with him by the time we get home. Knowing Fritz, he'll be on his way to Berlin right now."

Sophie could no longer listen. The stress of the proceedings had taken its toll. Without meaning to, she had started to block out her parent's words. Magdalena stroked her daughter's hair. Then she fished into her pocketbook and retrieved an unopened letter from the field hospital in Poland where Fritz was recuperating. Sophie recognized the pale green stationery.

"He loves you so much, dear Sophie."

Sophie clutched the letter in her hand and began to cry. Robert rushed over to his daughter.

"Now, now," Magdalena reassured her. "You'll see one another soon enough. He'll come to you immediately once he knows." Robert, unable to speak, nodded his head.

"One more minute," the prison guard shouted from behind the door.

Magdalena went to get up but fell back down again.

"Mother!" Sophie cried out. "You aren't well. Your heart again, isn't it?"

Magdalena didn't answer her.

"Jesus, Sophie. Remember Jesus. Don't forget him for a single second."

Her mother got up again, and this time, although she wavered, she stood on her own.

"And you, too, mother. You, too. Remember Him. " Sophie spoke calmly through her tears.

The door opened. Robert quickly ushered his wife out without looking back at his daughter. He couldn't.

Sophie put her hands out to be handcuffed. Thinking this unnecessary, the guard simply exited the empty room and waited for the prisoner to follow her.

Once inside her cell, Sophie took the unopened letter, sat down on the cot and held it, pressing it against her chest. The postmark from a hospital in Poland read February 12, 1943. She opened the letter. How many years had they been writing to one another like this? This was life's greatest treasure. These letters had shaped who she had become. She opened the letter, taking care not to rip the thin and wrinkled paper.

On Fritz's twenty-sixth birthday, a good doctor, he wrote, amputated two fingers from his left hand. He survived. He described how he was in the last plane to leave the surrounded city and the harrowing journey to the hospital. Fritz mentioned luck. Maybe, she thought, it was Providence. He used this word in a letter from the beginning of the war when he narrowly missed driving over a mine. Now he was calling surviving "luck." She wondered briefly about the difference. If it was all just luck, did she have it? She thanked God silently for Fritz's protection.

Fritz always told her everything, and like usual, she was amused and challenged by his news: *The nurses disconcert me. They are like little ladies that need to be flirted with, so their care is terribly based on favoritism.*

Sophie smiled. He expected people to be genuine, and if they weren't, he was disappointed. She read on, and the news made her angry.

I was at first sharing a room with a captain, an active officer. The type that gets on both of our nerves. We didn't talk much because he preferred to occupy himself with the pretty nurses while he complained about the less pretty ones. Perhaps the nurses noticed our not getting along—or maybe with his connections he got another room—because I was put into another room with a SS lieutenant! Despite that, we understand one another quite well.

Sophie wanted to tear the letter up. The very type of man who persecuted her in that awful courtroom. The very type of man who administered Hitler's perverse ideology. The ones who argued with Fritz about how to treat Jews. How could Fritz get along with a SS officer? He must be losing his mind. Now Fritz was sharing a hospital room with one of them? She corrected her thinking immediately. This war demanded a unique kind of understanding. She didn't know enough to judge Fritz now.

The damage to his hands and feet couldn't have been worse than the psychic damage of surviving Stalingrad. How much would all of this change him? Finishing his letter, she got down on her knees and this time asked God to help him.

She was so deep in prayer that she didn't hear the cell door opening. The female guard was back again. Sophie remained on the floor. The guard laid some pencils and paper down on the table and then putting her hand on the door knob, as she was about to leave the cell, said,

"The executioner and the guillotine are ready. You have one hour. If you wish, you may write your farewell letters now."

The words seemed to travel through space so slowly that at first Sophie didn't comprehend them.

"I have ninety-nine days," she stared back at the guard who did not respond.

"Ninety-nine days, right?" Sophie repeated, barely able to mouth the words.

Once again, the guard didn't answer and left without looking at her.

Sophie tried to get up but she couldn't. She could no longer feel her body. What did it mean when one has an hour left to live?

She got in the chair and smoothed out the sheets of paper with trembling hands.

Writing had always worked to save and explain her life. White pages were a present; an opportunity to make sense of everything. Writing was a release and her captor had just given her freedom back with these two blank pages. This life was over.

She set the pencil to paper and let it do her thinking. Writing rapidly.

Dear Fritz, she began and didn't stop once because she didn't want to cry. Over the past four years they wrote to one another as if they were each other's confessor. His letters had sustained her. They had also driven her further into reconciling her conscience with her actions. He challenged her to speak the truth. He encouraged her to be an artist—to paint, write, play the piano. She didn't stop to remember the softness in his voice when he spoke to her or the wideness of his smile. He would be so angry when he heard that she was the one to go back and distribute the rest of the leaflets. She was the one who got them caught. She was the one who informed on Alex.

She wrote until both sides were filled. This was her chance to tell him that their efforts had worked. The leaflets would wake the German people up. If you believed hard enough, there was nothing to fear. Now faith and trust would triumph over life's most difficult test—facing death. Fritz must have faced this many more times than she. Sophie wrote that she loved him always.

When she finished, she folded it neatly and put it in one of the envelopes, addressing it for the last time to Captain Friedrich Hartnagel at the hospital in Lemberg.

The letter to her mother, father, Inge, Elisabeth, and Werner was going to be more difficult. Her father understood why they couldn't have done anything differently. Sophie worried that her mother would blame their father. He had, after all, been the one to set the example. Would her mother be able to survive the loss of her two children?

When she finished, she looked up to see an older man with a full head of white hair clothed in black with a white collar. He had been let into the cell without her hearing him.

"My child," he said knowingly and reached his hand out to touch her. His voice was soft and filled her immediately with comfort. His worn and weathered face couldn't compete with the compassion revealed in his clear blue eyes.

Sophie looked up at him numbly.

"I don't care if I will be beheaded or if I will be hanged," she said forcibly.

"Then it is so," he answered. "You have completely understood."

He motioned to the cot and looked at her as a way of asking permission for him to sit down on it.

"Please, please come over and sit with me. I am Pastor Alt from St. Ludwig's Church in Munich."

Sophie got up from the table with the last of her strength fell down next to him.

"I've just come from seeing your brother. I need to tell you what we said. I don't know your journey towards God, so please forgive me if you already know as much as your brother."

Sophie nodded. Her heart hadn't stopped pounding through her chest since the morning, and it had begun to ache. She was so tired.

"How is my brother, Pastor Alt?"

He answered Hans was strong and would go to his death bravely.

"You must believe as much as he does because what you all have done couldn't have been justified without faith. Now you will make the ultimate sacrifice for it. For eternal freedom which has been granted to us through our belief in God."

Sophie remained quiet. She no longer had the strength to speak. She blinked her eyes and nodded, showing the pastor that she understood.

"Let us read Psalm Ninety, together, Moses' letter to man."
He opened his worn leather Bible with steady hands and sharing
the book with her, they began to read aloud:

Dear God, you are our refuge now and forever.
Teach us to think that we must die,
And that we become wise in knowing this.

Memories flashed in her mind. Fritz was teaching her how to drive
in his father's car, they were skiing together in the Black Forest,
walking in the woods. Together the pastor and Sophie read the
psalm's verses slowly and deliberately. When they finished, they
looked at one another with a peace that surpassed all understanding.

"We'd best start your communion now," Pastor Alt knew
their time was running out.

The prison called him more often over the last few months to
perform the sacrament. They hadn't told him that this one was
just a girl. It was all the same to the prison officials. The communion didn't change the fact that Sophie was barely a woman and
condemned to death for expressing her freedom of speech. Here
they were just two Christians joined together through Christ.

Pastor Alt got up from the cot and took the silver chalice and
bread from his carrying case. He intoned the liturgy:

Light from eternal light,
Peace to eternal peace,
Love to eternal love, which He gave to us.
Let us see You so that we can live a true life,

One with You, one among others, one with ourselves.
Our Father and Holy Ghost,
You give us eternal life.

Then he added something.

"No one has a greater love than she who sacrifices it for her friends," Pastor Alt said forcibly.

Sophie nodded. She didn't have to choke back tears. It was all over now but the beginning. Her pretty face had grown beyond her years. Fritz wouldn't have recognized her.

Her eyes appeared almost black from sorrow.

He continued, "You shall give your life for your friends. So many will be warned and saved from further unjustified bloodletting. Like one person who suffered for all mankind a dreadful death on the Cross—He died for us. Through this sacrifice He opened the door for us to eternal life so that no death can ever destroy us. You understand this, right, Sophie? So that death can't destroy us," he repeated.

"I know this, Pastor. I'm not afraid." Sophie managed to speak.

How did this young woman know all of this? Pastor Alt was ready to prepare her for the Kingdom of Heaven, but he had to be sure of one thing.

"You know that your earthly judges—your accusers—will also someday have to present themselves to the eternal judges and bow to them?" Their time together was almost over. They had to hurry now.

"Sophia Magdalena Scholl, the love and grace of Christ demands and makes it possible that we love our enemies as ourselves, and that we forgive those who have been unfair to us."

Sophie forced herself to sit upright. She was so tired now she could barely hold herself up at all.

"The Apostle Paul in Chapter Thirteen of his Letter to the Corinthians speaks of this brave and otherworldly type of love. He said, 'When I speak with men and don't have love, I would be a mute and empty shell.'"

He paused for a moment. Pastor Alt was having trouble continuing but he had to demonstrate through his strength how much he believed this to be the Truth. She was barely a young woman, yet she was so brave and wise.

"Love does not allow us to become bitter. It does not keep track of wrong doing. Sophie, do you have hatred in your heart towards the men who have unjustly and wrongly accused you?"

Oh God—would he understand if she did? There wasn't time.

"No," she answered without hesitation. "Wrongdoing can never be reciprocated with wrongdoing."

Her eyes brightened again. Pastor Alt thought he saw the beginnings of a tear. She was the girl dancing the waltz with Fritz. She was playing Schubert on the piano and swimming in Ulm's river. She was teaching her pupils at the kindergarten.

"Then you are fully prepared to receive eternal life. Whoever is able to die like this, dies well." The entire cell suddenly brightened and warmed with an invisible sun.

This time when they heard the keys at the cell door, Sophie stood up. She looked back at him and asked him to give Fritz and her family the letters.

Knowing that she didn't require assistance to walk to her execution, the guards didn't offer it. From the hallway he heard Sophie stop at Hans' and Christoph's cells and wish them good-bye.

There is always light

———

BERLIN, APRIL 1945

IT IS OUR DUTY TO give reason to Sophie's death. Fritz wrote to Elisabeth in the following winter, disobeying strict orders by continuing contact with the Scholl family. Sophie had miscalculated. Their idea of freedom had not taken flight. The country, and in particular the people of Ulm, blacklisted and shunned the remaining family. Shortly after his children's executions and together with Magdalena and two daughters in prison, Robert pleaded with his surrogate son. Fritz wanted to desert. Found innocent of co-conspiracy in Hans' and Sophie's acts of treason, but with a damaged hand, he was of little use on the front. His job reverted to the first wish he ever had about professional soldiering. Sent to train new recruits, men in their forties and fifties, Robert's words never stopped echoing in his ear, *some of us need to survive this war.*

One year later, Sophie's youngest brother, Werner, went missing in Russia.

Shortly after, the Red Army began their invasion, sweeping through Berlin with vengeance. Together with his company, Fritz waited for the enemy and death in the woods near the gutted city.

"Attention," Fritz summoned his men as the distant and errant artillery grumbled in the distance, getting closer and closer. Smoke columns like tornados billowed into the late afternoon sky. "The situation is hopeless." Fritz acknowledged their fear. Forty to fifty year-old-men had spent the last few days writing good-byes to their families. "If we do not raise a white flag, we will be killed in the next day or so, maybe even hours."

His lieutenant, Bauer, shook his head in agreement. A vote was necessary and this was what Fritz had learned at the military academy of Potsdam. As a younger man he never thought his life would come to this question. More than half of them did not have guns.

"Who here would like to continue living?" Fritz framed the question impartially. "Who among us wants to help re-build Germany as a free country? Who will surrender to the Americans?" One by one, slowly, and then in rapid fire, the enlisted men raised their hands. Fritz closed his eyes momentarily in relief. He was risking his life by disobeying Hitler's order to fight until the last man.

Raising his chin and smiling only with his eyes, he turned to Bauer who nodded in return. It was almost unanimous. All but two men wanted to take their chances with the Americans. They had to act quickly.

Fritz felt the coldness of a loaded gun pressing into the back of his head. To be murdered by his own soldier. Memories of life whirred past him and he heard Sophie's laugh. Without fully comprehending what was about to happen next, Fritz turned as his would-be assassin fell dead to the ground. There had been two shots. His protector, Bauer, stumbled forward, holding his stomach.

"Get him on a stretcher, now," Fritz ordered the men who had just witnessed their own saving. Without pausing to help his friend, he grabbed a branch out of the woods, running for the trucks lined up behind the building. "Follow me," he yelled again, pointing towards the trucks. Middle-aged soldiers piled in as fast as they could, forming a caravan. They made room for Bauer, covering him with their uniforms, begging him to stay conscious. Fritz threw his officer's jacket out of the speeding truck's window. Taking off his undershirt, he tied it to the branch. He handed the makeshift white flag to another of his men, who waved it bravely from the window.

ULM, SEPTEMBER 1945

Elisabeth stood alone at the altar inside the Münster Church, surrounded by ancient religious wooden carvings. Neither the pastor nor the groom had arrived yet. A light rain began to fall through a gaping hole in its colossal vaulted ceiling. Her borrowed silk dress rustled in the breeze blowing through the empty and partly destroyed church, one of the only structures that had survived relentless bombings.

Fritz ran the entire way to the center of town in his father's suit and brand new shoes. Bursting through the church door, he saw her, waiting. She was exactly who he hoped she would be. Their love for Sophie would form the center of their life together. Elisabeth's hands were empty. He motioned to her that he would be right back and hurried into the cemetery where his mother was buried after one of the city's last bombings. Autumn daisies were coming up. Sophie would have wanted her sister to have flowers. He bent down and picked some.

Waiting for Fritz to return, Elisabeth turned the wooden handle of an old dusty phonograph. A Bach symphony filled the broken church surrounded in rubble.

This time Fritz opened the massive carved door slowly and walked up the aisle calmly, handing his future wife the flowers, taking her other hand. They sat down and listened to the music. Pastor Alt and the rest of the Scholl family would be along shortly. For the first time since the war ended, they believed in the future.

————

IN MAY 1947, FRITZ HARTNAGEL received a letter from the American occupied forces in Ulm classifying him as a "mitlauefer (hanger-on)." This level of participation alleged that Hartnagel supported Nazism without directly taking part in its atrocities.

After Sophie's death, the Nazi party, secret police and military investigated Fritz for co-conspiring with the Scholl siblings. They forbid his interacting with the family and wearing the traditional black armband while he mourned their deaths. Accused now of sympathizing with the Nazis, he responded with a seven-page letter chronologically describing his life from 1933-1945.

Hartnagel stated that he left the Hitler Youth two years after joining it. Admitting to originally having a positive attitude towards the new National Socialist government as a soldier, Fritz explained. "I had idealistic expectations that were quickly disappointed by an officer core that was either consumed by Nazism or careerism."

The lengthiest part of Fritz's letter described his relationship with Sophie Scholl. He reported that together they learned about Christianity and encouraged by their new beliefs, they developed "a decisive way of thinking irreconcilable with Nazism."

Fritz concluded that during the war he sent money to his girl-friend for a "good purpose."

Four months later, the occupying American forces and a German de-nazification court cleared Fritz Hartnagel of "mitlauefer" status. They also determined that Fritz demonstrated ideological opposition to the Nazi regime through his actions.

Many thanks to Dr. Ellen M. Umansky, Carl & Dorothy Bennett Chair in Judaic Studies and Professor of Religious Studies at Fairfield University who prompted this additional research and writing.

———————

Die Geschichte von Sophie Scholl und Fritz Hartnagel (1937-1943)

von Alexandra Lehmann
Deutsch von Heinz Tophinke

IN DEUTSCHLAND IST SOPHIE SCHOLLS Name heute gleichbedeutend mit Freiheit. Als Gründungsmitglied einer studentischen Widerstandsgruppe in München trug sie 1942/43 zur Verbreitung antifaschistischer Flugblätter mit bei. Dieses Buch versucht erstmalig, Sophies Beweggründe klarzustellen, indem es ihre siebenjährige Beziehung mit dem deutschen Wehrmachtsoffizier Fritz Hartnagel aufdeckt.

Als Leiter von Nachschubkompanien sowohl an der West- wie an der Ostfront schrieb Fritz Hartnagel Sophie, wie er Zeuge von Gräueltaten der SS und der Wehrmacht wurde. Mit diesen Informationen eines Augenzeugen intensivierte Sophie ihre Untergrundtätigkeit mit ihrem Bruder und dessen Freunden.

Sie nannten sich zunächst die „Weiße Rose" und später „Der Deutsche Widerstand" und führten gefährliche Missionen aus, bei denen sie in vielen süddeutschen Städten insgesamt fünfmal Flugblätter verteilten, die zum Widerstand gegen Hitler aufriefen.

Am Abend von Sophies Verhaftung, „Verurteilung" und Hinrichtung durch die Guillotine überlebte Fritz gerade noch die Schlacht von Stalingrad, eine der schlimmsten der Geschichte.

Die Korrespondenz der beiden bewirkte mehr, als Scholl lediglich weiterhin im Kampf gegen den deutschen Diktator zu motivieren. Die Beziehung von Sophie und Fritz – zweier Menschen, die auf gegensätzlichen Seiten des Krieges gefangen waren – illustriert die moralisch komplexe Situation der Deutschen, die unter Hitler leben mussten, und sie ist letztlich auch eine Liebesgeschichte.

[Der Drang zum Handeln]

———————

München, Mai/Juni 1942

Mit Hans' Schlüssel sperrte Sophie auf und ging geradewegs zu einem Stapel Bücher, die planlos in der Ecke des Wohnzimmers lagen. Sorgfältig darauf bedacht, nichts durcheinander zu bringen, las sie rasch die geknickten Buchrücken. Schiller. Goethe. Sie setzte sich im Schneidersitz auf den Boden, öffnete das Schauspiel von Goethe und blätterte zu den unterstrichenen Seiten. Zweiter Akt, vierte Szene.

Sophie las die Passage laut:
[Des Epimenides Erwachen]

Hoffnung:
Nun begegn' ich meinen Braven,
Die sich in der Nacht versammelt,
Um zu schweigen, nicht zu schlafen,

Und das schöne Wort der Freiheit
Wird gelispelt und gestammelt,

Bis in ungewohnter Neuheit
Wir an unserer Tempel Stufen
Wieder neu entzückt es rufen:

Freiheit! Freiheit!

Zwischen den angegilbten Seiten des Buches entdeckte sie ein einzelnes Blatt Papier. Beim Lesen begannen ihre Hände zu zittern. Es war Hans' Handschrift. *Ein geistloses und feiges Volk verdient den Untergang. Vergesst nicht, dass ein jedes Volk diejenige Regierung verdient, die es erträgt.*

Eine Woge von Emotionen durchflutete sie. Das war eine Art schriftlicher Protest gegen Hitler. Was hatten Hans und Alex damit vor? Sophie war wie betäubt und wusste nicht, was sie als Nächstes tun sollte. Vor ein paar Tagen hatte sie mitgehört, wie Alex am Telefon mit seinem Nachbarn gesprochen und dabei vorgegeben hatte, ein Offizier der SS zu sein. Er hatte darum gebeten, eine Schreibmaschine benutzen zu dürfen, und behauptet, er müsse einige Mitteilungen nach Berlin schicken. Dafür wollte er die Maschine bestimmt nicht. Sie wollten offenbar dies abschreiben – aber um was damit zu tun?

In diesem Augenblick hörte sie Schritte.
Hans öffnete die Tür und fand Sophie am Boden sitzend, seine Bücher um sie herum verstreut. Er wurde blass. Unausgesprochene Fragen erfüllten den Raum. Sein Blick wurde eisig. Sie hatte eine Schwelle überschritten, und es war zu spät, um eine Entschuldi-

gung zu erfinden, die die Situation vielleicht weniger schmerzhaft gemacht hätte.

Sophie sagte nichts, sie sah nur zu ihrem Bruder auf.

„Verdammt, Sophie!" Hans war wütend. „Hast du denn keine bessere Meinung von dir?" Er griff nach einem medizinischen Text auf seinem Schreibtisch, rügte seine Schwester, weil sie die Vorlesung nicht besucht hatte, und schlug dann ohne ein weiteres Wort die Tür hinter sich zu.

Sophie seufzte tief. Die Scham und Verlegenheit, beim Schnüffeln in Hans' Sachen erwischt zu werden, schien nicht so schwerwiegend zu sein wie das, was sie gelesen hatte. Hans und Alex waren also schließlich und endlich im Begriff, etwas zu unternehmen. Fritz hatte ihr während des ganzen Krieges immer wieder davon geschrieben. Aus seinen Briefen wusste sie, dass die SS in Amsterdam demonstrierende holländische Zivilisten erschossen hatte, sie wusste vom Plan der SS, schwarze Kriegsgefangene in Frankreich zu töten, und sogar von ihren so genannten Maßnahmen zur „Bevölkerungskontrolle". *Es waren nicht nur Gerüchte gewesen.* Sie wusste es. Sie wusste es, und die Wahrheit hatte ihr Leben unfassbar gemacht. Es gab Morgen, an denen sie den Kopf nicht vom Kissen hochbrachte, so sehr war sie von Schuld erfüllt. Aber Hans würde niemals zulassen, dass sie ihnen bei ihrem Tun half. Er würde ihr sagen, das sei für eine Frau zu gefährlich. Alex und Hans begingen Verrat, und für Verrat konnte man mit dem Tod bestraft werden.

Sie würde warten, bis der richtige Zeitpunkt gekommen war, ihn zu fragen. Sie würde Hans im Beisein von Alex fragen. Dann hatte sie noch eine bessere Idee. Sie konnte ihnen *beweisen*, dass sie stark und klug genug war, um mitzumachen. Ihr Herz begann zu rasen. Sie wollte so sehr mitmachen, dabei sein, wie nichts anderes, das sie je gewollt hatte – sie konnte dies nicht einmal mit ihrem Wunsch vergleichen, mit Fritz zusammenzusein.

Sophie begann erneut zu lesen und dachte dabei immer aufgeregter über eine Möglichkeit nach, etwas zu tun. Sie konnte Hans verstehen. *Sind die Deutschen so tief in einen Todesschlaf gesunken, dass sie nicht mehr aufwachen können? Warum sind die Deutschen so apathisch angesichts all dieser entsetzlichen und unmenschlichen Verbrechen?*
Es ist nicht nur Mitgefühl für die Opfer der kriminellen Clique, was fehlt. Und nicht nur Mitgefühl muss er *spüren, sondern* er *wird Schuld fühlen.* Er *ist schuldig, diese „Regierung" weiterhin existieren zu lassen, und* er *ist sogar schuldig, sie überhaupt existieren zu lassen! Schuldig! Schuldig! Schuldig! Aber es ist nicht zu spät, diese widerliche und ungehörige Regierung aus der Welt zu entfernen. Wenn* er *nun handelt, kann* er *damit aufhören, noch mehr Schuld auf sich zu laden. Es ist die Pflicht jedes Deutschen, nun, da* er *weiß, was die Nationalsozialisten tun, es ist seine einzige und wichtigste Pflicht, diese Bestien zu vernichten.*

In dieser Nacht hatte sie nach einem vergeblichen Versuch zu studieren einen Traum, der sie überzeugte. Gott klopfte ihr auf die Schulter. *Nahm sie in die Pflicht.* Sie wachte gestärkt auf.

Heute würde sie aus der Universität Papier stehlen. Sie würde Hans beweisen, dass sie tapfer genug war. Sie brauchten mehr Papier. Sie mussten mehr Flugblätter schreiben und verteilen. Die Nazis kontrollierten den Papierverbrauch so genau, dass man einen speziellen Coupon brauchte, um große Mengen zu kaufen. Während Sophie zum erstenmal in ihrem Leben zur Universität radelte, hatte sie das Gefühl, dass eine wirkliche Veränderung möglich war. Die Pedale drehten sich wie von selbst, und mit ungeahnter Geschwindigkeit hatte sie nach wenigen Minuten das biologische Institut erreicht.

Die Flure waren verlassen. Sophie wusste dass der Professor den Vorratsschrank außerhalb des Vorlesungssaals nicht abschloss. Die Türen waren sogar nur angelehnt. Sie machte sich bereit. Sie musste in Sekundenschnelle eine Menge Papier stehlen.
Mit einem Blick nach links und rechts öffnete sie die Schranktüren und stopfte ihren Rucksack so voll, dass sie ihn gerade noch wieder verschließen konnte. Dann schaute sie sich erneut um, und da niemand zu sehen war, fasste sie sich. Mit einem tiefen Atemzug strich sie sich durch das lange Haar. Anstatt hinaus zu laufen, was nur Aufmerksamkeit erregt hätte, schritt sie ruhig aus dem alten, neoklassizistischen Gebäude.

Adrenalin schoss ihr durch den ganzen Körper. Während Sophie hastig die Leopoldstraße entlang fuhr, ging sie in Gedanken die Ereignisse durch, die zu dieser Aktion geführt hatten. Mit sechzehn hatte sie endlich bei einem Treffen des Bundes Deutscher Mädchen den Mund aufgemacht; sie hatte im Lager des Reichsarbeitsdienstes die Bibel gelesen, obwohl es verboten war, hatte die ganze Zeit über die so genannte ideologische Unterweisung abgelehnt, mit Fritz über seine Rolle in Hitlers Armee debattiert, war heimlich zum Orgelspielen in die Blumberg-Kapelle gegangen, hatte sich geweigert, bei der Winterkollekte zu spenden, hatte zusammen mit ihrem Vater verbotene Radiosender gehört und mit Carl Muth über Theologie diskutiert.

Irgendwie hatte all dies zu diesem Augenblick geführt. Sie war auf diese Arbeit vorbereitet. Sie fühlte sich dazu berufen. Sophie warf einen Blick hinter sich, um zu sehen, ob ihr Rucksack noch da war. Morgen würde Fritz nach München kommen, um sich zu verabschieden, deshalb wollte sie heute Nachmittag studieren, damit sie den Tag mit ihm verbringen konnte. Sie würde ihm ihr Geheimnis nicht verraten. Zum erstenmal seit Beginn ihrer Beziehung würde sie sich ihm nicht anvertrauen können. Sie wusste, dass das Verschweigen der Wahrheit dem Misstrauen Tür und Tor öffnen würde. Es war Fritz, der sie das gelehrt hatte. Trotzdem konnte sie es ihm nicht sagen. Obwohl er wieder an die russische Front zurückging. Obwohl es seine Berichte aus erster Hand gewesen waren, die ihr die Sicherheit gaben, dass das, was sie tat, das Einzige war, das man tun konnte. Jetzt. In München. Für Deutschland.

Sie hatten sich im Botanischen Garten, unweit von Schloss Nymphenburg, verabredet, wo Schwäne paarweise auf dem Kanal schwammen, der zu dem majestätischen, an Versailles erinnernden Palast führte. Statuen aus der griechischen Mythologie und immergrüne Pflanzen säumten die Kieswege des formalen

Gartens. Sophie radelte über die kopfsteingepflasterte Straße zum Hintereingang des Gartens. Sie freute sich darauf, exotische Pflanzen zu betrachten. München besaß einen der schönsten botanischen Gärten Europas.

Im Garten selbst fühlte sie sich gar nicht mehr wie in Deutschland. Dies war anders als alles, was sie kannte. Der Garten war wie ein Sinnbild für eine internationale Gemeinschaft, verschiedene Bäume derselben Spezies co-existierten und gediehen vollkommen friedlich miteinander. Sophie las die lateinischen Namenstäfelchen neben den zahlreichen Nadelbäumen und schaute dann auf, um ihre Unterschiede zu studieren. Sie sammelte sich, konnte jedoch nicht dem Impuls widerstehen, schneller den Kiesweg auf den Teich zu zu fahren, an dem sie sich treffen wollten. Als sie ihn erblickte, hielt sie den Atem an.

Fritz, in seine graue, abgetragene Uniform gekleidet, erwartete sie lächelnd bei einem Rhododendron-Busch, der gerade die ersten weißen Knospen zeigte. Sophie sprang von ihrem Rad, und sie umarmten und drückten sich herzlich. Seit ihrem ersten Treffen hatte sich zwischen ihnen nicht viel verändert. Das Gefühl, sich nahe sein zu wollen, war durch die Zeit des Getrenntseins nur gestärkt worden. Sogar ihre ständigen Diskussionen über den Krieg und Fritz' Rolle dabei hatte das Band zwischen ihnen gestärkt.

Sie hielt ihr Versprechen. Sie hatte ihn geliebt *wegen des Guten in ihm. Wegen dem, was ihn zu einem Menschen machte.* In diesem Augenblick erschien es ihr nicht einmal unmöglich, einen

Soldaten zu lieben, der schicksalhaft Hitlers verabscheuungswürdigem Plan ausgeliefert war. Der Krieg musste scheitern. Es war ihnen schließlich beiden klar geworden, dass eine Niederlage im Krieg keine Niederlage Deutschlands war, sondern die des Nationalsozialismus, und das waren zwei grundverschiedene Dinge. Fritz war im Begriff, sich Millionen dem Untergang geweihter Soldaten anzuschließen. Sophie fiel es schwer, ihn gehen zu lassen.

Er ergriff ihre Hand, und sie begannen ohne ein Wort, die kleinen Kieswege entlang zu spazieren, vorbei an den verschiedenen Blumen, die in Blüte standen oder gerade zu blühen begannen, und blieben zwischendurch stehen, um die dazugehörigen weißen Täfelchen zu lesen. Wie immer würde ihnen das Reden leichter fallen, wenn sie zusammen spazieren gingen.

Sie schlenderten durch das Arboretum und bewunderten die weißen Birken aus Nord- und Südamerika. Sophie sagte etwas, und Fritz erkannte, dass die Bedeutung dieser Worte zu ergründen vielleicht sein Leben lang dauern würde. Er hatte diese Eingebungen Sophies längst akzeptiert, er mochte sie inzwischen sogar. Vielleicht würde er sie ja eines Tages wirklich begreifen können. Sie blickte verloren auf eine Blutbuche, deren Äste nach unten wuchsen und den Boden berührten, und sagte dann: „Ich möchte einfach nur ein Stück Baumrinde sein – eine seltsame Vorstellung, aber sie verfolgt mich seit Jahren." Dann schaute sie in die Ferne und ging weiter. Sie setzten sich auf eine Bank neben einigen Felsen, die mit altem Moos und winzigen, mehrfarbigen Wildblumen bewachsen waren.

Sophie hatte nicht die Kraft, ihm von ihren Kursen, den Professoren oder der Universität zu erzählen. Oder gar von den Abenden mit Hans, Schurik, Christoph, Willi und Traute, wenn sie diskutierten und debattierten, was sie ins nächste Flugblatt schreiben sollten. Sie erzählte ihm nichts von der wichtigsten Sache, die sie in ihrem ganzen Leben gemacht hatte.

Stattdessen sprach sie über ihren Kontakt mit Professor Muth und ihr neues Interesse am Katholizismus. Sie wiederholte etwas, das Willi gesagt hatte, und erklärte Fritz, er sei der aufrichtigste von allen.

In Wirklichkeit bedeutet Christ zu sein ein schwieriges und ungewisses Leben, ein Leben voller Bürde, in dem man ständig neue Herausforderungen zu meistern hat.

Fritz hörte aufmerksam zu. Während er in Frankreich stationiert war, hatte er bemerkt, dass sein Glaube an Gott, der durch seine Liebe zu Sophie gestärkt wurde und auch durch Sophie existierte, zwei verschiedene Dinge waren. Um sie herum stand der Garten in der Blüte des Frühlings. Er klammerte sich an ihre Worte, als seien sie ein Seil, an dem er über dem Abgrund hing. Unter seinem gefassten Äußeren brodelten tosende Wasser, die im Begriff waren, ihn zu verschlingen. Er würde auf seinen Glauben an sie beide bauen, um zu überleben, und er brauchte diesen Glauben auch, um die richtigen Entscheidungen für seine Männer zu treffen.

Sophie unterbrach sich plötzlich, so wie sie es oft tat. Er wandte sich ihr zu. Sie hatten beide den gleichen Gedanken.

„Es ist durchaus möglich, nicht wahr, dass wir uns vielleicht nie wieder sehen?" Doch sie bedauerte ihren Zweifel augenblicklich und fuhr fort: „Verzeih mir bitte. Es tut mir leid. Natürlich werden wir uns wiedersehen. Lass uns nicht allzu ernst werden mit der Religion oder gar mit dem Krieg. Können wir nicht einfach alles vergessen, nur für einen Augenblick, hier an diesem Ort, wo die Bäume die anscheinend einzigen Wesen sind, die noch im Frieden leben?"

Fritz nickte mit einem Lächeln. Sie betraten das Gewächshaus mit seinen weißen Stahlstreben, das tropische Pflanzen, Obstbäume, seltene Orchideen und riesige Seerosen beherbergte. Die feuchte Luft roch angenehm. Ein älterer Gärtner in einer blauen Latzhose ging an ihnen vorüber und grüßte sie mit dem alten bayrischen „Grüß Gott" anstatt mit „Heil Hitler", lächelte ihnen zu und wässerte prächtig violette Pflanzen.

„Zu viel Wasser ist so tödlich wie zu wenig", sagte er und schob dann seinen Karren weiter den Pfad entlang. Sophie und Fritz setzten sich in das Café vor den vielfarbigen Rosenbeeten, deren Duft sie umhüllte. In den Ecken des mit Buchsbäumen bepflanzten Gartens standen weiße Statuen pummeliger Engelchen. Dieses Paradies war das Resultat der Koexistenz von Kostbarkeiten der Natur aus der ganzen Welt. Sie fassten sich an den Händen, lauschten den Vögeln und ließen sich von der Sonne wärmen.

Dann war es Zeit. Sein Zug nach Frankreich ging in fünfundvierzig Minuten. Spätabends würde er in Le Mans sein und am Morgen an den Don in Stalins Russland aufbrechen. Sophie hatte ihn nicht nach einem einzigen Detail zum vermutlichen Vordringen auf Moskau gefragt. Dafür war er dankbar. Er hätte ihr nur wieder sagen müssen, dass seine einzige Pflicht seinen Männern gegenüber bestand – was bedeutete, ihr Leben zu erhalten.

Er sagte Sophie, sie solle sich um ihre Mutter kümmern, der es nicht gut ging. Er versuchte noch immer, eine Begnadigung für ihren Vater zu erwirken, der noch zwei Monate im Gefängnis bleiben musste. Fritz war ein Teil der Familie Scholl geworden und fühlte sich ihr auf eine Weise verbunden, die er sich selbst nicht erklären konnte. Er umfasste Sophies Schultern und blickte ihr gerade ins Gesicht. Er wollte nicht, dass sie ihn zum Bahnhof begleitete. Sie hatten sich schon zu oft an allen möglichen Bahnhöfen in Deutschland voneinander verabschiedet. Er gestand sich ein, dass er genug davon hatte, sie allein unter all den anderen Frauen stehen zu sehen – Ehefrauen von Soldaten, Kindern, Müttern, Schwestern, Tanten, Großmüttern, Freundinnen. Es war ihm lieber, wenn sie noch eine Weile im Garten blieb, sich an dem Springbrunnen freute und zwischen ihren Lieblingsblumen saß.

Er bat sie, für ihn zu beten.

„Ich verspreche dir nicht, dass ich wiederkommen werde, Sophie", murmelte er. Dann küsste er sie, wandte sich abrupt ab und ging, ohne noch einmal zurückzublicken. Sophie schaute ihm nach, bis er verschwunden war. Sie weinte nicht. Ein Teil von ihr hatte solche Angst vor der Zukunft, dass es zu sehr schmerzte, so tief, so unerklärlich zu fühlen – und dass dies, obwohl sie es nicht denken durfte, sich nie zu denken erlauben durfte, das letzte Mal gewesen sein könnte.

Hans, Alex, Willi und Christoph trafen sich fast jeden Abend im Studio ihres Freundes in der Leopoldstraße. Heute hatten sie einen bekannten Münchener Schauspieler zu Gast. Hans weigerte sich, darüber zu sprechen, was Sophie herausgefunden hatte. Er benahm sich, als wüsste sie nichts. Er lud sie immer zu diesen Abenden ein, doch sie wusste, dass er damit beschäftigt sein würde, Gisela und Traute zu unterhalten. An letzterer schien er seit Kurzem etwas Interesse verloren zu haben. Es gefiel ihm, wenn Gisela mit ihren hellblauen Augen leicht ihre beneidenswerte blonde Mähne schüttelte und dabei unbeschwert lachte. Sie lachte wesentlich mehr als seine Freundin, die etwas zu sehr zum Nachdenken neigte.

Sophie versuchte, dem nicht zuviel Aufmerksamkeit zu schenken. Sie ging in dem riesigen Studio umher, bestaunte die umfangreiche Bibliothek und die übergroßen Fenster. Blau gedruckte Architekturpläne füllten Körbe und bedeckten jede freie Fläche an den Wänden. Das Studio gehörte einem gewissen Manfred Eickemeyer, einem Architekten, der im besetzten Polen arbeiten musste. Dann kam ihr ein Gedanke. Er musste es gewesen sein. Es musste Herr Eickemeyer gewesen sein, der ihrem Bruder von den in dem Flugblatt erwähnten ermordeten Juden erzählt hatte, das sie gefunden hatte. Alles begann, zusammenzupassen. Nach der Lesung zog Sophie ihren Bruder zur Seite und rettete ihn davor, mit Gisela und Traute gleichzeitig fertig werden zu müssen.

„Ich habe etwas für dich, Hans", flüsterte sie ihm zu und öffnete ihren Rucksack. Hans stockte der Atem; es kam ihm so unglaublich vor, dass er das Papier berühren musste. Sie hatten ihr letztes gerade aufgebraucht. Dies war genau, was sie benötigten, um neue Flugblätter drucken zu können. Er musterte seine Schwester mit einem durchdringenden Blick, denn er wusste, was sie ihn damit fragte. Niemals würde er die Verantwortung für die Sicherheit seiner kleinen Schwester übernehmen können. Was sie taten, war einfach viel zu gefährlich.

Dann, ohne zuzulassen, dass er etwas sagte, holte Sophie etwas aus dem Rucksack heraus. Es war ein Feldpostbrief aus dem russischen Donezbecken. Fritz war noch nicht einmal einen Monat dort.

„Hans, ich muss dir vorlesen, was Fritz mir gerade geschrieben hat. Ich weiß, dass es stimmt, was passiert. Ich weiß es schon lange." Hans sah sie verblüfft an.

Sophie räusperte sich und begann mitten im Brief: „*... Gestern musste ich wieder einen Abend in der Offizierskantine über mich ergehen lassen. Es ist wirklich zu schlimm, all der Wein, der sinnlos vergeudet wird, damit sie alle so schnell wie möglich ‚in Stimmung' kommen – die sich dann in Zoten, Lärm und zerbrochenen Gläsern ausdrückt. Wie arm diese Menschen sind, dass dies ihre einzige Freude ist, deren sie fähig sind ...*"

Sie verstummte. Dies war nicht der Teil, den ihr Bruder hören sollte, doch den nächsten Satz auszusprechen war nicht leicht. Sie lebte nun schon seit Jahren mit diesen Briefen und hatte ihren Inhalt nie jemandem mitgeteilt. Sie atmete tief und sprach die nächsten Worte sorgfältig und mit Nachdruck aus.

„Es ist entsetzlich, mit welchem Zynismus und welcher Kaltblütigkeit mein Kommandeur davon spricht, dass <u>alle</u> Juden im besetzten Russland ermordet werden."
Hans verbarg das Gesicht in den Händen. Sophie las weiter. *„Er ist noch dazu voll von der Rechtmäßigkeit dieses Tuns überzeugt."*

Sie faltete den Brief langsam wieder zusammen und wartete.

Zunächst wusste Hans nicht, was er sagen sollte. Er erwiderte stumm ihren Blick. Manchmal wurden die wichtigsten Vereinbarungen nur durch den Kontakt zweier Augenpaare getroffen. Dann berührte er Sophie leicht am Arm, nahm den Rucksack mit dem Papier, das sie so dringend brauchten, und sagte ihr, sie solle am nächsten Morgen ins Studio kommen.

[ENDE EXZERPT]

———

1. If being a member of a fascist youth organization was a condition for going to school and/or obtaining employment, would you belong to it?

2. Imagine living under a regime where propaganda surrounded you everywhere that promulgated a superior race. Imagine indoctrination from childhood to young adulthood – would you be able to think critically about this regime? If you answered yes, how?

3. Provided you knew this dictatorship was fundamentally wrong and transgressed basic human rights and freedoms, how would you steel or guard yourself against it - if free speech and personal freedoms had been confiscated?

4. Imagine you had chosen a career in the military. Upon graduating from a school like West Point or Annapolis, a dictator takes over your country, putting political opponents in jail and taking away rights guaranteed in your constitution. S/he also names him/her self as head of the armed forces. Would you continue to serve in the military? Why? Or why not?

Would you risk defection, knowing you could be killed and your family members' lives threatened and put in jeopardy?

5. War breaks out. You are forced to serve in the military as an officer in a dictatorship. You have two choices – defect under penalty of your death and family's or continue to fight? Why did you choose like you did?

6. If you decided to stay in this dictator's army, and eventually encounter situations in which you witness war crimes against humanity, what would you do?

7. Imagine yourself as a civilian living during worsening wartime conditions under a totalitarian regime. You receive eyewitness accounts of atrocities. Would you be able to start resistance against the dictatorship, even if upon capture, you and your family would be killed? How would you resist?

ACKNOWLEDGMENTS

———

I COULD NOT HAVE COMPLETED more than a decade of working on this book without the enduring inspiration provided by Sophie Scholl and Fritz Hartnagel's letters, the writerly wisdom of Vijay Seshadri, the support of my mother and father, and of friends and family, especially Sue, Maria and Helmut, Agnes, William and Christine, Jean-Pierre, Jennifer and Peter, and Tina. I am indebted to my patient best friends of the canine variety, Clara and Dinah, with whom I have taken long and wondrous walks that break many writer's blocks.

Many thanks to the Fulbright Association for its research grant and to Gene Sharp at Albert Einstein Institute, who inspired a deeper motivation and reminded me that civil disobedience and resistance must be taught. I greatly appreciate my German colleagues' dedication to preserving history at the White Rose Foundation and Institute of Contemporary History in Munich. I am grateful to St. Paul's German Church of New York, St. James Episcopal Church, the German Departments of Mt. Holyoke and Sarah Lawrence Colleges, Jewish Community Center on the

Hudson, and Fairfield and Western Connecticut State University for inviting me to speak on German resistance.

––––––––––

THE MOST IMPORTANT THING TO know about *With You There Is Light* is that Fritz Hartnagel wrote the five letters to Sophie Scholl in which he informed her of German Army and SS atrocities.

Sophie and Fritz's true story is important today because it helps us to comprehend the moral complexity of a people living under oppression and without personal freedoms. I chose to write about their relationship as narrative nonfiction because, after reading Fritz's letters for the first time in 2003, I discovered that, despite the enormous difficulty of putting it into words, their kind of love was the truer story. Many of the conversations quoted in this book are actual translated excerpts from their letters. They are gratefully reproduced here with the permission of S. Fischer Verlag.

Due to a deep familiarity with German culture (both my parents survived the war in the Eastern territories) and native language fluency, I was able to ask difficult questions during my research in the language in which this history happened. "Did the German people know?" or "how much was the German Army involved in the Holocaust?" were intensely personal questions. I base my answers evident in this story on my family of origin's individual history and the long, difficult hours spent speaking with family, German university professors, and archivists, as well as interviews with several eyewitnesses, including Elisabeth Scholl and Thomas Hartnagel.

Over ten years ago, I overcame an incident in graduate school when a professor asked if my grandmother deserved what happened to her as the Red Army descended upon Berlin in 1945. Twelve years later, when I guest lecture at colleges and universities on German resistance history during the Second World War, I get to answer different questions. Today's students are asking about what it was like to live under a dictatorship. I see this as a new and important concern for understanding what it is like to live in a totalitarian society and a sign of appreciation for living in a free one.

Captain Hartnagel was an extremely brave man. My grandfathers fought in Hitler's Army on the Russian Front, and my father, mother and aunt, as children, experienced the horrors of war. Writing this story was often painful. My mother's father never returned rom the prisoner-of-war camps in East Germany. Like my family of origin, Hartnagel was confronted daily by death as the Red Army surrounded the Sixth Army at Stalingrad and as it stormed through Berlin and the Eastern territories, seeking revenge.

Fritz Hartnagel risked his life by writing to his best friend. Because he was an officer, his letters were not censored. Sophie's family was punished before the war by the Gestapo for subversive acts against the Party, so she therefore was careful in writing her letters and diaries. Sophie's resistance is most evident, therefore, through her actions, but Fritz's desire to report the war crimes in letters, and its effect on his reader must not be underestimated or minimized. History has judged him both as a "co-conspirator in resisting the Nazis" and "a collaborator who sided with the Nazis."

Here were two people caught on opposite sides of war—convinced of their moral imperative to not only know the truth but to bring it into the light.

I am honored to have written Fritz and Sophie's story and appreciate your interest in it.

—Alexandra Lehmann, Ridgefield, CT

BIBLIOGRAPHY

Aicher-Scholl, Inge. *The White Rose, Munich 1942–1943*. Middletown: Wesleyan University Press, 1970.

Arendt, Hannah. *Origins of Totalitarianism*. New York: Viking, 1963.

Augustinus, Weg zu Gott. Eine Didaktische Lesehilfe zu den <Bekenntnisse> (I-IX) [Augustine's Way to God: A Didactic Reader to the *Confessions*]. Würzburg: Augustinus-Verlag, 1996.

Beevor, Antony. *Stalingrad*. London: Penguin Books, 1998.

Benz, Ute. *Frauen im Nationalsozialismus* [Women in National Socialism]. Munich: C.H. Beck, 1993.

Bernanos, Georges. *The Diary of a Country Priest*. New York: Carroll & Graf, 1937.

Bigongiari, Dino. *The Political Ideas of St. Thomas Aquinas*. New York: Hafner, 1957.

Breinersdorfer, Fred. *Sophie Scholl—Die letzten Tagen* [Sophie Scholl—The Last Days]. Frankfurt: S. Fischer Taschenbuch-Verlag, 2005.

Brockhaus, Gudrun. *Schauder und Idylle. Faschismus als Erlebnisangebot* [Fascism as a Way of Life]. Munich: Verlag Antje Kunstmann, 1997.

Buchheit, Gert. *Richter in roter Robe: Freisler Praesident des Volksgerichtshof* [Judges in Red Robes: Freisler as President of the People's Court]. Munich: List Verlag, 1968

Bruckner, Winfried and Nadine Haeuer. *Jugend im Dritten Reich: Damals war ich vierzehn* [Youth During the Third Reich: At That Time, I Was Fourteen]. Vienna: Jugend und Volk Verlagsgeschellschaft, 1987.

Douglas-Home, Charles. *Rommel*. London: Weidenfeld & Nicolson, 1973.

Funck, Marcus. "The Meaning of Dying: East Elbian Noble Families as 'Warrior Tribes' in the Nineteenth and Twentieth Centuries." In *Sacrifice and National Belonging in Twentieth Century Germany*. Edited by Matthew Eghigian. College Station, TX: Texas A&M University Press, 2002.

Funck, Marcus. „*Vom Hoefling zum soldatischen Mann. Varianten und Umwandlungen adeliger Mannlichkeit zwischen Kaiserreich und Nationalsozialismus.*" In *Adel und Moderne. Deutschland im europäischen Vergleich im 19. und 20. Jahrhundert.* [From Cadet to Soldier: Changes of Noble Manhood During the Kaiser and National Socialism] Edited by Eckart Conze and Monika Weinfort. Köln: Böhlau Verlag, 2004.

Gestapo Verhörprotokollen [Gestapo Trial Notes: Sophie and Hans Scholl, Alexander Schmorrell and Gisela Shertling]. February 20, 1943 and April 5, 1943. State Archives, Berlin, Germany.

Graf, Willi. *Briefe und Aufzeichnungen* [Letters and Diaries of Willi Graf]. Frankfurt: S. Fischer Verlag, 1984.

Haecker, Theodor. *Was ist der Mensch?* [What Is a Human Being?]. Leipzig: Oscar Brandstetter, 1933.

Haffner, Sebastian. *Anmerkungen zu Hitler* [Remarks on Hitler]. Munich: Kindler Verlag, 1978.

Hartnagel, Fritz. *Briefe aus Stalingrad* [Letters from Stalingrad to Sophie Scholl, July 13, 1942–February 26, 1943]. City of Ulm Archives, Germany. Unpublished and translated here for the first time.

Hillermeier, Heinz. *Im Namen des deutschen Volkes: Todesurteile des Volksgerichtshofes* [In the Name of the German People: Death Sentences of the People's Court]. Munich: Luchterhand Verlag, 1980.

Hirschfeld, Gerhard. *Nazi Rule and Dutch Collaboration: The Netherlands Under German Occupation 1940–1945*. Translated by L. Wilmot. New York: St. Martin's Press, 1981.

Hitler, Adolf. *Mein Kampf.* Munich: Zentralverlag der NSDAP, 1942.

Huber, Clara. *Kurt Huber zum Gedächtnis, Der Tod war nicht Vergebens* [In Memory of Kurt Huber, Death Was Not in Vain]. Munich: Nymphenberger Press, 1986.

Huse, Norbert. *Kleine Kunst Geschichte Münchens* [Small Art History of Munich]. Munich: C.H. Beck, 1990.

Jaspers, Karl. *Drei Gruender des Philosophierens: Plato, Augustin, Kant.* [Three Founding Fathers of Philosophy: Plato, Augustine, Kant]. Munich: R. Piper Verlag, 1957.

Kardorff, Ursula von. *Berliner Aufzeichnungen 1942–1945* [Berlin Notes]. Munich: DTV, 1994

Kersaw, Ian. *Hitler: Hubris (1889–1936).* London: Penguin Books, 1998.

Kersaw, Ian. *„Im Schatten des Kirchenkampfes"* [In the Shadow of the Church Fight]. In *Der Hitler Mythos: Volksmeinung und Propaganda im Dritten Reich* [The Hitler Myth: The People's Opinion and Propaganda in the Third Reich]. Stuttgart: Deutsche Verlag-Anstalt, 1980.

Kohl, Paul. *Der Krieg der deutschen Wehrmacht und der Polizei 1941–1944: Sowjetische Ueberlebende berichten* [The War of the German Army and Police 1941–1944: Soviet Survivors Report]. Frankfurt: S. Fischer Verlag, 1995.

Kopleck, Maik. *München 1933–194*5: *Stadtfuehrer zu den Spuren der Vergangenheit* [City Guide to the Clues from the Past, Munich 1933-1945]. Berlin: CH Links Verlag,

Lorent, Hans Peter de and Rainer Lehberger, editors. „*Die Fahne hoch*": *Schulpolitik und Schultag unterm Hakenkreuz* ["Flying the Flag": School Politics and Daily School Life Under the Swastika]. Cologne: Ergebnisse Verlag, 1986.

Leisner, Barbara. *Sophie Scholl: Ich würde es genauso wieder machen* [Sophie Scholl: I Would Do It Exactly the Same Way Over Again]. Munich: Econ Ullstein List Verlag, 2000.

Lill, Rudolf. „Über Hans und Sophie Scholl." In *Hochverrat? Neue Forschung zur "Weissen Rose"* [Treason? New Research About the White Rose]. Edited by Wolfgang Altgeld. Konstanz: UVK Universitätsverlag, 1999.

Mau, Hermann and Helmut Krausnick. *German History 1933–1945: An Assessment by German Historians.* London: Oswald Wolff, 1959.

Moncure, John. *Forging the King's Sword: Military Education between Tradition and Modernization: The Case of the Royal Prussian Cadet Corps, 1871–1918.* New York: Cornell University Press, 1991.

Möller, Horst und Dahm, Volker, et. al. *Die Tödliche Utopie: Bilder, Texte, Dokumente Daten zum Dritten Reich* [The Deadly Utopia: Pictures, Text, Documents and Dates of the Third Reich]. Munich: Institut für Zeitgeschichte, 1999.

Piekalkiewicz, R.S. *Stalingrad*. Munich: Suedwestverlag, 1977.

Pryce-Jones, David. *Paris in the Third Reich: A History of the German Occupation, 1940–1944*. London: Collins St. James's Place, 1981.

Salisbury, Harrison E. *The Unknown War in the East Front*. Vienna: Fritz Molden Verlag, 1978.

Schischkoff, Georgi. *Kurt Huber als Leibniz Forscher* [Kurt Huber as Leibniz Expert]. Munich: Buch Karl Schmidle, 1996.

Schneider, Michael and Winfried Süß. *Keine Volksgenossen: Der Widerstand der Weißen Rose* [Without their Countrymen: The White Rose Resistance]. Munich: Ludwig-Maximilians Universität, 1993.

Seaton, Albert. *The German Army 1933–1945*. London: Weidenfeld and Nicolson, 1982

Scholl, Hans and Sophie Scholl. *Briefe und Aufzeichnungen* [Letters and Notes]. Edited by Inge Jens. Munich: S. Fischer Verlag, 1984.

Scholl, Sophie and Fritz Hartnagel. *Damit wir uns nicht verlieren: Sophie Scholl, Fritz Hartnagel Briefwechsel 1937–1943* [So That We Don't Lose One Another: Letters of Sophie Scholl and Fritz Hartnagel, 1937–1943]. Edited by Thomas Hartnagel. Frankfurt: S. Fischer Verlag, 2005.

Shaw, Bernard. *St. Joan*. London: Penguin Books, 1924

Shirer, William L. *Berlin Diary: The Journal of a Foreign Correspondent, 1934–1941*. New York: Alfred A. Knopf, 1941.

Steinbeck, John. *The Moon is Down*. London: Penguin Books, 1942.

Studt, Christoph, ed. *Das Dritte Reich: Ein Lesebuch zur Deutschen Geschichte* [The Third Reich: A Compilation of Essays on Germany History]. Munich: C.H. Beck, 1982.

Ulmer Bilder Chronik, Band 5b. 1939–1945. Nazi Newspaper Articles. Assembled from destroyed newspapers by Hildegard Sander. Ulm/Donau: Dr. Karl Hoehn KG, 1989.

Vinke, Hermann. *Das Kurze Leben der Sophie Scholl* [The Short Life of Sophie Scholl]. Ravensburg: Ravensburger Buchverlag, 1980.

Vinke, Hermann. *Fritz Hartnagel: Der Freund von Sophie Scholl* [Fritz Hartnagel: Sophie Scholl's Boyfriend]. Zurich/Hamburg: Arche Verlag, 2005.

Voelkischer Beobachter [People's Newspaper]. Munich & Berlin Editions, 1933–1945.

Warmbrunn, Werner. *The Dutch Under German Occupation, 1940–1945*. Stanford: Stanford University Press, 1963.

Wiesemann, Martin, Falk Fröhlich and Elke Broszat, editors. *Bayern in der NS-Zeit* [Bavaria During the NS Period]. N.p.: Oldenbourg, 1977.

Welzer, Harald. *Auf den Truemmern der Geschichte. Gespraeche mit Raul Hilberg, Hans Mommsen, Zygmunt Bauman* [From the Rubble of History. Conversations with R. Hilberg, H. Mommesne, Z. Bauman]. Tübingen: edition diskord, 1999

Wickert, Christl. *Frauen gegen die Diktatur: Widerstand und Verfolgung im nationalsozialistischen Deutschland* [Women Against Dictatorship: Resistance and Persecution in National Socialist Germany]. Berlin: Gedenkstätte Deutscher Widerstand, 1995.

Woerterbuch zur Deutschen Militaer Geschichte [Dictionary of German Military History]. Berlin: 1985.

Zarusky, Jürgen. *Widerstand als "Hochverrat" 1933–1945*. [Resistance as High Treason] Munich: K.G. Sauer, 1998.

PHOTO: ©TUNDE JAKOB

ALEXANDRA LEHMANN RECEIVED HER BACHELOR of Arts, *cum laude*, from the State University of New York at Albany in Political Science and German. Her German fluency is born of heritage and studying *Germanistik* at universities in Wuerzburg, Braunschweig, and Munich. After nearly a decade of working in New York City as a copywriter and in Munich as a translator, she earned her Masters of Fine Arts in Nonfiction Writing from Sarah Lawrence College in Bronxville, New York. She completed her graduate thesis with Vijay Seshadri, comparing the letters and diaries of Sophie Scholl and Anne Frank. Yad Vashem in Jerusalem requested a copy for their library. With a Fulbright Scholarship, Alexandra began archival research in Germany for *With You There Is Light*. She won a fellowship to the Wesleyan Writers Conference and has guest lectured on German Resistance history at St. Paul's German Church in New York City, Mt. Holyoke College, and Fairfield and Western Connecticut State Universities. In June 2017, Alexandra began working with the White

Rose Foundation at the University of Munich furthering their initiative of bringing its traveling installation to the United States. She works as a writer and lives in Connecticut.

For more information about the author and upcoming readings, please visit www.alexandralehmann.com.